No Seat at the Table

CRITICAL AMERICA

General Editors: Richard Delgado and Jean Stefancic

Recent titles in the Critical America series include:

Rethinking Commodification: Cases and Readings in Law and Culture
Edited by Martha M. Ertman and Joan C. Williams

The Derrick Bell Reader
Edited by Richard Delgado and Jean Stefancic

Science for Segregation: Race, Law, and the Case against Brown v. Board of Education
John P. Jackson Jr.

Discrimination by Default: How Racism Becomes Routine
Lu-in Wang

The First Amendment in Cross-Cultural Perspective: A Comparative Legal Analysis of the Freedom of Speech
Ronald J. Krotoszynski, Jr.

Feminist Legal Theory: A Primer
Nancy Levit and Robert R. M. Verchick

The Emergence of Mexican America: Recovering Stories of Mexican Peoplehood in U.S. Culture
John-Michael Rivera

Law and Class in America: Trends since the Cold War
Edited by Paul D. Carrington and Trina Jones

The Sense of Justice: Empathy in Law and Punishment
Markus Dirk Dubber

No Seat at the Table: How Corporate Governance and Law Keep Women Out of the Boardroom
Douglas M. Branson

For a complete list of titles in the series, please visit the New York University Press website at www.nyupress.org.

No Seat at the Table

How Corporate Governance and Law
Keep Women Out of the Boardroom

Douglas M. Branson

NEW YORK UNIVERSITY PRESS
New York and London

NEW YORK UNIVERSITY PRESS
New York and London
www.nyupress.org

© 2007 by New York University
All rights reserved

Library of Congress Cataloging-in-Publication Data
Branson, Douglas M.
No seat at the table : how corporate governance and law keep
women out of the boardroom / Douglas M. Branson.
p. cm. — (Critical america)
Includes bibliographical references and index.
ISBN-13: 978-0-8147-9973-4 (cloth : alk. paper)
ISBN-10: 0-8147-9973-6 (cloth : alk. paper)
1. Women executives—United States. 2. Career development—
United States. 3. Corporate governance—United States. I. Title.
HD6054.4.U6B73   2006
331.4'81658400973—dc22   2006018398

New York University Press books are printed on acid-free paper,
and their binding materials are chosen for strength and durability.

Manufactured in the United States of America

10 9 8 7 6 5 4 3 2 1

Dedicated to Twelve Career Women:

*Jayne Barnard, Marilyn Berger, Elizabeth Boros,
Elizabeth Brackett, Martha Chamallas, Pat Chew,
Norma Hazlett, Elizabeth Hurtt, Lucy Isaki,
Therese Maynard, Marleen O'Connor,
Dawn Clark Netsch*

Contents

Acknowledgments

I wish to thank my research assistants, Jason Blake and Marcella McIntyre, class of 2002, Steven Chadwick, class of 2006, and Lauren Butler, class of 2007, School of Law, University of Pittsburgh, for doing much of the basic research in the law and business school libraries at the university. I thank my colleagues Jean Stefancic and Richard Delgado for reading, commenting upon, editing, and otherwise encouraging me to finish this book. My editor, Deborah Gershenowitz of New York University Press, spent free as well as work time giving me a list of extensive comments, most of which I incorporated in the book. She also listened, patiently, to my excuses and explanations. I presented portions of my findings at colloquia hosted by the School of Law, Loyola-Marymount University, Los Angeles, California, and the American Association of Law Schools Annual Meeting, San Francisco, California.

Introduction

According to Martha Burk of the National Organization of Women (NOW), who has led an attack against it, the last male bastion is the Augusta National Golf Club, which each spring hosts the Masters golf championship and to which, as of 2006, no women have been admitted to membership. That membership includes powerful business-men—corporate directors and CEOs of Fortune 500 corporations—at-torneys, statesmen, and the very wealthy, all male.

Strictly speaking, that Augusta National is the last male bastion may be true. But, after all, Augusta National is only a golf club. The last male bastions, the ones that really matter, have been, and continue to be, cor-porate boardrooms and the CEO suites that adjoin them. They remain male dominated—not impregnable, to be sure, but bastions nonetheless.

For much of the 35-odd years following the civil rights movement and the upheaval of the Vietnam War era, expectations for increased diversity in the boardroom and CEO suite have been high. Expectations ran high that the world could be changed for the better. Women and persons of color increasingly matriculated at and then were graduated from leading law and MBA schools. The new graduates were then hired by major law and accounting firms or joined corporate hierarchies, progressing upward through the ranks. In 1981, Jean Kirkpatrick became U.S. ambassador to the United Nations and Sandra Day O'Connor became the first female justice of the United States Supreme Court, after the 205 years of nation-hood and 109 male justices that had preceded her.[1] In 1960, when San-dra O'Connor began her law practice in Arizona, only 3.3 percent of lawyers and judges were women. "[W]hen [Sandra Day O'Connor] be-came the first woman to be nominated to the Supreme Court that per-centage had almost tripled."[2] Statistics in chapter 12 quantify how women registered even greater breakthroughs in medicine and other pro-fessions in the 1970s and 1980s. At time went on, too, there were also

1

high expectations that there would be an ample number of seats for women at the boardroom table. By the twenty-first century, a level of parity would be achieved.

That has not been the case, as this book demonstrates. Progress has come but the numbers, especially of women at the boardroom and CEO level, lag far behind expectations. Even in 2006, the actual number of women on the highest-level corporate boards in the United States is slightly over 550, the size of a high school's graduating class, and lower than the numbers Catalyst, Inc., the advocacy group for women in business, and other organizations report.

This book attempts to tease out implicit male biases in the deep structure of corporate governance. The analysis will unpack and shed light on the way patterns of male dominance reproduce themselves, over and over, from corporation to corporation, and how those biases, even though much more muted and subtle than they were twenty-five years ago, keep women from the executive suite and deny them seats at the boardroom table.[3]

I derived the research data summarized in this book from an in-depth examination of the 2001 and the 2005 proxy statements ("definitive 14A's") that large companies file with the Securities and Exchange Commission each year. In most cases, the data are from the five hundred largest corporations in the United States, ranked by annual revenues. *Fortune* magazine compiles the listing, known as the Fortune 500. In some instances, I have expanded the data to cover the Fortune 1000, which includes corporations ranking 501–1000 in terms of revenues.

The data demonstrate not only that the reported numbers of women on boards of directors lags badly behind the numbers once predicted but also that reality lags behind even the reported numbers. The silver lining, as demonstrated by event studies spaced four years apart in 2001 and 2005, is that some progress, although it is glacial progress to many, has been accomplished. The sequence of editorial reviews, editing, and printing does not permit inclusion of data that corporations filed with the SEC in Spring 2006 to determine whether emerging statistical changes constitute a "trend." Examination of that data will have to await another day and publication of another book.

After examining the data, in a series of ensuing chapters, this book documents, and explores in some depth, the explanations advanced for why women may not have progressed in the boardroom and the CEO suite in the numbers we would have expected. Those explanations require exploration of law (Title VII discrimination cases, and the prevailing corporate governance model, a portion of which is based in law), social psychology, linguistics, sociology, and other fields, to assess the state of America's boardrooms and to make suggestions on how the relevant actors might accomplish needed changes.

This book is not about employment discrimination. Other books cover that subject. Likewise, the book does not discuss sexual harassment, although harassment undoubtedly is a reason why some women have not advanced upward through the ranks. Rather, this is a corporate governance book, mostly about the demographics and composition of publicly held corporation boards of directors.

Many of the available works are advice or "how-to" books, which propose various one-size-fits-all recipes for success. Based upon empirical research in the social sciences, this book offers a new hypothesis: much more so than with men, with women, paradigm shifts occur as they move up the corporate ladder. The tactics that advance women initially are precisely the ones that will undermine their advancement through the higher echelons. The routes to the top that the literature recommends may be less rather than more likely to lead to the top. *Women have to follow pathways different than men in order to reach the boardroom or the CEO suite.*

Chapter 1 discusses the milieu in which women plaintiffs begin what has become an uphill advancement struggle for many of them. The chapter begins part 1 of the book, which consists of a series of chapters that describe some of the reasons why women in business have not advanced in the numbers one would expect.

Using the fact patterns of court cases under Title VII of the Civil Rights Act of 1964, chapter 2 describes acts and practices whereby corporate actors (bosses, supervisors, corporate officers, CEOs) build and then keep in place glass ceilings, floors, and walls, which confine women in business and inhibit their advancement. In doing the research, I retrieved electronically or photocopied two thousand published U.S. Court of Appeals Title VII cases from 1995 through 2005. I read in full text seven hundred of those cases. In chapter 2, I set forth the conclusions I reached from reading those judicial opinions. Those conclusions add to our understanding of why fewer women than expected have advanced to the level from which they could easily move into senior positions and onto corporate boards of directors.

The following chapters examine other reasons advanced for the failure of women to progress in the corporate world. Chapter 3 deals with the important subjects of childbirth, child rearing, work/life issues, and the phenomenon of women opting out of promising corporate careers altogether. In reading the large basket of court cases, I set aside representative cases describing discrimination against women based upon pregnancy or upon child rearing. I describe those cases in chapter 3.

Chapter 4 draws upon research in linguistics. Inflections and other speech patterns cause men to interpret certain female behaviors as expressions of emotion when in fact they are not. In turn, those false interpretations lead to stereotypes that women are too volatile to serve as upper-level managers, directors, or CEOs. These stereotypes persist in the eyes of certain beholders, in particular CEOs, directors on nomination committees, and full boards of directors. The result is exclusion of an unknown number of women from the wider pool of director candidates.

The opposite of the overly emotional stereotype is the "iron maiden" stereotype, which, in uncomplimentary fashion, those in West Coast high-tech industries have also come to label the "bully broad." Chapter 5 draws on behavioral psychology's observation of women in the high-tech sector, whose aggressive behavior on the job cause them to rise rapidly but then become sidetracked in their careers precisely because of the characteristics that enabled them to achieve high positions in the first place.

Part 2 transitions from the "why" to the "how." It distills the myths and the realities of women's progress toward seats at the boardroom table.

In the "how-to" books, of which the market contains many, the prevailing advice for women has been to be "patient, but not passive" as they work their way up through the ranks of a corporate organization. My evidence contradicts this advice. Very few women achieve board membership in this way. The best chance of being a female Fortune 500 company director is to be a tenured professor at Harvard University or a similar elite educational institution, an eye of the needle so narrow and permitting passage of so few as to not be a realistic pathway for women. Chapters 6 and 7 compare the advice with the evidence adduced in writing this book.

The original empirical research for this book, set forth in chapter 7, stems from data filed with the SEC in early 2001. Chapter 8 examines the 2005 data (filed in spring and summer 2005), noting changes and trends that have occurred in the meantime.

Chapter 9 draws again on sociological research to explain another myth. Some of the disadvantages women and persons of color face in the working world are not the result of any inherent cultural or other personal characteristics ("too emotional," "bully broad," and others outlined in Part 1). Instead, disadvantage results from organizational settings in which women and persons of color find themselves, namely, as tokens, or as minority members of a skewed group in which the dominant members are much more likely to think and act vis-à-vis the minority in terms of stereotypes. That chapter is subtitled "The Legacy of Tokenism."

Part 3 deals with the realities of the corporate setting. As "keeper of keys to the kingdom," or at least to the boardroom, corporations and their boards of directors regulate advancement.

Chapter 10 describes the U.S. corporate governance model, highlighting the individualistic and bold types of behaviors that the model prizes, for example, in the form of directors who will confront and remove underperforming or misguided CEOs. Chapter 11 continues this theme but from the perspective of women, or of women's perceived behaviors in certain settings.

Chapter 12 details further the paucity of women in CEO suites and boardrooms and outlines the rewards, financial and otherwise, for women who do make it to the very top of large corporate organizations. The chapter also focuses on women CEOs as well as directors. The largest pool by far from which male directors are chosen is the pool of sitting and retired CEOs. Professor Rakesh Khurana has termed the process whereby boards and consulting firms find CEO candidates "the search for the corporate savior." It is a process that by its nature tends to exclude women. Some have recommended that boards of directors reexamine this process. That is doubly necessary if capable women executives are to have equal opportunity to reach the very top and if the pool of suitable female candidates for director positions is to be enlarged.

What to do about all of this is the subject of part 4, "Getting a Seat at the Boardroom Table." Chapter 13 attempts to reconcile the paradigms outlined in earlier chapters. The conclusion is that no one model is suitable. Instead, women, unlike men, have to make several significant, conscious paradigm shifts as they advance upward in their careers. The realization that this is so, and that advancement requires more than having any one pathway or model in mind ("women must get line experience" or "women must have profit and loss responsibility") is an important finding. Documentation of the careers of the very few women who have succeeded, only later to be ousted, as CEOs of major American corporations (Jill Barad at Mattel Toy, Bernadette Healy at the American Red

Cross, Carleton Fiorina at Hewlett-Packard) confirms important hypotheses this book advances.

The conclusion ends with several sets of prescriptions. One set is directed at corporations: boards of directors and nominating or governance committees of those boards. No such committee should be operating today without the membership of one, and perhaps two, women members of the board. Another set of recommendations directs itself toward women who aspire to the boardroom and/or the CEO suite. In turn, they must be aggressive, then diplomatic and statesmanlike, and then aggressive once more, but in an entirely different mode than before, as they progress toward the top. A third set outlines what women might do in their public personae. Most important perhaps of all, the conclusion begins with an exposition on just why women's presence in the boardroom is so important, deserving of recognition as a hot and timely subject of our times.

This manuscript is up to date as of June 1, 2006. Any errors or omissions are those of the author alone.

PART I

Glass Ceilings, Floors, and Walls

1

Restraints on Advancement

It always happens at [conferences of businesswomen]. I speak, I listen, I hear the same words over and over—"baffled," "angry," "lost," "trapped," "stuck," "overwhelmed"—as each woman tells me she feels that she's gotten only so far in business and can't get any further.

—CNN executive and author Gail Evans,
in *Play like a Man, Win like a Woman* (2000).[1]

Donna Zahorik taught psychology at Cornell University in upstate New York. After several years of teaching and publishing, she applied for tenure but was denied. A colleague had introduced into faculty deliberations comments that Zahorik was "too feminine," "too unassuming, unaggressive, unassertive, and not highly motivated for vigorous interpersonal competition." The courts denied her claim of discrimination, finding that the comments related not to her gender but to the effect of Professor's Zahorik's personality on students.[2]

Sue Margolis, an engineer/manager at Tektronix, Inc., in Portland, Oregon, had fifteen years' experience. Performance reviews reported "results consistently met and sometimes exceed expectations." In a mini-reduction in force, Tektronix senior managers telescoped eight managerial jobs into seven, terminating the only woman manager, Margolis. Her supervisor rarely would recognize her in meetings. He told Margolis that he and others considered her to be "pushy" and "aggressive." "Sexual stereotyping . . . can serve as evidence that gender played an impermissible role in the employer's [adverse] decision," noted the federal appellate court.[3]

Employment of stereotypes, in which appearances rather than actual achievements matter, materially aids in keeping the glass ceiling in place. Senior managers rate one woman, such as Zahorik, as lacking in assertiveness, marking her low on "leadership potential." Managers rate another woman, such as Margolis, as "too pushy" and "overly aggressive," marking her low on "interpersonal skills." Neither woman advances and, in fact, both watch in horror as their careers shatter before their eyes. The glass ceiling endures.

Numbers

The glass ceiling is firmly in place. By 2005, only eleven women had become directors of Fortune 500 corporations by climbing the ladder at the corporation that employs them. Many of the rest bumped into the glass ceiling somewhere in their climb up the ladder.

Combined, the academic, not-for-profit, and governmental sectors provide the largest percentage of women directors, 37.2 percent of the 480 women holding board seats in 2000, as chapter 7 elaborates. In organizations in these sectors, the glass ceiling does not exist, or is more permeable. From them, some women then sidestep onto the boards of major corporations.

Many social psychologists, career counselors, and others who write "how-to" advice books for women in business assert that a glass ceiling exists. "Smashing the Glass Ceiling" or "Breaking the Glass Ceiling" are recurring titles.[4]

In May 2004, the Boeing Company paid $72.5 million in settlement of a class action brought by women who alleged that the company paid them less than men and promoted men more quickly to higher level positions. In July 2004, Morgan Stanley paid $54 million in settling a case that made similar allegations. Previously, Home Depot had paid $104 million and, in 2002, American Express had paid $42 million in settlement of sex discrimination claims.[5] Similar class actions are pending against other large corporations. Although women hold almost half of lower-level management positions overall, they account for only 8 percent of executive vice-presidents and above at Fortune 500 companies.[6]

Thus, the evidence supports the view that women in business "face a 'glass ceiling' that allows them to see, but not to obtain, the most prestigious jobs" within corporations.[7]

The Glass Floor

A related concept is the "glass floor." When they fall out of favor, or are actually demoted, men in the ranks of higher management frequently do not fall far. They rebound off the glass floor. Senior managers retain the underperforming manager in some nook or cranny within the executive suites from which the fallen executive crawls back to respectability and another senior management position. Time after time this occurs, as the court cases in the next chapter demonstrate.

A "glass floor" also exists for, and protects, CEOs. Much like major league baseball managers who, no matter how badly they perform, seem always to get rehired, so, too, have male CEOs who have been forced out found positions at other corporations. William Agee destroyed Bendix Corporation by making an ill-advised takeover bid for Martin Marietta. After the Bendix board deposed him, Agee found employment as CEO at Morrison Knudsen, the international engineering and construction firm, which Agee proceeded to mismanage into bankruptcy. The labor unions and employee-owners of UAL Corp., United Airlines' holding company, forced Stephen Wolf out as CEO. He left UAL, only to resurface as chairman and CEO at U.S. Airways. Many other badly performing CEOs nonetheless rebound off the glass floor.

Pundits hypothesize that female CEOs who have lost their high offices will bounce back up as well, but so far they have not. Although the numbers have been small, the deposed women CEOs (Jill Barad at Mattel Toy, Carleton Fiorina at Hewlett Packard, Linda Wachner at Warnaco Group) have been high profile. They have yet to reappear in other organizations.

The glass floor's existence, and the "pronounced trend" to replace CEOs with CEOs, of which it is a part, affects women in business if only because the phenomenon of men rebounding within the clubby ranks of upper management results in fewer openings for women to occupy and in which they could prove themselves.[8]

CEOs' and Economists' Views

Three-fourths of male chief executive officers of major corporations aver that no such thing as the glass ceiling exists, or so they opined to the Federal Glass Ceiling Commission in the mid-1990s.[9] According to Catalyst, over 80 percent of the CEOs they interviewed had an alternative explanation about why women have not advanced to the very top in their organizations, namely, women's lack of experience in line positions and with profit-and-loss responsibility.[10] Of course, CEOs themselves must bear a portion of the responsibility for women not being given line positions in which they could gain the requisite experience.

CEOs with those views find succor in the claims made by some that the glass ceiling, if it did once exist, is "cracking."[11] They find further succor in the work of conservative economists who have spawned a "human capital" literature.

Economists assert two propositions. One is that women have disadvantageous workforce positions because they "self-select" into jobs that require less education and lower levels of skill.[12]

The other is that labor markets, including markets for managers, and product markets are competitive. Gender discrimination, and the glass ceiling that is a component of it, does not exist because it could not survive in a competitive labor market. It is inefficient to exclude managers on the basis of sex. Firms that did so would not survive in product market, the Darwinian, dog-eat-dog world of business competition.

Instead women do not rise to the very top for other reasons: they self-select; lack line experience; allow themselves to get "stuck" in dead-end positions or positions with short promotion ladders; prefer to go onto the "mommy track" to raise children, and so on.[13]

Professor Richard Delgado has disputed the efficacy of labor markets. Not efficiency alone but baser motives, including destructive and/or oppressive tendencies, drive markets as well. Free markets are not likely to eradicate unfair discrimination. In fact, given the play for revenge, spite, prejudice, and the like to operate, the free nature of labor markets may aid in perpetuation of discrimination.[14]

Many women in business agree with a vice-president of NOW: "Women have been climbing the corporate ladder for thirty years now. We're well groomed for the executive suites, but too often we're all dressed up with no place to go."[15] "Everybody expected a lot more progress by now," echoed Irene Lang, president of Catalyst, Inc., in late 2004. "There are so many women in the work place. You just assumed this [cracking the glass ceiling] was a 20th-century battle, and by the 21st-century it would be over."[16]

Title VII Gender Discrimination Court Cases

Each year, in the federal courts of the United States, approximately twenty-five thousand women file claims of gender discrimination under Title VII of the Civil Rights Act of 1964.[17] Many of those cases involve out-and-out sexual harassment in the workplace. They have only tangential relevance, at best, to the glass ceiling and the glass floor. Further evidence of the glass ceiling's existence does come from a subset of those court cases in which women have bumped up against the glass ceiling, come away with contusions, and then sought redress in the courts. The cases are not plentiful, however, for at least three reasons.

One is that the procedure is cumbersome. Under federal law a woman, or any job-discrimination victim, must first make a complaint to the Equal Employment Opportunity Commission (EEOC), which only after an investigation issues a "notice of a right to sue" under the Civil Rights Act of 1964. Then, and only then, can plaintiff proceed to court, where she awaits further delays.

Second is that court cases are notoriously difficult. There is the further delay, which can mount up to three or four years, as understaffed federal district courts must give precedence to criminal cases. Even if a woman wins her court case at trial, in a Title VII case, on appeal a defendant corporation is *seven times more likely* than a plaintiff to overturn the result in the court below. Of any category of case filed in federal courts, the "most dramatic gap," by far, between plaintiffs and defendant corporations exists in employment discrimination cases, as an exhaustive recent study by law professors Kevin Claremont and Theodore Eisenberg at Cornell University demonstrates.[18]

The nature of discrimination cases themselves makes them "difficult to win." According to Stanford University law professor Deborah Rhode,

> "Disparate treatment" cases require proof that the employer intentionally treated similarly qualified women and men differently, and that the woman otherwise would have obtained particular jobs or benefits. For example, a female manager might attempt to demonstrate that she was left out of informal business networks and that she lost a promotion to a male colleague with lower performance evaluations. . . .[19]

Another principal category of court case is the "disparate impact" case, which requires "[p]roof that practices having an adverse effect on women are not job related and are not justified by business necessity. For example, a female applicant might show that qualifying tests disproportionately excluded women and demanded more physical strength than the position in fact required."

The cases require expert witnesses and have other costly features that quickly run into multiple tens of thousands of dollars that the plaintiff herself may have to advance because of ethical proscriptions on attorneys paying such costs themselves.

Third is simply that, at any level of management, such an EEOC complaint or court case constitutes professional suicide. That is doubly true at the upper levels of management with which this book deals. There are simply no court cases at that level because any aspiring woman who brought one would be labeled a troublemaker, blackballed, excluded for life from the corporate world.

For those reasons (cumbersome procedures, difficulty, expenses, adverse effects on jobs and careers), accounts of bumping up against the glass ceiling are underreported, at least in judges' opinions.[20] Accounts of bumping up against the ceiling once a woman has climbed a good way up the corporate ladder are rarer still, or simply do not exist.

Stereotypes

One element of the glass ceiling that results in wage discrepancies and other forms of disparate treatment before the fact, and may make discrimination cases more difficult to win after the fact, is the "secondary earner bias" under which women are stereotyped. Many men in power view married women's earnings as "somehow coming *after* that of her husband."[21] As they move up through the ranks, women may be perceived as not being as needy as men, who often, in the reverse of the stereotype, are viewed as the primary breadwinner for their households, whether that is true or not. Women may, therefore, consciously or subconsciously, be graded lower in the evaluation process leading up to a possible promotion or elevation to fill a higher-level vacancy.

Management scholars find that the "male breadwinner model" has been "outdated" for a number of years.[22] The AFL-CIO reports that 62 percent of working women contribute half, or more, of their households' income.[23]

Although it should have been relegated to the trash heap, the secondary-earner bias continues to operate, at all levels. One classic study of blue-collar women found that "[r]egardless of a woman's real contribution to the family, the husband is defined as the main breadwinner." The women in the study realized "that their husband's sense of manhood is contingent on the shared belief that his paycheck is 'supporting the family,' so [the] women define their work as 'helping their husbands.'"[24]

Subjective Promotion Processes

Another reason for fewer court cases is that as job candidates compete for high level positions, the process becomes more subjective: "[w]hich job candidates have the most impressive leadership skills, artistic creativity, or intellectual promise is often open to dispute. Because subjective criteria are particularly significant in allocating upper level positions, women are particularly likely to be under represented at the top," Professor Deborah Rhode has found.[25] Subjective criteria leave more room for unconscious prejudices to operate.

"Criteria for 'good decisions' or good management performance get less certain closer to the top. The connection between an upper management decision and a factor such as production efficiency several layers below or gross sales is indirect, if it is even apparent."[26] One executive termed this the "Law of Inverse Certainty: the more important the management decision, the less precise the tools to deal with it . . . and the longer it will take before anyone knows it was right." As a consequence of the subjective nature of the evaluation of management skills and performance, at the top corporate promotion processes "put trust and homogeneity at a premium." This accounts for the social homogeneity of business leaders for much of the twentieth century: "largely white, Protestant men from elite schools," concludes Harvard sociologist Rosabeth Moss Kanter.[27]

From a litigation perspective, it is much more difficult to challenge a "one off" selection for a high management position, laden as it is with subjective evaluation. There is no dependable yardstick. With sales persons or plant managers, evaluators have more objective criteria available, such as monthly and quarterly sales or production reports. If the evaluators ignore that data, or act in spite of it, a woman or person of color denied a promotion potentially has a better case to take to court.

Promotion Tournaments

Management scholars and behavioral psychologists liken the current promotion process in the upper ranks to a jousting or other tournament, consisting of a round robin of one-on-one competitions, until a winner emerges.[28] Enron emboldened a gladiator mentality among managers with its "Rank and Yank" tournament system. The corporation fired managers who ranked in the lowest 20 percent after annual evaluations, no matter how much the managers had improved their department's or unit's results in an absolute sense. General Electric Company CEO and management guru Jack Welch preached about the virtue of a more muted system he had installed that mandated that managers rank subordinates each year, dismissing managers who ranked in the bottom 10 percent, regardless of whether they had fared badly or not.[29]

Theories, summarized by Professor Marleen O'Connor, among others, allege that women are less likely to be eager to participate in the corporate promotion tournament because women are more likely to see that the tournament system is little more than a game.[30] If women do participate, they often come off second best because the qualities they exhibit and the ways in which they excel are not those a tournament system highlights or prizes.[31] Those who succeed tend to be men who combine qualities of loyalty, aggression, and fickleness.[32] They are loyal to a point, but then will be willing to substitute new objects for the old when their senses tell them that it may be in their best interests to do so. Scholars wonder, or theorize, about whether such "ethical plasticity" is more prevalent among men.

The corporate promotion tournament is an exemplar of what experts term second-generation job bias, those less blatant forms of discrimination that may go undetected by managers and by courts but that nonetheless disadvantage women and other minorities in the workplace.[33]

Vicarious Fault

In our system of jurisprudence, generally speaking, a plaintiff who seeks damages, or some other form of judicial relief, such as an injunction, must prove fault on the defendant's part. Thus, a plaintiff has to prove a lack of reasonable care (negligence), or slight care (gross negligence or recklessness), or knowing or intentional conduct.

A traditional exception to the rule of fault is the area of vicarious liability, in which a court holds a defendant responsible for the acts of others, who were at fault, and regardless of whether the defendant was at fault or not. Thus, a person who brings a dangerous instrumentality upon their land (tigers, explosives, great quantities of water) that, if it gets loose, is likely to cause great damage is liable for the damage caused. The latter is true even if the person exercised the utmost care in terms of precautions. Ergo, the terms "no fault" and "strict liability."[34]

A venerable area of strict liability is the acts of the employer, or master, for the acts of the wrongdoing employee, or servant, acting within the scope of his or her employment. Unless it finds that the servant was not even remotely serving the master's interests, which it rarely does, the law finds the master at fault, and hence liable, regardless of the precautions the master exercised or the warnings the master gave to the servant. One explanation is that, before the injury, through its control over the servant, and after the fact, through insurance and otherwise, the master is far more likely than the victim to prevent the harm that occurred or, after the fact, to compensate the victim for it.

Damages are important for several reasons. One is that they make the victim (the plaintiff) whole, or as nearly whole as can be. Another is that an award of damages deters the defendant, and others similarly situated, from the conduct. After having been made to pay out money, a defendant will be more likely to take precautions or to give warnings than he or she previously had been. These objectives, which we call "compensation" and "deterrence," are two principal goals of damage awards.

Employment discrimination law is different. It leans toward but does not follow vicarious liability and the law of agency, as briefly outlined. The victim of discrimination must prove a quantum of fault on the employer's part before the victim can obtain money damages, at least in cases in which plaintiff alleges she was a victim of hostile environment discrimination. Because the employer, rather than the supervisor or coworker, has the money ("deep pockets" in lawyer jargon), the nonapplication of straight vicarious liability concepts to employment discrimination cases is yet another hurdle for a plaintiff who seeks to vindicate a job discrimination claim based upon her sex, or for a lawyer who examines her case, or for both.

Michelle Vinson began her career as a teller-trainee at a Meridor Savings Bank branch. In four years, however, she worked her way up through the positions of teller, head teller, and assistant branch manager.[35] The courts all found that her promotions had been merit based.

But after her discharge, which she claimed had been in retaliation for her complaints, Vinson alleged sexual harassment by bank employee Sidney Taylor, a vice-president and manager of the branch at which Vinson worked. She alleged that she had intercourse with Taylor "40 or 50 times." "[T]aylor fondled her in front of other employees, followed her into the women's restroom . . . exposed himself to her, and even forcibly raped her on several occasions," she further alleged.

Mr. Taylor denied it all. The bank steadfastly clung to its explanation that it had discharged Vinson for poor performance. Seemingly siding with the bank, the district court disallowed evidence that Taylor had fondled other women at the bank, which the Supreme Court held important to Vinson's claim of hostile environment. The chance for Vinson to make out her claim of hostile environment outweighed any need the trial court had to maintain decorum, minimizing unseemly details that may have been revealed.

What the Court gave by upholding such claims, the Court took away with its pronouncements on the Meritor Bank's (and other employers') vicarious liability. The late Chief Justice Rehnquist opined that, along lines the EEOC suggested, courts should by and large follow an agency model but not completely, as the court of appeals had done. That court had taken literally the statute's language, which includes "agent" within the term "employer." A supervisor is an agent even if he lacks the power to hire and fire. His acts are imputed to the employer, regardless of fault on the employer's part, or so the court of appeals had held.

The Supreme Court corrected the misimpression that employers are always liable for sexual harassment or other forms of discrimination that supervisors may visit upon employees. The strict agency model does not apply to all employee discrimination claims. Instead, employers may escape liability by demonstrating that

- the employer had in place a reasonable grievance procedure to deal with claims of job discrimination, such as those based upon promotion or training decisions (disparate treatment) or upon hostile environment (disparate impact);
- a procedure would not be reasonable if it required or was likely to result in a requirement that the first responder be the individual about whom the employee complains in her grievance, which was the case in Vinson's claim against Sidney Taylor and Meridor Bank;
- the employer has a policy against discrimination, including discrimination based upon sex;
- employees had notice of and ready accessibility to the grievance procedure;
- the procedure was likely to produce a credible response, which would not necessarily be a response palatable to the employee but would not be a wooden gesture, either.

The truth is that the United States Supreme Court opinion in *Meridor Savings Bank v. Vinson* is much more succinct. Justice Rehnquist also expressly "decline[d] to issue a definitive rule on employer liability." He then did precisely that, albeit in brief and cryptic terms.

The bullet points above represent what any corporate counsel or corporate affirmative action officer takes from *Meridor Savings Bank* and subsequent Supreme Court decisions. In cases handed down the same day against Burlington Industries and against the City of Boca Raton, Florida (involving hostile environment claims by a female lifeguard), the Court came closer to the definitive rule Mr. Justice Rehnquist had said that the Court had avoided.[36] In cases involving "a tangible employment action, such as discharge, demotion or undesirable reassignment," normal agency law applies and the employer is strictly liable.[37]

In other cases, namely, those in which women make out claims of a hostile environment rather than any particular adverse employment action, the Court elevated the *Meridor* guidelines to the status of an "affirmative defense."[38] Thus, if the defense is able to show that, despite a hostile environment and resulting discrimination, it had in place a reasonable grievance procedure, of which employees had notice, and plaintiff had failed to use it, the corporate defendant will sidestep liability.

Counsel or corporate officer will put antidiscrimination policies and grievance procedures in place. They will cause persons throughout the organization to post placards and otherwise give notice. They will insure that grievances procedure function in a meaningful way and are not merely pretexts or gestures. In doing those things, counsel and corporate officers will reduce substantially, if not eliminate altogether, the prospect of employer liability for sex and other forms of discrimination.[39] In turn, the prospect of no employer liability, or only a dim chance of one, will insure that fewer claims based upon hostile environments and the discrimination that results from it are brought in the first place.

Restraints of the more subtle as well as the blatant kind circumscribe the work environment for many women managers. Restraints bring readily to mind the glass ceiling that, through no fault of their own, restrains women's upward mobility, and the glass floor that, more indirectly, crowds women out of the climb toward the top. Glass ceilings and floors continue to exist, despite claims to the contrary. The court cases give further evidence of the fact.

2

Glass Ceilings and Floors
The Court Cases

Glass-ceiling discrimination cases do emanate from law, accounting, and other professions. The facts of those cases give us a good idea of other raw materials—acts, practices, and behaviors—that go into the making of a glass ceiling. While the glass ceiling affects more middle-than high-level women managers, in the long run it is the glass ceiling and its durability that prevent great numbers of women from progressing upward into the pool from which nominating committees and boards of directors choose directors and senior executives.

A listing of those glass ceiling devices, which I derived from a reading of over seven hundred court of appeals Title VII cases, would include (1) retaliation against women who complain of treatment they perceive to be discriminatory; (2) upper-level hostile work environments for women; (3) sand-bagging (silently refusing to help or support) by male counterparts or subordinates of capable or aggressive women managers as they advance; (4) targeted "reductions in force" to sidetrack or curtail the careers of women who advance too rapidly; (5) the new boss phenomenon; and (6) utilization of stereotypes of women to find a lack of (or too much) femininity—that is, the basing of an adverse employment action upon a woman being "overly masculine" or "overly feminine" (almost a "you can't win" phenomenon).

1. Retaliation. Women stand a better chance of recovery on a claim for the retaliation by coworkers and superiors that frequently follows sex discrimination than they do for the sex discrimination itself. For that reason, perhaps, retaliation suits increased 72 percent between 1992 and 1998.[1] These retaliation suits recount the facts of cases that reveal glass-ceiling nitty-gritty, the first bit of which is the retaliation or the threat of retaliation itself.

In a law case chapter 10 further describes,[2] after a four-week trial, a jury awarded plaintiff Jennifer Passantino $100,000 in back pay, $2 million in front pay (salary she would have received had her career progressed over her expected working life of twenty-two years), $1 million in emotional distress damages, and $8.6 million in punitive damages, for a total of $11.7 million.

Title VII of the Civil Rights Act of 1964 caps punitive damages according to the size of the employer's business. Even a large company such as Johnson & Johnson benefits from a relatively paltry cap of $300,000. So the trial judge in Passantino's case had to reduce her total damages to $3.4 million, but he then awarded her $580,000 in attorneys' fees and reimbursement of costs she had paid. The legislative cap on punitive damages is another obstacle that EEOC cases encounter but that other cases do not and constitutes an impediment, for some cases and for some attorneys, at least.

In another retaliation case,[3] after an experienced female technician complained that a less qualified male had been promoted ahead of her, her supervisor began greeting her as "Trouble." He retaliated, denying her promotion by changing job specifications for further openings so that she would never be able to hit the "moving target."

After fifteen years' service, the only tenured woman professor in the business school of a large state university discovered that her salary was 31 percent less than that of her male peers and 13 percent less than that of male junior faculty. Once she filed an EEOC complaint, the sole woman professor was told by the business school dean that he would reassign all her courses; that she "was going to be out of there"; and that she should not bother to attempt to speak at faculty meetings because he would not recognize her.[4]

Retaliation by the male members of a work group or job classification may be part of what sociologists term "boundary heightening." The dominants in the group take actions to emphasize their common characteristics while as the same time they take actions to emphasize differences and isolate a token even more.[5]

A subset of the retaliation cases involves women who become pregnant or overburdened with child-care responsibilities. When adverse employment actions occur, and they complain, these women are frequently subject to retaliation. Several of those cases are reported and analyzed in chapter 3.

2. Hostile Environment. These are the cases in which the boys leave up the *Playboy* centerfolds in the fire house or locker room even after a woman coworker complains. These are the crude jokes and sexual reference and innuendo cases that ordinarily occur in the blue collar environment, not in the management ranks. But not always.

Gail Abeita worked in a management position with TransAmerica, a catalog sales company (women's apparel, cosmetics, and jewelry) that employed 330 persons. Her work bought her into constant contact with the company's president, Avrum Katz.[6]

Katz did not know when to quit. Four years into her seven years of employment, Abeita got a greeting from Katz one morning: "[O]h, yellow dress and yellow shoes, yellow underwear, too?" Whenever an attractive female employee came by, after she had passed, Katz would say to no one in particular, or to Abeita, "I'd really like to lay the pipe to her," or "I'd really like to lay her." Asked by a subordinate what he wanted the subordinate to do with an attractive model hired for the day, Katz retorted, "Well, that doesn't matter. It's what I'd like to do with her that's important." Katz persisted in showing Abeita the Frederick's of Hollywood catalog, pointing at a particular model "who was wearing practically nothing" in the photos. Abeita complained. The executive vice-president told his boss, Katz, that his behavior "was inappropriate and unprofessional and had to stop." But it continued.

TransAmerica suffered a downturn in its business. In 1991 it reduced its workforce from 330 to 214. In early 1993, Katz let go a male vice-president to reduce overhead costs. Katz, and TransAmerica, fired Abeita in June 1993.

Abeita had complained to Katz of lower pay for comparable work by women and of his refusal to promote women to executive positions within the company. She thought that her complaints were the immediate cause of her dismissal. But she failed to check the "retaliation claim" box on her EEOC complaint and, on that technicality, lost any retaliation claims she may have had.

She also failed on her claim of disparate treatment because her lawyer did not produce evidence that gender played any role either in her dismissal or in TransAmerica's failure to fulfill salary promises Katz had made to her. A male vice-president had been let go before her. Abeita also offered no proof that salary promises to similarly situated males were kept while promises to her were not.

The appeals court did hold that she had stated a hostile environment claim. "[V]erbal conduct alone can be the basis of a successful hostile environment claim." The verbal conduct must be more than the "mere banter of a group," as was true in a case in which men at breakfast sales meetings said in the presence of the plaintiff, and another female coworker, "Nothing I like more in the morning than sticky buns" and that a land development adjacent to a Hooter's restaurant should be named "Hootersville" or "Twin Peaks."[7] Sexual comments must not only be more than mere banter in a group. They must be "commonplace, ongoing and continual."

In another hostile environment case,[8] the only female sales manager, Joyce Quinn, was sexually accosted by her supervisor; subjected to discussions about "strip club" escapades by her coworkers; and at a golf course outing tackled and pinned down beneath her supervisor while two of her clients watched.

Gail Abeita's and Joyce Quinn's cases seem rare ones. In this day and age, one would have thought that senior managers in midsize and larger companies would know better, refraining from the type of locker room behaviors to which the supervisors in these cases seem to have been addicted.

3. Sandbagging Advancing Female Coworkers. Title VII of the Civil Rights Act of 1964 prohibits an employer from "discharging any individual, or otherwise . . . discriminating against any individual with respect to his compensation . . . because of such individuals' . . . sex."[9] One form discrimination takes that often results in lack of promotion, or even demotion or discharge, is sandbagging of women by male coworkers.

Sandbagging consists of attempts to hamstring, or forestall altogether, the target worker in achievement of her objective, whether it be achieving a promotion, reaching the top, or completing a single task. After the fact, sandbagging consists of downplaying the target's accomplishments, or robbing her altogether of credit with her supervisor or other superiors.

Sandbagging occurs because males feel that a woman is not a team player; or that she has gotten as far as she has through affirmative action and favoritism toward women; or that she has simply risen too fast within the organization; or that she fails to act or dress according to the stereotypes men have of women in the workplace. Sociologists find the practice frequent in work groups or job classifications in which a coworker is the only female or minority group member or in which, beyond tokenism, the minority group members are greatly outnumbered by the dominant group (skewed distributions).

To use a phrase from the Vietnam War, describing what enlisted men would do to an unpopular officer, in the workplace men may "frag" a female or minority coworker, providing reports or information to her late, or not at all. They may gang up, savaging her one after the other when she gives a presentation in a meeting. They may confirm their attendance and then not show up for meetings she convenes. They may act out impulses as alpha males, interrupting her and putting her down, especially when in a group. They may appropriate her work and label it as their own.

All of these behaviors reinforce the glass ceiling. Victims may find it all bewildering. They may be seriously harmed and may smart for days from comments or outcomes that, for men, are but part of a game and quickly forgotten. At least two of the "how to" advice books for women in the workplace ascribe it all to the difference in our society between the upbringing that of boys and of girls.

Sociologists Pat Heim and Susan Golant note that parents teach boys of a hierarchical, competitive world in which there are winners and losers. Boys play teams sports in which they learn to obey the coach, be a team player, accept defeat, and come back the next day ready to play again:

> Girls live in a "flat" social structure. They play games in which power is shared equally. There is never a "captain doll player" or a winner in a game of nurse. Boys' games are goal focused. A boy would never say, "Let's get started with the game and figure out where the goal line is later." Finally, boys play in large groups; relationships between each other are secondary to reaching the goal. Girls play one-on-one with best friends. . . .[10]

According to Heim and Golant, authors of a self-help volume for businesswomen, "[t]he impact of these differences on the business world is profound":

> Men continue to perceive business as they do sports. It is a hierarchical game with goals. [W]omen see business as a web of relationships that moves forward in a continuous process. Relationships with co-workers are tools men use to get the job done. For women, such relationships are

a key part of their personal lives. [Men] view everyone in the organization as either above or below them. Women tend to see co-workers,
from executives to mail clerks, as being more on an equal footing. In
fact, a key tenet of the female culture is that power is always shared
equally and no one is ever better than or above anyone else.[11]

These explanations seem based upon a 1950s world in which the upbringing of girls was different. Today, girls play many competitive team
sports—softball, soccer, basketball, field hockey, even ice hockey and
rugby—from first grade through university days. At least half a generation of those women are now in the workplace. So the boys' "play hard-
ball" scenarios do not have the explanatory power they once did.

Mary Ann Luciano ran recruitment and retention programs for Olsten, Inc., a large temporary employment agency. Her performance ap-
praisals were excellent. She received a job offer from U.S. West, one of the
baby bells created from AT&T's court-ordered breakup (and now part of
Qwest, Inc.), with the title of vice-president and a $75,000 salary. The
CEO at Olsten's, William Olsten, matched the U.S. West salary, promoted
Luciano to VP Field Marketing, and promised a promotion to full vice-
president in one year, contingent upon acceptable performance reviews.[12]

Thereafter a senior vice-president, the vice-president for human resources, and Luciano's supervisor met to formulate a new job description
for Luciano. The participants in this meeting "resented her rapid rise up
the corporate ladder, and the group drew up an impossible job description to ensure that her performance would be unsatisfactory," or so a
court later found. They assigned to her additional duties, such as implementation of a new sales program and management of the incentive program designed to reward top salespeople.

Just before the year was up, and the promised promotion in the offing,
CEO Olsten retired. Under the new CEO, the jealous coworkers started
piling it on. They named Luciano the director of a newly established marketing advisory committee and director of direct mail and telemarketing.
They promised her but did not provide additional staff. Three years after
she had spurned the U.S. West offer, and after more than two years spent
on the treadmill her coworkers had crafted for her, the company informed
Luciano that it was terminating her employment. Her responsibilities
were to be divided between two male executives, one of whom was recruited from outside the company. Although as well or better qualified
than the two men, she was not given an opportunity to compete for one

of the new positions. Human Resources "rebuffed her inquiries about a regional director vacancy without investigating her qualifications."

Mary Ann Luciano's case is unusual in that she introduced evidence of both a glass floor and a glass ceiling at Olsten's. On the glass ceiling element of the case the jury heard testimony that

(i) William Olsten admitted that when he promoted Luciano . . . senior men in the company complained that she could not do the job; (ii) senior vice-president Ramsey stated, "Mr. Olsten shouldn't have promised her the vice presidency"; (iii) [her supervisor] Bingham . . . admitted that "there certainly wasn't any intention on my part to consider her for promotion to vice-president"; (iv) Bingham intentionally gave Luciano an impossible workload without commensurate support staff; and (v) Luciano was denied the promised review [and promotion] despite the fact that she capably performed jobs that were previously or subsequently performed by [three male senior vice presidents]. Proof that the glass floor existed consisted of evidence that[m]ale employees with poor performance records were treated more favorably than higher performing women such as Luciano . . . [F]red Henry, Henry Pittus and Joseph Steffanelli[,] . . . responsible for over a $3 million loss to the Company[,] were nevertheless given promotions, salary raises and transfers to better positions. . . . [G]ereshlak was fired as vice-president of marketing due to deficient performance, but was rehired . . . later into a higher position of senior vice-president of the Northeast Region, and [was promoted again] even though his performance was again found to be unsatisfactory.

Mary Ann Luciano recovered damages in court, although, again, the court reduced the $5 million in punitive damages the jury awarded her to $300,000. To obtain $480,000 in total damages, she endured several years of discovery, pretrial motions, a month-long trial, and an appeal in which Olsten's was represented by Mayer, Brown and Platt, a powerful national law firm.

4. The Targeted Reduction in Force. The mini-RIF is a device that senior managers have utilized to keep the glass ceiling in place. "Reduction in force" (RIF) has become a term of art in employment law. Skilled human resources executives know how to go about accomplishing it. If a company terminates an employee, eliminating her position, the termination is adjudged to be part of the ubiquitous restructurings one has to be

prepared to encounter in corporate life. She probably has no claim. If the position was eliminated and the employee not replaced, it is a "reduction in force." By contrast, if the company hires or promotes a male to take over the woman's position, as Olstens did with Mary Ann Luciano, the woman has the makings of a prima facie case of employment discrimination.

In Elizabeth Bellaver's case, her employer, Quanex Corp, thought it had done it right, using a mini-RIF to end her career at Quanex.[13]

After receiving her MBA at Kent State University, Bellaver was recruited to become marketing manager for Nichols Homeshield, a manufacturer of aluminum products used in making of windows. Bellaver and her family moved west to St. Charles, Illinois. In 1988, the company promoted her to the position of "Product Manager, Engineered Products," with responsibility for give product lines. In 1992, the company promoted her again, to "Product Manager" for twelve lines. In 1996, the company promoted her to "Business Development Manager," with responsibility to prepare market research, identify growth opportunities, and direct new sales efforts.

Bellaver received high praise in her annual evaluations, always being rated "excellent," "outstanding," and "exceeds expectations." In 1996, her supervisor, Michael Penny, general manager of her division, noted that her "problem solving [and] decision making skills leave nothing to be desired."

Shortly after Bellaver's trip west, Nichols Homeshield had been acquired by Quanex Corp., which also acquired a similar manufacturer one hundred miles away, in Chatsworth, Illinois. Quanex began the process of eliminating redundant employees, consolidating functions between its two Illinois plants. The waves of pink slips constituted legitimate reductions in force, as follows: six in 1991, six in 1992, ten in 1993, five in 1993, none in 1994, one in 1995, none in 1996, and in 1997 Elizabeth Bellaver, after ten mostly successful years in various jobs.

Bellaver's employment history was only "mostly" successful because throughout her performance evaluations ran a current of dissatisfaction with her interpersonal skills. In her 1993 evaluation, Michael Penny called her a "bright and talented employee [with] excellent judgment" who was "making progress in her interpersonal skills." "In dealing with others," he noted, "she is continuing to be direct and demanding but less offensive." In 1994, Penny wrote, "Elizabeth is working to improve her interpersonal issues that cause harm to, or at least impact, team performance." Her 1995 and 1996 evaluations contained similar references. Her principal problem was that she did not suffer fools gladly, especially among subordinates. One earlier review was more revealing: "[A] poor listener. Not too tolerant of the less bright. Does not always allow two-way communication. Insensitive often to social environment." Two male employees were listed by name as having complained about Bellaver's treatment of them.

Every coin has two sides. The Nichols Homeshield human resources manager, Patricia Shaw, who herself had been a victim of reduction in force in 1992, testified that Bellaver was a good all-around manager but that "male engineers at the company viewed a woman's presence negatively." "That attitude reflected a double standard," she said, "because the same traits were viewed positively in men." She testified that the male engineers treated Bellaver "unfairly as a woman" and that the company had "a good ole' boy network [that] attempted to keep women out of the male dominated world."

When Quanex formally merged its two Illinois facilities into one corporation, it brought in a new vice-president and general manager. He conferred with Michael Penny, who had complained that he "was tired of continually mopping up the blood after [Bellaver's] interactions with people at the plant." After conferring several times, they fired Bellaver, assigning her responsibilities to two male employees as well as two newly hired telemarketing specialists.

At trial, Quanex successfully invoked the reduction in force defense. Bellaver's pink slip was but one of many in a long process of contraction. She could not point to "a similarly situated employee outside of the protected class who was treated more favorably." In other words, no male received better treatment than females (the "protected class"); men and women alike suffered from the integration by Quanex of its Illinois facilities.

The appellate court disagreed. The trial court had ignored evidence that the corporation left untouched male employees with the same, or worse, evaluations of their interpersonal skills. Quanex had admitted to manipulating the term "RIF" as a pretense for eliminating another female employee in 1992, human resources manager Patricia Shaw. The court saw through the pretense:

> Bellaver's duties were not really eliminated at all; they were merely redistributed among male employees. The prototypical RIF involves a com-

pany that perhaps once employed 100 engineers, but because of a business slowdown or change in product lines, needs only twenty engineers. The rest of the positions are eliminated, not absorbed. There does not seem to be a question that Quanex no longer needed someone to market the HFP line.

The court had seen the pretext before, and undoubtedly would see it again: "[w]e have held that the inference arises in single discharge cases, sometimes called 'mini-RIFs,' where the terminated [female] employee's duties are absorbed by other employees not in the protected class [men]." The mini-RIF can be utilized to keep the glass ceiling intact.[14]

5. The New Boss Phenomenon. New bosses often throw their weight around, establishing their authority, if not their swashbuckling management style, in the first few months in command. In my review of employment discrimination court cases, I found that, in a disproportionate number of cases, woman managers run afoul of a new boss under whom the denouement (termination, firing, faux reduction in force) takes place. Change of bosses seems to be a point of particular vulnerability, or indeed a purposeful strategy whereby adverse employment actions are implemented, for women managers. New bosses delivered the coup de grace to Jennifer Passantino, Mary Ann Luciano, and Elizabeth Bellaver.

The new boss's arrival provided the occasion for latent sexual prejudices to surface in the case of Deborah Zimmerman.[15] Associates Financial hired Zimmerman as an associate vice-president for business development director (BDD). She was one of fourteen BDDs, each assigned a region of the United States. They, and their staffs, marketed financial services wholesale to dealers in goods (Laz-E-Boy, PC Warehouse), who then provided financing to retail consumers. Zimmerman had "decades of experience selling financial services to dealers." Associates recruited her for the job.

After one month, Zimmerman endured one change of bosses. Eleven months later still another vice-president of operations, Stephen Haslam, was appointed as her boss. In the fifty-first day in his new position, Haslam summoned Zimmerman, whom he had never met, to Dallas, where he fired her, allegedly because she "didn't have a good relationship" with one of her supervisors, Senior Vice-President Steve DiUbaldo. DiUbaldo later testified that he had never spoken to Haslam about Zimmerman. Haslam's explanation was laid bare as pretext.

Zimmerman had also always exceeded her performance goals, in the most recent quarter by "a modest amount (about six percent), earning a performance bonus of $1,635" in addition to salary. She was also on the verge of signing two large retailers to contracts with Associates.

One week after he fired Zimmerman, Haslam fired the second of the three female BDDs. He replaced Zimmerman with a slightly younger male employee. At trial he stated that Zimmerman was fired for "inferior performance," although she had met her performance goals. He also stated that she refused to use his "new methodology for contacting dealers," but provided no documentation as to what that methodology might be. He testified that he threw out Zimmerman's and other BDDs' documentation thirty to sixty days after he fired her but that it made no difference because she had kept copies of her weekly and monthly reports as well as her bonus statements, which she had introduced into evidence at her trial. He (or Associates' lawyers) missed the point: records of other BDDs would have shown whether Zimmerman's performance was or was not, on a comparative basis, inferior.

Haslam and Associates lost. They were held liable for $215,000 in back pay and damages and $1 million in punitive damages. Again, the court had to reduce the punitive damages to $300,000, making the final judgment $452,979 in Zimmerman's favor.

Why corporations continue to litigate cases in which the evidence is weak or transparent, or the pretexts for discrimination flimsy and the costs of litigation high, seems mysterious at first blush. It may be just old-fashioned pig-headedness. Or defending losing cases to the bitter end may be a manifestation of that noble sentiment many large corporate law firms espouse: "We will defend each and every one of our clients—to their last dime."

In any case, for women managers in the workplace, installation of a new male boss may herald a time of particular vulnerability, which can result in their termination.[16]

6. Lack of (or Too Much) Femininity (Nonadherence to the Stereotypes). Women must walk a tightrope. If they appear too feminine, superiors evaluate their femininity as "lack of confidence and assertiveness." Superiors rate them low on such qualities as "leadership potential." They hit the glass ceiling, or are stopped well short of it.

By contrast, if women adopt, or come naturally by, male behaviors, bosses mark them down, as they did Elizabeth Bellaver, on interpersonal skills. A woman who is confident or assertive in the workplace is denominated a "bully broad." She is then shunted off into some dead end position. Worse yet she is demoted, terminated, or made the target of a mini-RIF.

This tightrope phenomenon, whipsawing women managers from "not confident and assertive enough" to "bully broad" and "man in a pants suit," is the subject of several glass ceiling court cases.

As a senior associate in the well-known Philadelphia law firm Wolf, Block, Schorr & Solis-Cohen, Nancy Ezold had paid her dues as the only woman in a 28-lawyer litigation department. It was time for the firm to consider her for entry into the high-paying circle of partnership. The partners refused to admit her, finding her to be "too assertive," preoccupied with "women's issues."[17] The partners further evaluated her negatively for being "too demanding" of those with whom she worked. The partners admitted to partnership male associates who had been evaluated as "not demanding enough" and rated lower than Ezold. The partner in charge of the litigation department had told her "it would not be easy for her at Wolf, Block because . . . she was a woman [and] had not attended an Ivy League law school."

The grandparent of stereotyping cases went to the United States Supreme Court, which found ample evidence of discrimination and that discrimination was a motivating factor in the denial by Price Waterhouse, the worldwide accounting firm, of partnership to Ann Hopkins. It took Hopkins seven years and five levels of judicial decision making, with rulings by two trial courts, two appellate court panels, and the Supreme Court (the zeal of the defense being due to the "defend you to your last dime" phenomenon). In the end, the appellate court took the exceptional step of not only awarding Hopkins money damages but also affirming a trial court order that Price Waterhouse's partners admit Hopkins to partnership.[18]

Ann Hopkins rose to the level of project leader at Price Waterhouse. She labored in the firm's Office of Governmental Services in Washington, D.C., where she "played a key role in Price Waterhouse's successful effort to win a multi-million dollar consulting contract with the Department of State." She was viewed as a "highly competent project leader who worked long hours, pushed vigorously to meet deadlines, and demanded much from the multidisciplinary staffs with which she worked."

Partners' comment sheets also criticized her interpersonal skills, one suggesting that she was "overbearing and abrasive":

> One partner described her as "macho"; another suggested that she "overcompensated for being a woman"; a third advised her to "take a

course in charm school." Several partners criticized her use of profanity. [A]nother partner suggested that those partners objected to swearing only "because it's a lady using foul language." Another supporter explained that Hopkins "had matured from a tough-talking somewhat masculine hard nosed manager to an authoritative, formidable, but much more appealing partnership candidate."

Many of those behaviors would go unmentioned in a man's evaluation forms or, indeed, some would be praised by Price Waterhouse partners (among whom 662 of 665 were male).[19]

The PW Policy Board discussed Hopkins, voting not to admit her to partnership, even though she had billed more hours and brought in more business than any other candidate for partnership that year. Denial was not an "up or out" event for her, though. The board voted to "hold" her candidacy with the possibility that it might reconsider the following year.

Afterward, a supportive male partner took Hopkins aside, telling her to "*walk more femininely, talk more femininely, dress more femininely, wear makeup, have [your] hair styled, and wear jewelry*" (italics in court's opinion). In other words, with a woman, outstanding results did not matter. Appearances did.

Ultimately, Price Waterhouse made a decision not to repropose Hopkins for partnership the following year. She sued and each court that considered her case agreed that "sexual stereotyping," not merits, "thoroughly infected the decision making process among Price Waterhouse's partners" when it came to considering a woman for promotion to partner. Nonetheless, Hopkins and her lawyer faced seven years of technical, nitpicking legal arguments by Price Waterhouse and its lawyers.

Coda

That, then, is part of the mosaic fitted into the glass ceiling. Reading any number of the employment discrimination cases demonstrates that the glass ceiling, and its flip side, the glass floor, remain firmly in place in many organizations. They forestall women's upward progress. Many never come within shouting distance of directorships and other senior positions. That may be doubly true, given that the reported sex discrimination cases at middle or high management levels are rare, possibly representing only the tip of an iceberg. At higher managerial levels, the stakes for a female manager, if she should lose, and the problematic nature of employment discrimination cases, especially when more subjective upper-level promotion and transfer decisions occur, indicate that many cases never advance beyond the thinking or discussion stages. Law case opinions reinforce the deductive reasoning in the previous chapter, which illustrates how seemingly innocuous or even meritorious practices, such as the promotion tournament based upon merit, in reality become tools of second-generation sexual discrimination.

3

Prices of Motherhood
Stereotyping, Work/Life Issues, and Opting Out

Work/Life Issues

Over the three decades of the 1960s, 1970s, and 1980s, the proportion of married couple families with both spouses in the workforce tripled, from 28 percent in 1960 to 54 percent in 1990, reaching an apogee at 60 percent in the mid-1990s.[1] Yet "[i]f child care worries are increasingly shared by men and women, child care work is not. Women still do the bulk of all household tasks. Of the women employed full time, 76 percent still do the majority of the housework . . . ," according to sociologist Catherine Ross.[2] This stressful tension between work at work and work at home takes its toll on women, as another statistical snapshot shows: employment among mothers of very small children has been falling steadily.

For example, over the five years from 1998 to 2003, employment among mothers with children younger than one year has fallen from 57.9 percent to 53.7 percent.[3] The trend is more pronounced among more highly educated and upwardly mobile women. They are departing from the workforce, including the ranks of the professions and upper middle management, to bear children, only to postpone or forego altogether a return to professional or management positions. An in-depth *New York Times* piece has described the latter phenomenon as the "Opt-Out Revolution."[4]

Many other working women are making a different choice, one to forego children altogether. In the United States, the number of women over forty who have no children has nearly doubled, to one-fifth of that age group.[5]

The One-Child Alternative

Women who seek to rise to the higher levels of corporate organizations can do so while at the same time having and raising children. They often, however, limit their child rearing to one child, as, for example, exemplars such as Andrea Jung, CEO at Avon Products, or Carleton Fiorina, formerly CEO at Hewlett Packard, have done.

Aspiring women managers and professionals must have excellent day care available sixty to seventy hours per week to be able to work after hours, on weekends, and on out-of-town trips. They must be able to afford child care by others, which has become increasingly expensive, especially in urban settings. They must limit themselves to the maternity leave provided by their employers, and no more, going on a severely truncated "mommy track" of two or three months' duration.[6]

If women executives follow that child bearing prescription, at age thirty-six their income will be 99 percent of the income of their male counterparts. Even then bosses and coworkers may subject themselves to criticism. Toward the end of her three-month maternity leave, one female physician overheard a male coworker say, "She's sure milking the system for all it's worth."[7]

"More" Alternatives: More Children, More Time Off

Women who do "more" in the way of child rearing pay a steep price. The "more" may be extension of maternity leave beyond what the employer corporation allows. The "more" may be the birth of a second child, with a concomitant geometric increase in child rearing responsibilities. The "more" that may prove fatal to career aspirations may be a subsequent leave of absence to attend to children, or a refusal to travel out of town, or to work after hours or on weekends. At age thirty-nine, career women who have in any of those ways pursued the mommy track will earn only sixty cents for every dollar their male counterparts take home in pay. On average, over her lifetime, a college-educated mother who goes onto the mommy track in any of its various forms will earn $1 million less than an equally educated and capable male.

Male Leadership Attitudes

Pronouncements on these issues feature a significant amount of hypocrisy. Typical is a statement by Lawrence Summers, former secretary of the treasury and former president of Harvard University, who has stated that "[r]aising children . . . is the most important job in the world," but later opined that women academicians were not achieving tenure in fields such as math and science because "women with children are reluctant to work the 80-hour weeks that are required to succeed in those fields." He suggested the possibility that differences in men and women long attributed to socialization might be "innate."[8] These (ofttimes contradictory) statements by men caused author Ann Crittenden to note, "[L]ip service to motherhood still floats in the air, insubstantial as angel dust."[9]

Crittenden says further that "[r]aising children may be the most important job in the world, but you can't put it on your resume." Not only is child rearing not rewarded. In many sectors, corporate America penalizes it. Child rearing and household management are considered to have no economic or job-enabling value. "[T]he United States is a society at war with itself. . . . We talk endlessly about the importance of family, yet the work it takes to make a family is utterly disregarded."[10]

Largely because of male attitudes, a stigma attaches to leaves of absence or part-time endeavor that may be necessary to accommodate child bearing and child rearing by women managers, professionals and other female employees. Many employers realize that the corporate organization benefits in the long run when the organization permits a maternity leave and two to three years' part-time work but retains the employee for a thirty year career. When an employee leaves, the corporation loses institutional memory associated with that employee; loses customer or client relationships; loses productivity while the departing employee's position remains unfilled; and suffers a loss in the collegiality and morale of those left behind. The corporation also incurs significant costs in replacing the employee a cost personnel experts peg at 150 percent, or more, of the departing employee's annual salary.[11]

Employers and their managers know these things. Despite the common sense of it, however, male managers and supervisors tend to see not the long- but the short-run view. "Part-time work is highly stigmatized in many departments. . . . Part-time [employees] report isolation, loss of status within their departments, negative comments from supervisors, colleagues and clients, loss of desirable assignments, elimination of advancement opportunities, and relegation to sub-par office space." Law Professor Joan Williams, who heads the Project for Attorney Retention (PAR), which, in a series of reports, examines reasons for the lack of opportunities for women first in law firms and then in corporate law departments, concludes that "[l]ong hours, macho attitudes, competition for limited advancement, and a management that is not itself in a position of [doing the needed] juggling . . . combine to create a culture that rejects or undermines part-time policies."[12]

Opting Out

So what happens? Because of the economic loss they suffer, the hypocrisy they see, or the difficulty of coordinating job and family they encounter, most women in business penalize themselves. They take time out to rear children, the cost be damned, returning to the workforce only when the children have reached high school or college. Or they may stay in the workforce with a part-time position. Or they may retain their position but place severe restrictions (articulated to others or only mental) on their participation (no out-of-town travel, home by 6:00 P.M. every day), which often is fatal to their chances for subsequent promotions.

As one woman executive recounted,

> My erratic work schedule worked well for me and my son, but it was hard on everyone else at my office. I missed meetings; I bowed out of last-minute crises; I won't travel; I couldn't stay late. In short, I was not the kind of employee who could be counted on in a crunch. Dependable, yes, hardworking and competent, yes, but highly restricted. I was passed over for projects I would have liked. . . .[13]

Mommy Tracks

And passed over for promotions as well, according to career women who go on that particular form of the mommy track.

In a paean to family values, women who have chosen (or been forced to accept) one of the alternatives also face (or are forced to accept) another reality. They subordinate themselves to their husbands' careers. If their husbands accept a transfer, they follow, abandoning altogether whatever chance they had for promotion. Opera diva Beverly Sills left New York and the Metropolitan Opera to follow her husband to Cleveland, Ohio. She felt that "my only alternative was to ask Peter to scuttle the goal he'd been working toward for most of 25 years. If I did that, I didn't deserve to be his wife."[14] No "good wife" wishes to rob her husband of the masculinity men associate with the primacy of their careers within the family unit.

For still other educated women who begin in business, at some point it becomes not "family then career" but "family—no more career." Knowing the odds they face in seeking promotion or even survival in their current position, women with children simply quit fighting. They opt out completely, at a high cost both to society and to themselves. The number of children being cared for by stay-at-home mothers increased 13 percent in the 1990s.[15] Many women who look up at the top in their organizations are increasingly deciding that they do not want to do what it take to get there. In fact, this phenomenon affects even the top: *Fortune*'s examination of 108 businesswomen who in recent years had appeared on its annual list of the fifty most powerful women in business revealed that twenty of those women had voluntarily relinquished their positions.[16]

The Leaky Pipe

We have advanced only so far. Women have been pursuing and receiving MBAs, law degrees, and other advanced degrees in numbers for thirty years. In unprecedented numbers, they then enter the workforce. But it is like a leaky pipe. There is a torrent at the supply end but only a tickle at the tap end. The "tap end" of course consists of the ranks of upper middle and upper management from which women could spring upward into positions as corporate directors and CEOs. The Harvard Business School survey of women MBAs from the classes of 1981, 1985, and 1991 found that fifteen or more years later only 38 percent of them were working full time.[17] The leaks in that pipeline, and the resulting losses, both societal and personal, are the "price of motherhood," the title of an excellent book by Ann Crittenden. "[A] 70s feminist peering in the window would be very confused at best and depressed at worst," *New York Times* author Lisa Belkin muses. A Princeton and Duke Law graduate who left her law firm to rear two small children states, "This is what I was meant to do . . . I know its very un-p.c., but I like life's rhythms when I'm nurturing a child."

"One of the misleading impressions [of] the women's movement is that it swept away women's traditional lives, like a sandstorm burying the artifacts of an ancient civilization. The media constantly remind us that women have become doctors, lawyers, merchants . . . ," Ann Crittenden postulates as a reason why society seems so unaware of women's fate.[18] Yet, of married women with school-age children, 28.4 percent are not in the labor force at all. An additional 20 percent work only part time. Only about half of all women with school-age children, numbering eighteen million strong, work full time.[19]

Children and families have not suffered because of women's entry in great numbers into the working world, despite what conservative politicians and religious leaders maintain. Instead, women fulfill multiple roles. It is "career and family," not "career over family." Women juggle both balls by employing a number of artifices.

They delay having their children. They have fewer children. But they invest more time in the children they do have. As women become better educated, they spend more, not less, time with their children. All of this amounts to a phenomenon that has paralleled women's increased presence in business and in the workforce, the shift "from quantity to quality" in human reproduction.

College-educated women in business talk more and read more to their children than their own mothers ever did. They take longer and better vacations with them. They negotiate rather than demand blind obedience to household and family rules. The results are children with more independence, capable of critical thought. Overall, however, the further result of work-life tensions is that fewer women progress in their careers to the point at which higher-ups consider them in the pool from which corporate directors and senior managers are chosen.

Work versus Life

What gets squeezed? Between career and child rearing, the first thing to go is housework. One child of a career woman thought that everybody got dressed in the morning in front of the clothes dryer.

The second thing to go is cooking. In the 1960s the average meal took two and a half hours to prepare. Now it's ready in fifteen minutes.[20] Some families may go a week or longer without sitting down together for dinner. A career woman has her teenage son put the empty pizza boxes out on the garbage only on pickup day so that the neighbors won't know just how dependent her family has become on Pizza Perfecta.

The third thing to go is leisure. There is no longer any time for long walks, bridge games, tennis doubles, and so on for the career woman with children. One woman executive would combine leisure and face time with her children by having her teacher husband bring the children to a city park near corporate headquarters. In fair weather the family would eat lunch at a picnic table and spend an hour together.

And the squeeze gets more severe. Through the 1990s, U.S.-style "turbo capitalism" has steadily lengthened the work day and the work week for white collar employees and managers. We now have the most productive managers in the world, who have the heaviest workload in the industrialized world, exceeding that of even Germany and Japan. For all workers, the average number of hours worked per year climbed to 1,980 in 1995, from a post–World War II low of 1800 in 1982. For higher paid managers, the increase has been more dramatic.

Despite the women's movement, and the increased entry of women into professions and business, "one thing has stayed the same: it is still women who adjust their lives to accommodate the needs of children, who do what is necessary to make a home, who forgo status, income, advancement, and independence" by having children.[21] That fact alone has great explanatory power in explaining the paucity of women on boards of directors and in CEO suites.

A large subset of women who have opted out cite not the gravitational pull of bearing and rearing children but the changing and more burdensome nature of work. Author Lisa Belkin quotes a woman manager who has opted out: "[I]t was not a change I made only because my children needed me. It's more accurate to say that I was no longer willing to work as hard—commuting, navigating office politics, having my schedule be at the whim [of someone else], balancing all that with the needs of my family."[22]

Of the three factors behind the opt-out phenomenon (unfair treatment in the workplace, gravitational or genetic pull toward rearing children, and the changing nature of work itself), a surprisingly high percentage of opt-outs "talk not about how the workplace is unfair to women, but about how the relationship between work and life is different for women than men,"[23] a seeming combination of the second and third factors.

The result is a "quiet exodus" of highly trained women from corporations, consulting, accounting, and law firms. Today young women finish college, go to MBA or law school, acquire skills, develop seniority, accept transfers in order to climb the ladder, work endless hours, make partner, get promoted to the ranks of senior management, and postpone children until their biological clock seems to be winding down. When they do give birth, "they are expected to treat the event like an appendectomy."[24] Despite it all, ultimately they still opt out, exiting corporate America, or becoming a part-time "consultant," or finally resigning themselves to the less demanding staff or "pink collar" job.

The Studies

The 1970s and 1980s produced young women who were determined to "have it all": meaningful careers and promotions, family and children, athletic fitness, travel, and luxurious vacations. How successful have they been?

The answer is not very, at least by objective criteria. One study followed one thousand two hundred college-educated women from 1969 until the mid-1990s, when they had reached the ages thirty-seven to forty-seven.[25] Fewer than 20 percent had managed to maintain both career and family by their late thirties or early forties. The percentage of women who had been graduated from college between 1966 and 1979 and who reached midlife with career intact and children was between 13 and 17 percent of the sample. The women who did not have children were twice as successful in achieving a career as were the women with children.

Another study queried 902 women who had obtained law, MBA, and other professional degrees from Harvard between 1971 and 1981.[26] Fully 25 percent of the Harvard MBAs had left the workforce entirely by the early 1990s. Although 82 percent of the mothers had taken a minimum maternity leave of four months or less, ultimately 70 percent cut back on their careers anyway as their first child grew or after a second child was born.

Subjectively, these talented women—the best our universities could offer—felt "blind sided," in that they never had imagined the difficulty of combining career with family. Many said they had been forced out of the best jobs after they had become mothers. They lamented a corporate culture in which employers are not content with "a dedicated high performing employee. They want your soul." The emphasis on "face time" in the office and the 24/7 work culture (twenty-four hours per day, seven days per week), prevalent throughout corporate America and not just the Silicon Valley, are workplace realities that cause well educated, highly talented women who elect also to have children ultimately to throw up their hands and opt out.

The "Big Four" accounting firm of Deloitte and Touche has for some years had roughly 50 percent of new hires that are women. By 1992, however, the percentage of partners that are women had crept up to only 5 percent.[27] Women reported that asking for a flex-time schedule was akin to committing professional "hari-kiri." Most female CPAs reported that they were afraid that motherhood would damage their careers.[28]

Women have numbered in excess of the 40 percent mark (50 percent in the late 1990s) of law school graduates since the mid-1980s. Normal partnership tracks require seven or so years as an associate before consideration for partner. Yet only 13 percent of the partners, and 7 percent of the equity partners (owners), in the nation's 1,160 largest law firms are women.

A principal reason is the "female brain drain." Workplace demands, the need for face time, the 24/7 culture, the lack of acceptance for flex-time work schedules exist in those settings as well, causing women with children at some point to abandon the partnership track or to quit "the big time" of law or accountancy altogether.

And, in some lines of work, it is getting worse rather than better.[29] In law and accounting firms, the need for expensive computer equipment, high-rent offices, nonlawyer support staff, and other costs has vastly increased overhead. The result is a demand for professionals to bill more hours. From the early 1980s, when expectations for lawyers in large law firms were sixteen hundred or so billable hours per year, requirements (not expectations any longer) have risen to over two thousand hours per year. To bill two thousand hours per year, or forty hours per week for fifty weeks, requires sixty to seventy hours per week of office time. Many women with children simply cannot keep up with the demands. A result is that the rate of elevation to partnership for women actually declined, falling further behind that for men, in the 1990s.

The Economic Value of Child Rearing

The flip side of the 24/7 workplace culture and the demand for face time is the lack of economic value accorded motherhood. As long ago as 1870 it became official, when Francis Walker, an economist who headed the U.S. Census Bureau and who later became president of MIT, solemnly pontificated, "We may assume that speaking broadly [a wife] does not produce as much as she consumes."[30] Ergo, householding and child rearing would not be considered when in the 1930s economists began calculating gross national product.

One hundred thirty years after Francis Walker that remains true. The notion of the "unproductive housewife" persists. Domestic labor is accorded no recognition in the political economic calculations. Those realities have tremendous negative consequences for women who take a "time out" to attend to children.

Economists in other countries have calculated the additions to gross domestic product unpaid work represents, even though most of that work occurs in the home and may be only partly visible. In 1994 the Australian Bureau of Statistics calculated the value at 48 percent of GDP. Other studies have found the percentages to be as high as 55 percent in Germany, 40 percent in Canada, and 46 percent in Finland. In the United States, Nobel Prize–winning economist Gary Becker is the only advocate of treating parenting, which is after all the means whereby valuable human capital is replenished, as economic production.[31] The official United States position, and the position adopted by most male law firm partners, senior accountants, economists, and corporate higher-ups, is that child rearing and other forms of domestic labor have no economic value.

Not only is child rearing uncompensated and unrecognized, but also career women who do it often suffer penalties in the workplace. Not only do they suffer penalties, but those penalties are also disproportionate, starkly revealing the discrepancy between what we say we value (families and child rearing) and what we actually value, in terms of pay, promotions, and flexibility in the workplace.

The Legal Prohibition against Discrimination

In 1978, Congress enacted the Pregnancy Discrimination Act, or PDA, which amends Title VII of the Civil Rights Act of 1964. Title VII now defines the term "because of sex" as including "because of or on the basis of pregnancy, childbirth, or related medical conditions." As amended, Title VII commands that "women affected by pregnancy, childbirth, or related medical conditions shall be treated the same for employment-related purposes."[32] When these provisions are read into the fundamental command of Title VII, then it is unlawful for an employer "to fail or refuse to hire or to discharge an individual, or otherwise to discriminate against any individual with respect to his compensation, terms, conditions, or privileges of employment because of . . . sex," which includes pregnancy.

Evidence that disproportionate penalties are visited upon women who become pregnant or overburdened by child care responsibilities thus may be gleaned from a portion of the Title VII court cases. In these cases, women have paid something approaching an ultimate, or at least a very high, "price of motherhood."

Childbirth: Case One

Celia Zimmerman graduated from Princeton University and obtained her MBA from Southern Methodist University. On the basis of her experience in the financial sector, the chief executive officer of Direct Federal Credit Union, David Breslin, hired Celia as manager of financial planning. Her first sixteen months on the job were "a tour de force," in the court's estimation. Zimmerman performed not only her own job but also that of her direct supervisor, Controller Joseph Capalbo, who was on an extended leave due to the death of his wife. During that period, Zimmerman attended eighteen of twenty board meetings, making presentations at several of them, and was promoted to director of finance.

Sixteen months into her employment Zimmerman notified the CEO that she was pregnant. The next day he trimmed her responsibilities and reduced the size of her staff. Her baby was then born prematurely, causing her to take a six-month pregnancy leave.

Upon her return to Direct Federal, she discovered that the CEO and controller had stripped of her management role. Back on the job, Controller Capalbo had assumed her responsibilities. The company moved her to a small office, which she shared with a noisy wire transfer machine. Managers excluded her from the senior management retreat, which previously she had organized. The CEO shunned her, refusing to recognize her at meetings. Capalbo assigned her projects unrelated to finance, such as facility redesign, or to monotonous tasks beneath her skill level, such as underwriting twenty to thirty home equity loans per day. She received her first "poor performance" review, contrasted to earlier reviews praising her as a "team player" and a "role model."

After she filed an EEOC complaint, the CEO called plaintiff out in a public meeting, stating that "she was not woman enough to come face-to-face with me." The CEO and Controller Capalbo continued to tinker with her job description, assigning more menial tasks and tasks unrelated to her finance expertise. Through discovery (questions and requests for production of documents and other things, which parties are authorized to make to one another in litigation), CEO Breslin obtained plaintiff's journal. Attorneys often advise workers who believe discrimination may be occurring to record in a journal instances of what they believe to be discriminatory treatment. Breslin tried to turn Zimmerman's coworkers against her by reading to them (not always accurately) entries she had made in her journal.

Plaintiff sought psychiatric help to cope with stresses related to her job and treatment by her superior. Her physician-psychiatrist diagnosed severe depressive disorder, put her on medication, and advised her not to return to work. Three months into her medical leave, Direct Federal terminated her.

Oddly enough, a jury found against her on her basic Title VII claim but did find for her on her retaliation claim. The jury awarded Zimmerman $330,000 in compensatory and $400,000 punitive damages, which the court of appeals upheld.[33]

Childbirth: Case Two

GAP, Inc., hired experienced store manager 39-year-old Joanna Laxton not only as a manager but also to open a new store in its Old Navy chain. On her first day at work, Laxton informed the regional assistant manager that she was pregnant. The regional assistant manager became visibly angry, berating Laxton for not appreciating the fact that the baby would be born around Thanksgiving, a busy time for GAP stores.

After working 12–15-hour days, Laxton opened the new store on time. The store earned strong revenue, and won a national sales contest in its first month of operation. Laxton received monthly $1,000 performance bonuses. Nevertheless, Laxton also received a "Written Warning" and a "Final Written Warning" (strike two) for petty violations, such as leaving the store by the back door on one occasion, in violation of GAP company policy, or spending $85 to treat her store personnel to pizza, which exceeded by $10 her discretionary spending allowance.

While Laxton was working seventy hours per week, the regional assistant manager recruited the zone human resources manager and then the zone trainer to prepare official warnings to Laxton and to visit the store. GAP then faxed a "Final Written Warning" (strike three) to Laxton at her home on her day off, a Saturday. The following Monday a GAP auditor arrived at her store from headquarters to fire Laxton, replacing her with a male manager. He testified that he had never before been called upon to fire an employee, and it was not a normal part of his job. GAP took the unusual step of faxing the final warning to Laxton's home so that it would be in hand when the auditor arrived on Monday to fire her. The auditor then denied knowing she was pregnant, but contemporaneous photographs showing that Laxton obviously was pregnant were admitted into evidence at trial.

A jury awarded Laxton $484,000 in damages, an amount tinkered with but basically upheld on appeal.[34] It seems astonishing that a national company such as GAP would side with bureaucrats in its organization (regional assistant manager, zone human resources manager, store auditor) against a hard-working store manager, relying on pretexts such as $10 overspending, to "gang up" on an employee whose pregnancy might in the future inconvenience a manager who would have had to find a temporary replacement during the busy season. Yet these types of pregnancy discrimination cases arise with frequency, almost in parody of the movie *Dumb and Dumber*.[35] They also demonstrate how pregnancy can terminate completely the rise of a woman manager as she moves upward through an organization. She never gets within shouting distance of the point at which she legitimately can begin to think of upper management.

Child Rearing: Case Three

Other pregnancy cases center around child care and employers' inflexibility with regard to female employees' temporary needs following childbirth.

Shireen Walsh worked as an account representative for National Computer Systems. She gave birth to a son who in infancy had medical difficulties. Walsh's supervisor docked Walsh for arriving at 7:37 A.M. (seven minutes late) on a day when the child had been sick. The woman supervisor, Barbara Mickelson, denied permission to leave at 4:30 because

Walsh's son's day care center closed at 5:00 P.M. Evidence was that other account representatives regularly left at 3:45 P.M.

The supervisor put an "Out—Sick Child" sign on Walsh's cubicle when Walsh missed work, yet she never placed notes on other absent representatives' cubicles. Supervisor Mickelson openly referred to Walsh's son as "the sickling." The supervisor informed Walsh that she must make up "every minute" missed for her son's medical appointments. Neither Mickelson nor any other supervisor forced other employees to make up time for those kinds of absences. "At one point, Mickelson threw a phone book on Walsh's desk and told her to find a pediatrician who was open after hours." As a result of the stress the supervisor placed upon her, Walsh fainted at work and was taken to a hospital. Upon her return to work the following day, Mickelson greeted her, "you better not be pregnant again." Thereafter Mickelson steadily increased Walsh's workload and directed profanity toward her on a regular basis.

The court of appeals affirmed judgment of $625,525.90 entered upon a jury's verdict in favor of Shireen Walsh.

Child Rearing: Case Four

The school setting, one would guess, would be one in which supervisors would demonstrate a degree of flexibility to accommodate subordinates' child rearing responsibilities. It was not so in the case of Elana Back, who served as school psychologist at a New York State public school with the bucolic name of Hillside Elementary. In her first two years at Hillside, Back's supervisor rated her "outstanding" and "superior." Back then took maternity leave, returning to Hillside three months later. Thereafter the school principal and the district personnel director did a complete about-face.

They inquired about how Back was "planning spacing her offspring," told her to wait until her son was in kindergarten before having another child, and entreated her with "please do not get pregnant again before I retire." The principal told her "that she did not know how [Black] could perform [the] job with little ones." "If my family was my priority . . . maybe this was not the job for me," Back reported being told on more than one occasion. "They stated that once I obtained tenure, I would not show the same level of commitment I had shown because I had little ones at home." The district director of personnel and the school principal re-iterated to her that her job "was not for a mother."

Upon applying for tenure, Back received a negative evaluation. The evaluation stated that, although her written evaluations were uniformly positive, "informal interactions with her had been less than positive" and certain parents and teachers had "serious issues" with Back. The personnel director then became hostile, falsely accusing Back of mis-handling cases and removing positive letters from Back's personnel file. There followed the first negative formal evaluations ("below average" markings), followed by termination of Back's probationary appoint-ment.

Raising an issue germane to the corporate setting as well, the court of appeals "asked whether stereotyping about the qualities of mothers is a form of gender discrimination." It concluded that the "plaintiff has as-serted genuine issues of material fact in her gender discrimination claim" and remanded the case for trial in the district court.

It seems incredible that, in the pregnancy and child rearing discrimi-nation cases, a law (the Pregnancy Discrimination Act) can have been on the books for over twenty-five years. Yet, within organizations such as a public school district, the global retailer GAP, National Computer Corp., or a federally chartered credit union, persons in authority proceed bla-tantly to discriminate against women who have chosen to bear children, or devote even modest amounts of extra time to their children when the children are of tender years. The court cases continue to come forward, if not as a rushing river, then as a steady stream, raising questions about the efficacy of laws and their ability to transform, completely at least, behav-iors everyone seemingly should decry. The cases also constitute evidence as to what many aspiring women face, or believe they might have to face, if they take a few years' time in a 40-year career to have children and to devote some time to raising them.

Return to the Career Track

A development yet to play out in full is the return of opt-out mothers to the workplace and employees' and coworkers' reception of them. For many women, absences taken to rear children are not permanent. "It's not black and white: it's gray. You're working. Then you're not working.

Then maybe you're working part time or consulting. Then you go back." Childbearing and child rearing are merely chapters; they're not whole books.[36]

This is a hot-button issue in the work-life debate at present: How liberal will employers be in permitting women to return to the workforce and under what conditions will they permit such returns? One legacy of the high-tech and dot-com boom has been that nonlinear career tracks have become much more acceptable. Employers are less put off by resumes with gaps and zigzags.

Related issues arise as women revert back to full-time labor not only from leaves of absence or part-time work but also from job sharing, compressed or unconventional work schedules, and other flexible arrangements more enlightened employers provide. "Returning to full time would mean either firing the job share partner or increasing the . . . department's personnel budget—neither of which is likely to be feasible."[37] Those are difficult "crunch type" questions for even the most enlightened or liberal of employers.

There is also an equity issue. How will women returning to the profession or other workplace after a 3-, 5- or 7- year hiatus be integrated with those who did pursue a linear career path? Part of the answer lies in the team-production and collaborative nature of work in the modern world. In many companies, managers and professionals move from team to team with higher-ups assembling ad hoc teams suited to the task at hand. The upward linear progression in the workplace is a thing of the past: "Now the logic of corporate careers is less likely to resemble the bureaucratic pattern of an orderly progression of ever-higher level's and more remunerative jobs. Instead, people are more likely to move from project to project, rewarded for each accomplishment, like professionals," notes sociology professor Rosabeth Kanter.[38]

An irony of the modern workplace is that while some features (the 24/7 management culture, high overhead to support) may drive women and mothers from it, other features (team production and collaborative work environments) may ease the return of women to the workplace after children have reached a degree of independence.

A related, and unanswered, question is whether corporate hierarchies will permit women returning to the workplace to resume not only work but also ascension to positions as senior managers and candidates for corporate boards of directors.

Persistent Pay Disparities between Men and Women

In Leviticus, God instructs Moses to tell the Israelites that women, for purposes of tithing, are worth thirty shekels while men are worth fifty—a ratio of 60 percent, recounts Ann Crittenden.[39] From 1930 to 1980, "the value of women in the workplace eerily reflected the biblical ratio: [t]he earnings of full-time working women were only 60 percent of men's earnings." In the 1980s this condition began to change. "By 1993 women . . . were earning an average of seventy-seven cents for every dollar men earned," but by 1997 the gap had widened again, with women's earnings falling to 75 percent of men's.

Yet those statistics are for women who work in job classifications that contain both women and men, undoubtedly influenced by Title VII's proscription of discrimination on the basis of sex. When pay for women who work in exclusively female occupations is lumped with women's pay in joint occupations, the average earnings of all female workers in 1999 was 59 percent that of men, right at the biblical ratio.[40]

A survey of Stanford Business School MBAs, class of 1982, who were still employed, found that women earned on average $81,300 while men earned $139,100, a ratio of 58 percent. By the late 1980s, 1974 women graduates of the University of Michigan Law School earned 61 percent of what their male counterparts earned.[41]

Still another survey of two hundred female MBAs focused on a group who had made only slight detours down the "mommy track." These women had, on average, taken 8.8 month off for child rearing activities. They were, however, less likely to receive promotions and earned 17 percent less than their female counterparts who had had no gap in employment with their companies.[42]

An Attitude: Motherhood Does Not Matter

The penalties women suffer for slight deviations from the career track are "strikingly harsh." The question that arises is, why?

Many career women report that bosses, male and female, believe that mothers who work part-time or take time out for child rearing responsibilities have a "recreational" attitude toward work. They also report that "face time" matters more than actual productivity in many companies, so women who leave promptly at the end of the work day or who have taken "time-outs" suffer. Of course, the majority of women who do those things do them to attend to their children and their activities.

Many more women in business are choosing not to have children. Of female college graduates, 28 percent are childless by age forty. The Catalyst, Inc., female MBA study found that only 20 percent of the female MBAs had children while 70 percent of the male MBAs did.[43] The percentage of all women who remain childless is also rising, from 8 percent in the 1950s to 10 percent in 1976 to approximately 18 percent today.[44]

Why Motherhood Does Matter

The future supply of human capital may be inadequate. In many industrialized nations, including all the nations in the European Union, the birth rates have fallen below the death rates, and dramatically so.[45] So the supply of human capital is not being replenished. Increases in productivity do not fill the gap. The result will be that standards of living will fall. Other nations, in East Asia or elsewhere, will leapfrog other states in terms of per capita income and standards of living. The United States may not be far behind nations such as Spain or the Netherlands, where demographers and sociologists have begun to evaluate, and bemoan, the consequences of falling birth rates.

Corporate America seems to regard child bearing and child rearing as just a lifestyle choice that some women may make, just as other women dedicate leisure time to improving their tennis game or to training for a marathon. Bearing children and raising them well, however, is not just another lifestyle choice. It is far more important than playing tennis or running a race. It is the source of human capital, a sufficient supply of which is critical to the society as a whole. No corporate executive, male or female, should tolerate the attitude that "well, it's their choice" when women in the organization take time off or "time out" for child rearing.

Prescriptions

Besides such a zero tolerance policy within corporate organizations, what other sorts of solutions will lower or eliminate altogether the price of motherhood? What kinds of things can corporations do to eliminate the "built-in headwinds" that mothers face on the career track?[46]

Consider the recommendations contained in Ann Crittenden's book, the "Price of Motherhood," for a comprehensive proposal:[47]

1. Give Every Parent the Right to a Year's Paid Leave.
2. Provide Equal Pay and Benefits for Equal Part Time Work.
3. Eliminate Discrimination Against Parents in the Workplace.
4. Facilitate Women's Return to the Workplace and to the Promotion Ladder under Conditions Equitable to All.

After analyzing work/life issues in law firms and in corporate law departments,[48] professor of law Joan Williams offers a more detailed-oriented set of recommendations:

1. Individualized Flexibility. Best-practices employers allow many different types of flexible schedules, including leaves of absence, part-time work, job sharing, sabbaticals, telecommuting, and the ability to "buy" time off through acceptance of less pay for periods of time. They maintain web sites that outline options available to employees.
2. Keep an Open Mind, with the Attitude That Any Job Can Be Done Flexibly. Williams's group found corporations in which personnel on flexible schedules were doing every job previously thought of as suitable only for traditional full-time endeavor.
3. Fairness: Make Alternatives Available to Everyone. This approach avoids even the appearance of favoritism. It also recognizes that, although they may not have children, single, gay and lesbian, and other, employees have parents, siblings, significant others and visitors who may make demands on the employee's time.
4. Employ Part-Time Parity: Proportionality. Employees in flexible arrangements should have, insofar as is possible, pay, benefits, bonuses, and opportunities for advancement, but some of these benefits will differ for them in that they will be distributed only on a proportionate basis. They will not be denied altogether.

5. Equal Advancement Opportunities. The pervasive notion is that employees cannot advance as managers or supervisors unless they adhere to a standard schedule. Professor Williams offers evidence that this notion is misguided. Some companies may slow the part-time employee's progress along the advancement track, but they do not derail it altogether.

6. Equal Job Security. Those employees in flexible job schedules should not necessarily be the first laid off or fired or face the prospect of having to adhere to a standard schedule or else be fired.

7. Measure and Reward Quality Performance. An old saw states that "you manage what you measure." If evaluation processes measure face time and 24/7 availability, those are the quantities employees will produce and the quality of output will be left to chance. Effective evaluations measure "effectiveness, judgment and quality of work so that the amount of time spent in the office becomes less meaningful." Professor Williams, along with countless human resources managers, finds that 360-degree reviews in which superiors, peers, subordinates, customers, and others evaluate employees more accurately gauge what most employers actually wish to manage.[49]

Women in the workplace and executives, male or female, sympathetic to the necessity of permitting women the flexibility to balance child rearing and careers, need to keep constantly in mind the importance of child bearing and child rearing to a society. They must also be aware that, especially over the longer haul, child bearing and rearing bear little relationship to job performance and to the overall value of a female employee to a corporate organization. Until the "price of motherhood" is lowered or eliminated, and many of the "built-in headwinds" buffered, the ultimate goal to which corporate America pays lip service—greater representation for women on boards of directors and in CEO suites—will remain a totem of hypocrisy.

4

In a Different Register
Women in the Governance Model

The Stereotype

As will be amplified in chapter 10, the model for governance in the United States demands of directors a rugged individualism. Independent directors are to confront and, if necessary, remove underperforming CEOs. In critical matters, such as adopting takeover defenses or planning the corporation's overall response to a hostile takeover bid, the independent directors must take charge, convening in executive sessions to make the decisions on the corporation's behalf.

Men may not perceive women, even ones with records of long-standing service to the corporation, as possessing the requisite quantum of rugged individualism to function well in the new governance milieu. For example, an early analysis of female attorneys' trial practice techniques by Messrs. Conley, O'Barr, and Lind, which finds "that women's language is really powerless language," has been particularly influential.[1] In the authors' view, "[w]omen's tendency to be indirect is taken as evidence that women don't feel entitled to make demands," according to linguist Deborah Tannen.[2]

In a like vein, as recently as 2002, in a Title VII glass ceiling discrimination case, the CEO and CFO of a large Pacific Northwest grocery chain refused even to countenance promotion of two long-serving women executives to officer positions, on grounds that women generally are "too emotional."[3]

Studies in linguistics show that many women speak and act in ways different from those of men. Thus, because they speak "in a different register," and even though it may not be the case, male board and committee members may perceive women as lacking the confidence and assertiveness necessary for board service and senior management positions.

Similarly, because many women speak with rising intonation in their declaratory speech, men may perceive women as more emotional and less dispassionate than men, even though, again, that may not be the case. The how-to books, such as that by Catalyst's Sheila Wellington, advise women in business to "lower the pitch of your voice" and not to "show emotion."[4]

Early on linguist Erving Goffman demonstrated that women smile more and do so more expansively than men.[5] This fact places women in a double bind. "[W]omen are expected to smile more than men are. Furthermore, women are seen as severe and lacking in humor if they rarely smile. . . ."[6] Men perceive women who smile too much as "frivolous" and "hare-brained."

This chapter raises the question of whether a disconnect exists between the modern model of corporate governance and the speech and actions of women.

Assertiveness and Individualism

Corporate statutes have long provided that a corporate director who is present is deemed to have consented to a matter voted upon unless she takes affirmative steps to see that her "no" vote is recorded in the minutes of the meeting, or she files a written dissent with the secretary of the meeting immediately after the meeting. And, in the current governance regime, a director can expect to have many more matters come to a formal vote than would have been the case twenty or thirty years ago.

A centerpiece of U.S. corporate law is the "business judgment rule." One salient feature of the rule is that the directors must have made a judgment or decision—the rule does not protect directors who do nothing.

Experienced directors complain that many boards reach decision by consensus or a process of accretion over several weeks or months. The business judgment rule, with its emphasis on making a formal judgment or decision, forces directors to act as a legislative body, bringing matters to formal votes and voting them up or down, with recordation of who voted in which way. The modern rule has brought excessive play acting, a certain amount of confrontation, and a necessity for more individualistic behavior to the boardroom.

What do the business judgment rule and deliberative processes in corporate boardrooms have to do with women on boards of directors? The contention here is that the last twenty years' events have transformed the lens through which nominating committees and senior executives evaluate potential nominees for the board or women coming up through the ranks, seemingly destined for senior executive positions or service as independent directors on other boards.

At the same time, the great increase in the number of independent directors necessary and the decline of the insider-dominated board, term limits on board service in many companies, the decline in number of male trophy directors, and similar developments should open many more boardroom doors for women. But that has not occurred.

Early Linguistic Research

In 1975, the linguist Robin Lakoff of the University of California at Berkeley made the claim that there is a distinctive "women's language" that differs from male speech.[7] She argued that women who use this mode of speech appear less assertive and confident than those who use male speech patterns. Lakoff went on to assert that this "women's language" not only reflects women's subordinate position in society but also reinforces that subordination, including what feminists term "economic subordination," much of which occurs in the workplace and in the corporate management hierarchy.[8]

Lakoff's pupil, Georgetown's Deborah Tannen, also theorized "that systematic differences in women's and men's characteristic styles often put women in a subordinate position in interactions with men."[9] Tannen, however, had reservations. She thought that context (the "framing") often was as important as gender in the speakers' use of linguistic strategies. In other cases, other facets of the situation, such as body language or cultural traits, overwhelm and trump the strategy examination of linguistics alone reveals.[10]

Lakoff's, and later Tannen's, contentions sent many researchers off on the trail to test their theories. Researchers contrasted the speech of women of different age groups.[11] Others examined the speech of a generation or two gone by.[12] Another researcher conducted empirical studies on the effect of women's speech in the courtroom.[13]

A professor of criminal law, Janet Ainsworth, applied Lakoff's and other linguists' theories to the subject of custodial interrogation of women by the police.[14] Ainsworth's ideas in "In a Different Register" have application to corporate governance. They are useful in analyzing subtle influences not only in the way men may evaluate women for service on corporate boards but also in the way higher-ups may evaluate men differently than women as women move up through the executive ranks.

In English, men and women do not speak different dialects, as they do in some other languages, but gender does correlate with the use of different linguistic registers. A register is a characteristic way of speaking that is adopted by certain members of a speech community under specific circumstances.

Use of a particular register depends on the context of the speech occasion. A register may be associated with certain settings or situations, or it may be correlated to social role or relationship. Not all women share the speech characteristics of the register and some men will exhibit that register of speech, but researchers have shown that a particular register is gender linked. Sociolinguistic research on gender and language supports the claim that women disproportionately use a characteristic speech register.

Some contexts will maximize gender differences in language. One context relevant to the corporate setting occurs when there exists a power disparity between the speaker and the hearer, as in female subordinate to CEO, or rising woman executive to a member of the board of directors or the nominating committee.

Other contexts minimize gender difference. An example linguists use is of an impersonal, formulaic interaction, such as making an inquiry at a public information booth.[15] A linguist with blinders on may record "pass the food" as an interruption at the dinner table. Many linguists think interruptions to be more the province of male speakers and of attempts to dominate conversations. All present at the dinner table, however, would regard "pass the food" as an aside or overlapping bite of language.[16]

Characteristics of the female speech register that may have application to women's role in corporate governance include (1) avoidance of imperatives and the use of indirect interrogatories instead; (2) increased use of modal verbs; (3) use of hedges; (4) rising intonation in declaratory statements; and (5) silence or quiescence in the face of adversaries or aggressors.

1. Avoidance of Imperatives. Users of the female register avoid using the imperative, substituting interrogative forms. As Lakoff states, "An overt order . . . expresses the (often impolite) assumption of the speaker's superior position to the addressee, carrying with it the right to enforce

compliance, whereas with a request the decision on the face of it is left up to the addressee."[17]

The imperative is the most starkly assertive of grammatical forms. In adult speech it may seem to be the prerogative of the male:

Place the order. (male)
Hire X as a consultant. (male)
Should we hire X as a consultant? (female)
Get it done this week. (male)
Can you get it done this week? (female)
Meet with me at 10:00 A.M. Friday morning (male)

Demands phrased in the interrogative form sound less presumptive and more tactfully deferential than baldly stated imperatives. Modern interpersonal relations allow for less use of imperatives by either males or females but, because the exercise of power represented even in the occasional use of imperatives is considered "unfeminine," "women are socialized from earliest childhood to avoid directly ordering other people to do things." In corporate settings, bosses may perceive reticence as a deficiency most women exhibit.

The widespread American association of indirectness in conversation with female style is "not universal." In Japanese and other Asian cultures it is the indirect manner that is more nearly universal. A Greek father may use the indirect with his children. A European aristocrat communicates with servants and subordinates only in an indirect manner. "Indirectness, then, is not itself a strategy of subordination. Rather it can be used by either the powerful or the powerless."[18] In American business, however, the tendency is strong, if not universal, to associate indirectness in conversation with subordination.

2. Increased Use of Modal Verbs. Users of the female register make far more frequent use of modal verbs such as "may," "might," "could," "ought," "should," and "must."[19] Those verbs hedge the pragmatic impact of a sentence or phrasing, making the speaker appear perhaps less confident or assertive when that may not be the case at all.

You might hire X as a consultant.
You should meet with me Friday at 10:00 A.M.
The audit committee ought to discuss that.
You could travel to Houston next week.

Strong modal verbs "such as 'should,' 'ought,' or 'must' carry the implication that the statement is the product of surmise, deduction, or process of elimination rather than an unmediated statement of fact," Professor Ainsworth notes.[20] Again, penultimate perceptions that a subordinate or coworker lacks confidence or acts upon surmise, while having their foundation solely in speech patterns, may lead to ultimate perceptions of women that put them at a disadvantage in corporate governance settings or selection for promotion.

3. More Frequent Use of Verbal Hedges. Users of the female register make more frequent use of qualifiers called hedges, lexical expressions that function to attenuate the emphasis that otherwise the statement might carry. Speakers use hedges such as "about" or "around" with respect to numerical quantity to render the statement less precise and thereby less contestable. Hedges such as "kind of" or "to some extent" soften the assertion by qualifying the application of the idea expressed, thus undercutting assertiveness.

Other hedges, such as beginning expression with the qualifier "I think" or "I suppose," or using "maybe" or "perhaps," convey the sense that the speaker is uncertain about the statement. Alternatively, those hedges convey the notion that the speaker prefers not to confront addressees with bald assertions.[21] A similar hedge, castigated by businesswoman Gail Evans in her how-to book, is "I'm sorry," as in "I'm sorry to interrupt you" or "I'm sorry that our profits forecasts have been revised." "The word *sorry* is a female addiction. We use it so often, to express so much, and in many contexts it has virtually no meaning. It's just something we say, the iceberg lettuce of conversation, a kind of verbal filler."[22] Lakoff observed that women use hedges more frequently than men do.[23] Frequent use of hedges "arise[s] out of a fear of seeming too masculine by being assertive and saying things directly."

Boardroom actors and CEOs may misinterpret hedged speech by female subordinates or director candidates as signs that the speaker is lacking in the confidence and assertiveness for which modern corporate settings and board service call.

4. Rising Intonation in Declaratory Statements. Users of the female register exhibit a further "paralinguistic characteristic: its speakers use rising inflection in making declarative statements."[24] Ordinarily, English speakers use rising intonation to signal a question or to express incredulity.[25]

The use of rising intonation in ordinary declaratives when the speaker does not intend to express uncertainty or incredulity is a gender-linked trait.[26] American men tend to pronounce their sentence endings at the lowest level of intonation that they customarily use whereas women frequently adopt a rising "sentence terminal." Women also exhibit a much greater dynamic range of intonation, four or five separate levels of intonation while men seldom use more than three levels of intonation.

Rising intonation at the end of declarative sentences and use of a greater range of levels of intonation indicate emotion, or extreme emotion, in male speech. Male addressees may assume that the same is true in female speech when that is not the case at all. Men in boardroom or corporate positions hearing female speech with rising or slightly rising intonation may be reinforced in preconceived and sexist notions that "all women are emotional" or that women bring to business decisions and corporate settings an inappropriate level of emotion.

This assumption is more than trivial. As one volume of advice for women by Catalyst's Sheila Wellington puts it

Eschew emotion. Certain behaviors work against you in the workplace. . . . Emoting about anything, be it your own screw up, frustration at yet another photocopier jam, work poorly presented by your staff . . . is one sure way to make others uncomfortable in the workplace. Keep your cool; emotionalism makes you look unreliable and unsteady and reinforces the stereotypes about women that men already hold.[27]

Professor Ainsworth concludes that "[t]he overall pragmatic effect of the female register is the substitution of indirect and tentative locutions for strong and assertive modes of expressions."[28] Speakers utilize the female register to convey uncertainty, soften the presumptiveness of direct speech, or preempt opposition from the addressee. Pioneer Robin Lakoff, upon whose work Professor Ainsworth and others have drawn, sums it up:

Men's language is the language of the powerful. It is meant to be direct, clear, succinct, as would be expected of those who need not fear giving offense, who need not worry about the risks of responsibility. . . . Women's language developed as a way of surviving . . . without control over economic, physical or social reality. [To survive under those conditions] it is necessary to listen more than speak, agree more than confront, be delicate, be indirect. . . .[29]

Cognitive psychologists tell us that we tend to hear what a speaker says to us as though we had said it and to hear what we think the speaker said rather than what she actually may have said. Men in positions of power hear emotion in the female register when there is none; they detect lack of confidence or assertiveness when the reality is that there is not.

In its doctrine and its models, corporate governance presumes that actors will utilize direct and assertive speech—a mode of expression characteristic of men. Gender bias results in the treatment of prototypically male behavior (confident, assertive, powerful) as a synonym for *all* human behavior, at least on the rarified level upon which corporate boards act and on the pathways to get there.

5. Silence or Quiescence in the face of Adversaries or Aggression. Overall, Deborah Tannen finds that "male speakers tend to be competitive and more likely to engage in conflict (for example, by arguing, issuing commands, and taking opposing stands) and females tend to be more cooperative (for example, by agreeing, supporting, and making suggestions)."[30]

Implications of the Theory

The unwitting incorporation of a male normative standard in business and corporate settings may be nearly invisible, but it is not inconsequential. Women whose behavior fails to conform to the behavioral norms encoded within the governance norms are penalized on the route to the boardroom, reaching the destination far less frequently than would be predicted on the basis of the demographics.

Drawing a broader conclusion yet, the characteristically male preference for assertive speech, rather than suggestion, innuendo, implication, or inference, may be seen as but one instance of a more generalized male preference for assertive behavior in corporate and business settings that goes back 150 years. As sociologist-turned-historian Stephanie Coontz observed,

> In eighteenth-century Europe and early nineteenth-century America . . . [t]o men were assigned all the character traits associated with competition: ambition, authority, power, vigor, calculation, instrumentalism, logic, and single-mindedness. To women were assigned all the traits as-

sociated with cooperation: gentleness, sensitivity, expressivism, altruism, empathy, personalism, and tenderness.[31]

Women are assigned those traits whether they possess them or not. Then the unstated but real preference for the assertiveness and competitiveness men are presumed to possess by those in executive suites hamstrings women in many areas of corporate life and not merely on the route to the boardroom.

Prescriptions

Women rising in businesses should not necessarily change, wearing power suits and becoming "bully broads," in the lexicon of one popular work.[32] Male directors, directors on nominating committees, CEOs, and others who evaluate women in business settings should become aware that they may be evaluating through a lens colored in a manner that creates inaccurate perceptions of female behavior and often puts women at a distinct disadvantage in corporate life.

The changes necessary may be subtle. One firm found that hiring of qualified women MBAs increased when the company lengthened interview times from thirty minutes to an hour. Women were much more likely to speak out about their talents and accomplishments in the longer interviews.[33]

Another prescription may be to refrain from sidetracking women into the "soft" side, or "pink-collared" sector, of business, where a different register and qualities such as less assertiveness or competitiveness are perceived by male superiors as advantages, or at least not disadvantages.

Thus women have a greater presence in human resources and staff positions. Feminist scholars have demonstrated that, when women have occupied a field in great numbers, a "male flight" from that field occurs. For example, women now dominate the residential real estate agent market while men continue to dominate the more lucrative commercial sales areas.[34] Feminization of a field signals that the field has begun to deteriorate in status, within a corporation or among trades.[35] Presence on the soft side of business or in a field that is thought to have "deteriorated" holds women back when they seek promotion later or aspire upwards toward the boardroom.

Combination with Other Realities

When one blends in the material from an earlier chapter, "Prices of Motherhood," with the information in this chapter, as well as with additional traits males presume all women possess, the gauntlet women must run to the boardroom or the CEO suite lengthens. The ideal worker takes little time off and certainly none for child rearing and household management. Though this ideal-worker paradigm does not define all jobs in the corporate setting, it does define the good ones.[36] The good jobs will be positions that require fifty to seventy hours' work per week, and they will not be on the soft side of business, into which organizations are far more likely to shunt women.

Women may be ideal workers, but they may be constrained by the field they occupy (soft side of business), the register they use (different), the traits they are assigned (not assertive, emotional, intuitive), and the other roles they are required to play (mother, household manager).

This chapter draws on the work of Professors Lakoff, Tannen, and Ainsworth, among others, applying their teachings in the field of linguistics to women in the corporate environment and to corporate governance. The chapter adds to the mix food for thought on why women have not succeeded to board and CEO positions in the numbers we expect. "In a Different Register" (this chapter and the title of Professor Ainsworth's seminal article) may also point to a disconnect between the prevailing corporate governance model and unstated presumptions of male behavior and inaccurate perceptions of women, which are based upon appearances rather than reality, on the one hand, and reality itself, on the other, as women progress through corporate life and are evaluated on the road that may lead to the boardroom.

5

Bully Broads, Iron Maidens, Queen Bees, and Ice Queens

The last chapter dealt with a long-standing stereotype of women that is based upon language they may use that may be antithetical to their interests in the workplace or the boardroom. Women may strike others as emotional as individuals or on particular occasions whether they are or not. Stereotypes develop on the basis of appearances that are often contrary to reality.

This chapter deals with more recently developed stereotypes of women in business, at the other end of the spectrum. Generally speaking, under this set of stereotypes, women are criticized less for being timid or emotional than for adopting male behaviors; for harsh, overly assertive conduct; for excessive zeal and loyalty to the company; and for unrelenting pursuit of perfectionism by their subordinates as well as themselves.

When these latter stereotypes are applied to them, women progress in the organization but only to a point. The stereotypical behavior that raised them up to middle management then begins to work against them. Higher-ups grant no further promotions. Superiors shunt them aside into a dead end track, or terminate them altogether.

The Bully Broad Hypothesis

The Women's National Basketball Association started out in the late 1990s with mostly women coaches. Very quickly, owners and general managers weeded out a good percentage of the women coaches and replaced them with men. One of the principal reasons, social psychologist Jean Hollands reports, is that many of the first-generation coaches were what, in infelicitous terms, Hollands labels "bully broads."[1] What made the women succeed as players, and in coaching at the lower levels of the sport, did them in when they reached the upper echelons of coaching: "Why have . . . the women washed out as coaches? For the same reason that they have washed out in the corporate . . . world. . . . Women can't get away with the harsh command-and-control style that many male coaches and managers can."[2]

In corporate promotion tournaments, and other evaluative rituals that women, as well as men, must go through as they ascend toward upper management, superiors view overly aggressive women as accomplished but deficient. Bully broads are perceived as lacking the diplomatic and strategic skills and outlooks that higher-ups deem necessary to reach the higher rungs on the ladder.

The Iron Maiden Phenomenon

When a woman (or other minority) is the only one, or one of only two, of her type in an organization—say, a group of middle managers who meet periodically—she will be a token, subject to a set of performance pressures unlike those that dominant members of the group experience. Because the token stands out, the dominants will heighten the boundary between the token and the dominants, emphasizing rather than minimizing differences.[3]

The token (women) may react in several ways. One reaction is to attempt to become one of the boys. Joke telling (or at least not being off put by ribald stories), participation in and viewing of sports contests, and other assimilative behaviors may aid a token woman in becoming an insider, one of the boys.

Another reaction is to resist pressures that might trap a token into a role (one of the boys, for example). The dominants often perceive this sort of behavior as tough. In her work, "Men and Women of the Corporation," Rosabeth Moss Kanter terms this perception of a woman by the dominants as the "iron maiden" perception.[4] If a token woman insists on full rights in the group, displays her competence in a forthright manner, cuts off sexual innuendos, refuses merely to be one of the boys, and so on, she will be regarded with suspicion and distance by the dominant male members of the group. The dominants and superiors will accord her bully broad–like status whether or not the underlying reality calls for such treatment. Women who resist role encapsulation, such as behaving like one of the boys, often are stereotyped as iron maidens, more militant and aggressive than they really are. At some point, male coworkers will leave them to flounder on their own. Within their group, they will find no peers sympathetic to them when they encounter problems. Coworkers and higher-ups may abandon them.

The Queen Bee Stereotype

The assertiveness and ambition with which these stereotypes deal often bring promotion. The Queen Bee syndrome occurs when the first woman to reach a certain job classification or management level tries to exclude other women from the same level, status, or job classification. She may treat women subordinates coldly. "Once some managerial women get a taste of power, they may be afraid to share or delegate it because they fear they're going to lose it, so they hold on. They stay aloof," author Carol Gallagher posits.[5]

Queen Bee behaviors are often cited as examples of "women's cruelty to women." They rise up out of insecurity and, often, a warped sense of competition. Organizational psychologists observe that some women in business compete not just to win but to conquer or to crucify opponents, real or perceived. Men and women "who have been involved in healthy competition (such as participation on sports teams) typically know how to compete more effectively than those who do not."[6]

The Ice Queen Stereotype

Women who remain silent but appear judgmental in the extreme and who are rigid, feeling that their way is the only way to accomplish a task fit under this stereotype, as has been described by Jean Hollands. "[The Ice Queen] is reserved and steely. People shy away from her because they expect her to judge them." These women tend to remain silent, "afraid of revealing their real feelings because often they are perceived as being negative" as well as judgmental.[7] They frequently "turn their frustration on to other people. They always look to the other person as being the source of the problem."[8]

The advice books for women in business (titles include "How to Succeed in Business"; "Smash the Glass Ceiling"; "Play like a Man, Win like a Woman"; "Learn the New Success Rules for Women"; "Get the Corner Office"), of which there are dozens, are filled with colorful descriptions of stereotypes of behaviors women should avoid.[9] The four just reviewed, however, for the most part capture the substance of the descriptions and advice.

The advice books are right. Women in business should seek to avoid the behaviors and the characterizations upon which the stereotypes build. Women will find it easier to avoid those behaviors if they better understand why many women in business act in the ways they do.

Insecurity and Overcompensation

Managers do not necessarily have to adopt a confrontational style, yet that is the overcompensating management style the Bully Broad or the Iron Maiden may adopt. It is the style of a wet-behind-the-ears army lieutenant. Yet, partly out of insecurity, and partly because the technique worked for them in the lower management ranks, many middle-level women managers continue with a confrontational leadership style. An important point to be made, however, and one that Hollands fails to recognize, is that the style may not be sex based at all but rather is the result of organizational settings in which many women managers find themselves. Thus it is that stereotypes such as the Bully Broad, Iron Maiden, and Queen Bee are generated.

This genre of women and other middle managers worry too much about getting the job done, and not enough about the people with whom they work or over whom they have authority. There may be complaints by subordinates to Human Resources or to the manager's supervisor. Despite the faults, Carol Gallagher observes that "companies and individuals alike get seduced by the worker who seems to produce more than anyone else. They are the stars, so it is difficult to find fault with the star just because people are complaining all around her."[10]

"Bully Broads" are "intense intimidating dynamos. . . ." However, "[i]ronically, these remarkably capable and talented women who aspire to power are handicapped by the very courage it took them to rise through the ranks." There is a high burnout rate among them.

They also only go so far up the ladder of an organization. They "[a]re often loved, praised, and promoted until they become a liability, and are [then] eventually ostracized or dismissed."[11] These women managers focus on the goals and the results, rather than on the people and relationships, and thus do not fare well over the longer haul. They are in a hurry to get the job done. They do not even notice when people get run over in the process.

Earlier we considered the increasingly subjective nature of the promotion process as managers rise toward the top of an organization.[12] "Criteria for 'good decisions' or good management performance also get less certain closer to the top." Professor Kanter finds that a result is that those in charge of the promotion process will tend to put "trust and homogeneity at a premium."[13] Due to the vacuum created by the subjective nature of the evaluative process, they also will tend to rely much more on stereotypes such as Bully Broad, Ice Queen, Queen Bee, and the like. Women managers seeking promotion then carefully avoid stereotypical behaviors.

The Advice

Jean Hollands bases her conclusions on training and counseling she has done for female managers at Cisco Systems, Intel, Hewlett Packard, Wells Fargo, Netscape, and many other northern California–based companies. Aggressive women who rise rapidly through the ranks have to undergo a difficult transformation. They must become more statesmanlike, more strategic in their thinking and actions. If they continue to emulate their male counterparts, or some of them, they are very likely to plateau or be marginalized within the corporations for which they work.

Hollands has developed rules by which women middle managers should live. Some are trite, and bear little discussion. For example, "Don't Tick Off the President [or] the CEO" (rule 1) seems to go without saying. A perfectionist may correct the CEO's grammar without seeing that such an action may be suicidal. An overly aggressive manager may be critical of the CFO, oblivious to the fact that board members and the CFO have worked together for twenty years.

Another obvious precept is to refrain from harsh and judgmental words such as "stupid, incompetent, ignorant, or lazy."[14] Aggressive women managers must mask impatience with coworkers or customers. They must drop from their vocabularies altogether labels that are deprecating or insulting. Attack phrases ("I could kill him," "Let's hammer them") evidence overaggressive attitudes that the manager must shed as she moves up through the ranks.

Some advice that Hollands dispenses is familiar, found in the myriad advice books on the market, such as "Create Allies (Lots of Them)."[15] Aspiring female managers may be contemptuous of coworkers, regarding them as relatively passive and too prone to engage in small talk. Fast-track female managers may not learn that "[i]n the new management era, collaboration [with coworkers and others] is a fact of organizational life." They simply do not "grasp the notion of collaboration at a gut level." Mentors and support groups within an organization become increasingly important over the longer haul.

These rules are important, but with a caveat, which is never given. It is important for women to adhere to some, or most, of these precepts to get to what sports fans refer to as the next level. As they break through that level toward the very top, however, as chapter 13 demonstrates, the paradigm shifts again. Some of the very behaviors women managers may have avoided creep back into the picture, albeit in mutated forms. To become a senior manager, or win a seat at the boardroom table, women managers must show a different form of risk taking or aggressiveness, or they must exhibit aggressiveness combined with diplomacy, or they must adapt some similar form of new behaviors that will position them for selection at the very top.

Other Rules

Some other standard prescriptions for women managers, formulated by Jean Hollands and others are as follows.

"Keep in Mind That 85 Percent of the Rest of the World Is Conflict Avoidant."[16] Corollaries that flow from this principle are that aspiring managers "should dress out of power periodically." They should work to drop mannerisms such as folded arms and cross facial expressions.

"Don't Burn Bridges—Ever."[17] Some individuals burn bridges because they crave finality and hate ambiguity. "[They] prefer a harsh ending over no conversation at all. Or [they] cut people off [telling themselves] 'I don't need her.'" Bully broads hang up on telephone operators who take too long. They are sentence finishers for others in conversations and in meetings. This is strong type A behavior that a manager rising through the ranks must eliminate.

One (later terminated) aggressive executive described her manner of burning bridges to author Carol Gallagher:

> I am brutal on incompetent males and females. I basically would not continue the relationship. I just won't work for or with those people. And I have to be honest—I've crushed them before I severed the relationship. I don't want them anywhere near my organization. . . . I walk away and refuse to participate in anything they do. I take opportunities . . . to publicly disgrace them. I distance myself physically as well as professionally.[18]

"Perfectionism Kills."[19] Perfectionists seem to have no "discernment software" programmed into their heads. "Everything and everyone has to be lined up in order, right, straight, correct, and complete." In small jobs, perfectionism may serve a ministerial employee well as he or she goes about tasks at others' direction. As one rises in the ranks, supervising others instead of being supervised, perfectionism has the reverse effect. Criticizing everyone and everything may cut short a career or cause a diversion into a nonline or nonsupervisory position. "[B]alanced employees who pace themselves will not wear out" and will have a greater chance of success in the long run.

A perfectionist who sets the bar extremely high for her subordinates "often sees her staff become more frustrated than motivated." In that way, perfectionism disempowers subordinates. Perfectionism also disempowers the superior. She will refrain from taking strategic risks out of fear that she will be unable to achieve perfection. Perfectionism is linked to isolation and its pursuit generally is "a career limiting move."[20]

"You Don't Own the Company."[21] Excessive loyalty to the company may easily tip over into rigidity and overcommitment to the organization and its goals. As an example, Hollands describes "Nancy,"

> [who] took on all the problems of the company. Each employee seemed to be her personal challenge. She was furious when people left the company. [O]verblown expense accounts were her prime targets for rage. She was Chief Technical Officer, not Chief Financial Officer, but . . . *everything* was [her] personal battle.

In spite of Nancy's loyalty to the company, she was placed on probation. She had intimidated too many employees and the real CFO was fed up. Of course, she didn't see it that way, here she was, trying to save the company's resources, and all she got back for her fierce loyalty was probation.

"Avoid All or Nothing Thinking."[22] A coworker or supervisor may be a platonist: it is "their way or the highway." Such persons tend not to rise high in an organization. The woman manager about whom Hollands writes "believes there is one right way and it is only right to take that right way. All or nothing folks such as these believe that life is black and white." They use words such as "always," "never," and "absolutely." With them, you are in or you are out. There is no gray area, no capitulation, no compromise. They tend always to be in a critique mode when supervising or reviewing the work of others.

By contrast, those who rise in organizations bring a practical, big-picture management style to the table. They sense when to "cut and paste and when to go for 100 percent perfection." Women managers who aspire to the highest levels of management learn to sketch out and follow (albeit not slavishly) a decision tree. At times, they have learned even to be "open to the beauty of chaos theory." They have learned not always to judge or be in a constant critique mode.

Sex-Based Responses to Organizational Settings

Years ago sociologists and organizational theorists advanced Bully Broad, Queen Bee, and similar behavioral models. In 1937, psychoanalyst Karen Horney authored *The Neurotic Personality of Our Time*. In her work, she contended that the traits associated with these phenomena are not sexually related but merely universal human responses to the organizational settings in which women often find themselves, as tokens, the first or one of a few of their kind, and in lower-power leadership positions.

People, such as traditional women managers in low-level positions, who have the ability to do so, attempt to dominate others when they feel anxious or helpless, inferior or insignificant. As a protection, the psychologically powerless turn to control over others. They want to be right all the time; they are irritated at being proven wrong. They cannot tolerate disagreement. They become critical, bossy, and controlling. When people are rendered powerless in the larger arena, they may tend to concentrate their power need on those over whom they have even a modicum of authority.

That the neurotic response is to organizational settings rather than being sex based is corroborated by research Stanley Hetzler conducted in the 1950s with lower ranking air force officers, all of whom were men.[23] Officers of lower rank who had little advancement potential favored directive, rigid, and authoritarian techniques of leadership, seeking control over subordinates. Subordinates were their primary frame of reference for their own status assessment so they found it important to "lord it over" their subordinates.

These behaviors produce a vicious cycle that spirals downward. Relatively powerless authority figures who use coercive and demeaning tactics provoke resistance and aggression, which prompts the authority figure to become even more coercive, controlling, and behaviorally restrictive. Low-power leaders, Professor Kanter summarizes, attempt to "control their subordinates, keep them from learning or developing their own styles, jump in too quickly to solve problems, and 'nitpick' over small things their subordinates do differently."[24]

One refuge of the low-power leader is excessive rules orientation. Relative powerlessness, coupled with accountability, the position in which many women managers may find themselves, provokes a cautious, low-risk, play-it-safe attitude. Getting everything right is the response of those who lack other ways to impress those above them. So, in turn, they demand this ritualistic, by-the-book conformity from subordinates.[25]

Attitudinal Surveys

In her pioneering book, Rosabeth Kanter concludes, "[N]o research evidence makes a case for sex based differences in either leadership aptitude or style."[26] Yet in numerous studies in the 1940, 1950s, 1960s, and 1970s both men and women workers expressed strong disinclinations to work for women bosses. A 1965 *Harvard Business Review* survey of one thousand nine hundred male and female executives reported that two-thirds of the men and one-fifth of the women stated that they would feel uncomfortable working for a woman. Very few of either sex (9 percent of the men and 15 percent of the women) felt that men would feel comfortable working for a woman.[27]

A 1940s study found that 99.81 percent of a large sample of women workers preferred a male supervisor, for the following reasons:

1. Women bosses are too jealous. Their positions go to their heads. They boss for the mere sake of bossing, to remind you that they are in charge.
2. Women bosses take things too personally. They are not businesslike.
3. Women bosses are overly concerned with efficiency and routine details. They bother about small petty things.
4. Women bosses supervise too closely. They delegate only superficially.
5. Women bosses find more fault. They are too critical.[28]

These characteristics of less desirable leadership styles do not correlate to sex or bully broad contexts at all. The portrait painted by these surveys of workers and others has one central characteristic. Professor Kanter concludes, "*It is a perfect picture of people who are powerless. Powerlessness tends to produce those very characteristics attributed to women bosses.*"[29]

Again, though, skewed or not, what the studies show is that many of the behaviors attributed to bully broads or other women managers (iron maidens, ice queens) do not relate to sex but to the organizational settings in which the bulk of women managers historically have found themselves.

The times have changed. Increasingly, women do advance upward in organizations. They move from relatively powerless leadership positions. What one finds from surveying the literature is that there exist bewildering arrays of seemingly contradictory sociological analyses/explanations and how-to advice for women in business. How to reconcile the advice and the various explanations is the key.

If they are to reach the boardroom and the executive suite, or at least the pool from which candidates for those more lofty positions emerge, women must go beyond mastery of some or all of the rules, tedious at times, about behavior. They must also have a grasp of the why's and wherefore's behind the suggestions for behavior modifications. Beyond that, and perhaps most important of all, women must realize that the path they must follow may take many twists and turns as they move toward the higher ranks. Different times, and different positions, will place premiums on different behaviors, or different aspects of a set of behaviors, much more so than with male counterparts. There is no "one size fits all."

PART II

Climbing the Corporate Ladder
Myths and Realities

6

Routes to the Top
The Advice

Goals

The highest peak, of course, is the CEO suite. Eight women now in office have scaled that height among Fortune 500 corporations and, overall among publicly held companies in the Fortune 1000, the number is fifteen. The next level is the boardroom, to which women in business might reasonably aspire. Within this paneled sanctuary, members of the board enjoy Chippendale furniture, catered luncheons, prestige, and name recognition in business and other spheres.

The standard advice for women is to work their way to the top, moving up through the ranks of large businesses in phases. The journey may require a lateral move or two, from one corporation to another, often with an accompanying promotion. Although from there on the advice on just how to get to the top is contradictory, as the chapters on the "Bully Broad"[1] and a "Tale of Two Women" show,[2] the theme that does emerge is to work one's way up the ladder in a corporate setting.

The Standard Advice

Pamela Thomas-Graham, the CEO of CNBC.com, an NBC subsidiary, advised younger women to do three things.

The first thing is to aim high. Thomas-Graham exhorts would-be superachievers to have no fear. "If you have to be the first, be the first, and take it as a challenge, not something to discourage you."[3] She was the first woman of color from her high school to apply to Harvard College, which she did even after a guidance counselor attempted to dissuade her.

The second thing—and here Thomas-Graham echoes advice found in much of the literature—is to find mentors. In fact, the advice is that mentors are like stocks. Women in business should build a diversified portfolio of them. Thomas-Graham "has had a mentor to coach her in public speaking, and one to help her weigh her early career opportunities." She had mentors from college, from graduate school, and from McKinsey & Co., the prestigious consulting firm at which she began her career.

The third thing is to maintain balance. Thomas-Graham sits on several for-profit and not-for-profit boards of directors. She rises at 4:30 each morning to write murder mysteries. She and her spouse are raising a 3-year-old son, although as the chapter "The Price of Motherhood" shows, the views on parenting and pursuing a corporate career simultaneously are mixed.

Each year *Fortune* publishes its list of "America's Most Powerful Businesswomen."[4] In the 2001 version, the subtitle was "Patient but Not Passive." Examining the careers of fifty women, the authors began with their conclusions:

> For some 30 years—ever since women started jockeying for power in the workplace—patience has gotten a bad rap. [Women in business] have felt the need to make bold pronouncements and rush to action. . . .
>
> Now, in more muted times, patience may be about to reap its own reward. In FORTUNE's annual survey . . . we see the emergence of women who came to power slowly. . . . [T]hey stayed with a company, steadily building influence there, and rose to power through determination and insider knowledge, not promises and self-promotion.

Andrea Jung, who now is CEO of the remade Avon Products, followed this pattern but interspersed it with two lateral moves. She began at Bloomingdale's, followed her boss and mentor to I. Magnim, and then finally climbed the rest of the ladder at Avon. The six years she then spent as the head of marketing at Avon "gave her the knowledge to revive the troubled company faster than anyone expected when she became CEO."

Jung also emphasizes the importance of a mentor: "The first woman CEO at Federated Department Stores had been my mentor at Bloomingdale's. She's the first person to whom I attribute a lot of my success. She believed in me."[5]

Catalyst, by and through its long-time president, Sheila Wellington,[6] dispenses the same or very similar advice. Three keys to successful advancement are networking, choosing the right conduit to the top, and finding mentors. Rosabeth Moss Kanter notes, "If sponsors are important for the success of men in organizations, they seem absolutely essential for women. If men function more effectively as leaders when they appear to have influence upward and outward in the organization, women need even more the signs of such influence and the access to real power provided by sponsors. . . ."[7]

Networking

Surveys of women in business indicate that "exclusion from informal networks . . . [is felt to be] one of the top barriers to success" for women. Wellington notes,

> We women watch men leave together for lunch as we bolt down a cup of yogurt at our desks. Then, at day's end, we see men heading out together for drinks and more talk, while we go pick up the kids, pick up dinner, pick up the dry cleaning. . . . During these informal networking sessions, men are building their lifelong contact base.[8]

In an informal network, besides enjoying socialization, members can offer practical advice on how to close a deal, deal with a particular personnel problem, or "handle a looming disaster." Within one's circle of contacts, a woman in business "can exchange information about your specialty, your industry, the economy." Information is power. An informal network is often the forum in which women will obtain information.

Some women in business, feeling that the networking needed is with men rather than women, take up golf, or begin watching Monday night football, as means of entry into a network comprised largely of men. Sociologists find those behaviors typical defensive reactions when women and other minorities find themselves in positions as tokens, as the only one, or one of only two, of their kind in a work group, job classifications, and so on.[9]

While not necessarily to be condemned, those steps are often not necessary. Seeking out and befriending other women across the organization may lead to successful networking. The techniques job placement counselors espouse also work well within organizations. Making a point of having lunch or coffee with a new colleague each week and obtaining from her another name or contact snowballs the size of one's network within and without the firm.

"A network grows exponentially," observes Wellington. "The best personal network forms a river of people into which more and more helpful people flow from various tributaries all the time."[10] A career counselor gives her observation that older, successful businesswomen "have an existing and integral group of individuals—friends, colleagues, professional and personal mentors—who are there for them over time and for whom they are available, too."

The experts point to bad networking as well. "For years, books . . . had focused on those bulging Rolodexes and the need for female managers to glad-hand their way to the top." In this model, which Carol Gallagher describes (but scorns),

> [N]etworking connotes pressing the flesh, handing out business cards, and developing rather superficial relationships at social functions and "networking" gatherings. [O]f the initial seventy [highly successful] women interviewed, *nearly all scorned this approach.* Although you may meet hundreds of people by attending conferences, membership functions, and breakfast forums, the relationships you form there are often too shallow to be meaningful or even helpful.[11]

Some of the better conceived advice speaks in terms of "building alliances" rather than mere networking. That advice urges formation of key, longer lasting alliances with 20–30 persons, no more than 10–15 percent of whom are in one's own business unit, with the rest divided evenly between those without the organization and those within but across the breadth of the entire company.[12]

Networking occurs outside the firm through participation in civic and community endeavors. "Nonprofits make an excellent training ground and stepping-stone for future work on corporate boards."[13]

Choosing the Right Career Path

A second ingredient of success within a single organization is choosing the right conduit toward the top. "Most organizations have two paths. One path includes the jobs that involve running the businesses; these are line, or operational jobs. The other path is the staff side—the human resources, legal, communications, finance functions that support those in the line jobs." According to Catalyst's Wellington, "I can't stress this enough: working in a line position as early as you can will give you the experience in management and revenue responsibility that is critical to advancement."[14]

Line jobs are difficult for women with children. The hours are less predictable and the stress may be much greater than in staff jobs. Also, the male corporate mentality may be a pretext but it seems real nonetheless. Eighty-two percent of male CEOs say that lack of significant general management or line experience is the most crucial factor restraining women in their quests for top positions. According to one CEO, "[it's] not that women haven't been in the pipeline long enough to advance: it's what they've done while they are in the pipeline."[15]

The advice that women must not only advance but advance along the "right" career path has become repetitive. "[The] major obstacle for women is not getting the key business experience that will allow them to claim the top positions. [O]verall women and [male] CEOs agree that a lack of profit and loss experience is the biggest barrier preventing women from rising to the top of corporations," was the conclusion a major Catalyst study reached.[16]

Women's groups have come to refer to support work done by staff, and undervalued in many corporate settings, as "invisible labor."[17] The staff work often is essential but, in the final analysis, given only lip service. The assisting woman staff person may be applauded and told "we couldn't have done it without you," but when the higher-ups distribute promotions and rewards, they distributed them to the "rugged individuals" who assertively promoted their own ideas and to those who had "line" responsibility. Often such lip service marks the height of intracorporate visibility for invisible labor.

What is a staff job in one organization may be a line job in another. In a consumer products company, marketing and brand management positions may be considered line rather than staff jobs. Some positions— human resources, corporate secretary, shareholder relations, corporate foundation positions—are sidings that while they do not derail the career train may leave it stranded where it sits. On the other hand, a human resources position nearer the operational heart of the company, at a plant or other facility away from headquarters and the rest of the staff, may be an astute career move in early midcareer. In her study of Indsco (Industrial Supply Corporation), sociologist Rosabeth Kanter found that, despite knowledge of the prevailing wisdom about the importance of line responsibilities, "[c]areer paths automatically flowed from a [certain] position because the job provided a person with exposure, visibility, and connections. Central headquarters jobs could have that potential so people lined up to move to headquarters almost regardless of the specific opening."[18]

Exposure, visibility, and connections may then be a quasi-substitute for line experience. A combination of the two may be better yet.

One reason for the greater representation of women in staff positions is that, despite their best efforts, senior managers shunt women into staff roles from which they find it difficult to emerge. Once in human resources, for example, always in human resources. This is what Wellington refers to as "glass walls." Everyone knows of the glass ceiling phenomenon women in business encounter as they attempt to rise to the very tops of organizations. By contrast, glass walls "represent invisible barriers that prevent women from moving between functions and getting the experience of the variety of responsibilities that organizations require for upward movement."[19] Glass walls are as real as glass ceilings.

Nonetheless, Wellington's strongest imperative is that "[c]ertain jobs, no matter how good they are, won't take you to the very top of most organizations. If you have set your sights on the pinnacle . . . you must have some experience with the bottom line. That means a line job—one with profit and loss responsibility."[20]

An Essential: High Quality Mentors

The last principal ingredient in the prevalent formula for routing one self to the top is finding one or more mentors. "Everyone Who Makes It Has a Mentor" was the title of a well-known piece in the 1978 *Harvard Business Review*.[21]

Mentors can provide many of the same things that members of an informal network may provide. They may advise on how to close a deal, handle a particular personnel problem, or put out this or that brush fire. They also may provide broader strategic advice or information: suggesting possible steps for the woman executive ultimately to reach her goal or examining the political landscape within the company and advising the woman executive how to deal with it to move through and beyond the ranks of middle management.

Marie Knowles, the CFO at Atlantic Richfield, opined at a Catalyst conference, "[Mentoring] is the thing women don't get [in corporate settings]. We don't get told to stop doing that or 'Gee, you're really good at this, but you need to be thinking about developing that skill, too.' Or 'Do you know how much you ticked off that person in that meeting.'"[22]

Many times the capable mentor may be close at hand. "Good bosses make great mentors. Where it works, that's the best mentorship you can have," relates Anne Mulcahy, who later became CEO of Xerox.

Sheila Wellington distills her thirty years' learning on the first page of her book:

> [T]he single most important reason why . . . the equally talented men tend to rise higher than women is that most men have mentors and most women do not. . . . Mentors are more important to career success than hard work, more important than talent, more important than intelligence. Why? Because you need to learn how to operate in the work world . . . and mentors can teach you how. . . . [T]hat translates into a person who can hook you up with the experiences and people you need to move ahead. . . . Mentors can show you the ropes. And pull strings.[23]

For women in business this may be difficult, for "[w]hen women train their sights upward, they often see no one else in senior management who looks like them. Even in organizations that have made women's advancement a priority, there aren't enough women mentors to go around."

Of course, it is extremely helpful for an ambitious woman to have a female mentor, but many (though perhaps not all) of the functions mentors perform may be performed by a male mentor, who may become an avuncular or patriarchal figure to the mentee. In fact, the British use the term "office uncle."

Reservations about Mentors

A few caveats about mentoring are in order. Mentors disappear. They transfer to another location or move on to a competitor or other company. They may be victims of downsizing or a reorganization. Mentors may also become overprotective, especially if they have become the kind uncle or father figure whose faults Rosabeth Kanter identifies:

Many women object to the protectiveness that they perceived in their [sponsors] that "encased" them "in a plastic bubble," as one put it, and rendered them ineffectual. Anyone who is protected loses power, for successes are then attributed to the helpful actions of others, rather than the person's own actions. Women complained about the "people who want to move walls for me instead of saying, 'Hey, here's a wall. Let's strategize working through it.'"[24]

Certain sponsors may then engage in "negative mentoring," advising a woman to move sideways into human resources or other staff positions, out of a well intentioned conclusion that their mentee needs sheltering from the sudden storms that arise in line or other staff positions. Most of the "how-to" advice for women in business recommends that women retain the ultimate decision over their career choices and, hence, destiny.

Mentors, or sponsors, often provide "the occasion for lower-level organization members to *bypass the hierarchy:* to get inside information, to short-circuit cumbersome procedures, or to cut red tape. . . . [They] also provide an important signal to other people, a form of '*reflected power.*' . . . Proper use of a mentor or sponsor, however, may be an elusive thing, capable of abuse by the mentees, who must "be careful about the way they use the reflected power of the sponsor." For example, Kanter emphasizes, "You can't use it with your own manager or you get into trouble."[25] A "fast tracker" or "rising star" should never use sponsorship to run roughshod over the chain of command.

What is to one person mentoring may be to another person a "star system." In many corporations' management ranks such a system holds sway. Stars of the first magnitude, those managers within one or two reporting levels of the CEO, have one or more stars of lesser magnitude in the organization whom they champion. Merit becomes largely irrelevant. The young or lesser star rises because she is the favorite of stars of the first magnitude. Rosabeth Kanter notes,

> Sponsorship is sometimes generated by good performance, but it also can come . . ."because you have the right social background or know some of the officers from outside the corporation or look good in suit." . . . Boy wonders rise under certain power structures. They are recognized by a powerful person because they are very much like him. . . . When women acquired sponsors, the reasons were often different from the male sponsor protege situation. In one case, officers were looking for

a high performing woman they could make into a showpiece to demonstrate the organization's openness to women.[26]

But the leading star may fall, temporarily or permanently, from the firmament, in which case the lesser star may fall even further. The whims of the CEO may determine who is in favor that day, that week, or that month. The system very much resembles the king's court at Versailles.

Both from corporate-governance and from career standpoints, a star system in a corporation is a snake pit. Backstabbing and rumor mongering are common. For example, this author observed first-hand a star system in operation at a major forest products giant, during the tenure of an eponymous member of the founding family as CEO. A thirty-something MBA, who had risen rapidly from the ranks, fell from favor after his ascendent star fell from on high and left the company. Other rising stars then pulled the knives and went after their fallen brother, predators pouncing on a wounded animal. The victim was gone from the company in nine months, consigned to working for a firm importing automobile tires from China.

So, any rising woman manager should ask herself whether what she sees is a good-faith mentoring system, a corrupt "star" system, or something in between. She can then act accordingly. She should be aware of the possible detriments, as well as the benefits, and the ins and outs of mentoring.

Negative Advice: Careers to Avoid

Empirical studies in business management literature advise on what women should avoid and demonstrate why they should do so. For example, even though "an increasing number of women choose entrepreneurship [over careers with firms] out of frustration with demanding and inflexible work environments,"[27] women must be aware that the choice may be a pronounced one. Professor of business Joan Winn finds that "business ownership [is] not compatible with raising a family." On the other hand, she also demonstrates that entrepreneurship may seal off for women any route they formerly had toward the top of major corporations.[28]

That, then, is the current and standard advice for women in business who wish to rise toward the top and, possibly, push on through the glass ceiling. Build a network, find good mentors, choose the right conduit or career path toward the top. Stay within one or possibly two organizations. Be patient but not passive. Merit and hard work will be rewarded. That is the advice. Now let us look at the evidence.

7

The Road to the Top
The Evidence

Being patient but not passive and working one's way up through an organization internally may be the worst route to the top for women, at least when the top is defined as a seat in the boardroom. In the Fortune 500, in 2001, excluding the five CEOs who sat on their own companies' boards, there were only nine women "inside" directors in 2001.[1] They held seats at United Parcel Service (52), PepsiCo (94), Pepsi Bottling Group (237), retailer Kohl's (293), Avon Products (310), Southwest Airlines (316), Security Pacific Life Insurance (354), Caremark RX (384), and Maytag (395), the appliance manufacturer.

In truth, as discussed in chapter 11, the trend of the last twenty years has been decidedly away from inside directors. Publicly held corporations will have two or three at most. In a bygone era, but not so long ago (twenty or twenty-five years), insiders would have been a majority, or at least a critical mass, of directors serving on the board.[2] This turn away from inside directors affects men and women alike. It also renders obsolete the advice to patiently work up vertically through an organization, at least if an ultimate objective is a board seat. Be that as it may, the evidence seems to show that more men are likely to gain a board seat through climbing the internal ladder than will women.

The Preferred Route

And the best way for a woman to become a director of a Fortune 500 company?

Be a tenured professor at Harvard—in law, economics, business, or even medicine. Thirteen women professors from Harvard held twenty-one Fortune 500 board seats, according to proxy data filed with the SEC in 2001. The other Ivies had six women professors altogether, each with one board seat, from Cornell, Columbia, Dartmouth, Penn, Princeton, and Yale.

The women presidents of Penn and Brown, Judith Rodin and Ruth Simmons, respectively, come on strong both as high-salaried university presidents and as holders of multiple board seats. Rodin, then the second most highly compensated university president in the United States, earned a corporate-size $698,325 in pay and benefits in 2000.[3] When Rodin's four directorships (Aetna Insurance [63], American Airlines' holding company AMR [98], Electronic Data Systems [106], and Young & Rubicam) are added to Simmons's four (Goldman Sachs [42], Met Life [47], Pfizer [53], and Texas Instruments [163]), Rodin's and Simmons's incomes head toward the $1 million mark and the rest of the Ivies pull closer to Harvard's total number of directorships.

The other significant competitors to Harvard are not close. In academe, they are led by Georgetown, with three women holding Fortune 500 board seats, followed by the University of California at Berkeley, the University of Chicago, Cooper Union, and George Mason, with two each.

Research Design

The methodology for my study entailed sending four law student research assistants into the University of Pittsburgh Business School library and then online to the SEC's EDGAR (Electronic Data Gathering and Retrieval) database, where they could access 2001 proxy statements.[4] The students employed a seven-column spreadsheet: (1) Company Name, *(2)* Fortune 500 Rank, (3) Board Size, (4) Number of Women Directors, (5) Name of Woman Director, (6) Background (Day Job) of each woman director, and (7) Other Boards. In mid-2005, another group of students repeated the process, utilizing data filed with the SEC in Spring 2005. This chapter analyzes that data for, among other things, trends.

The 2001 spreadsheet totals show that there are 5,821 director positions at Fortune 500 companies, more or less. The number changes over time because, as noted earlier, very few corporations have boards of fixed size. In some cases, the number of directors is fixed by the bylaws (the internal written governance rules every corporation must have), but the directors themselves have power to amend the bylaws and thus to increase or decrease the number of positions. In other cases, the bylaws provide for a variable-range board size, say, from nine to thirteen directors, within which the board allows the number of seats to fluctuate.[5]

Of those 5,821 board seats, 678 of them, or 11.6 percent, were held by women in 2001. When one counts the names, however, the numbers are smaller. There are only 480 women holding board positions in the Fortune 500 in 2001. This is the case because quite a few women, such as Presidents Rodin and Simmons, hold several directorships, and a few women, such as Anne McLaughlin, hold so many (nine) that they may be classified as trophy directors.[6]

Specifically, thirty of the 480 women hold four or more board seats and collectively represent 151 board seats, or 22.3 percent, of the board seats women held. Some of them, such as Anne McLaughlin, are candidates for the appellation "super trophy director."

McLaughlin, now Anne McLaughlin Korologos, a former secretary of labor and former chairperson of the Aspen Institute, and Jackie Ward, identified by proxy material as CEO of Computer Generation, Inc., tie for the 2001 lead among Fortune 500 women directors, each holding nine directorships. McLaughlin Korologos sits on the boards of Fannie Mae (26), Microsoft (79), AMR (98), Kellogg (269), Nordstrom (324), Vulcan Materials (593), Host Marriott (882), Harmon International Industries, and Donna Karan International, Inc. Ward sits on boards at Bank of America (13), Sysco (105), SCI Systems (230), Flowers Industries (387), Equifax (707), Matria Healthcare, Premier Technology, Profit Recovery Group International, and Trigon Healthcare.

The runner up is Rozanne Ridgeway, a former assistant secretary of state for Europe and Canada with the rank of ambassador, who, according to 2001 proxy material, sits on eight high-powered boards: Boeing (15), Sara Lee (96), Minnesota Mining & Manufacturing (118), Emerson Electric (126), Union Carbide (284), Nabisco, New Perspective Fund, and the Verizon subsidiary Bell Atlantic.

Number of Women versus Number of Seats Held

The number of women holding prestigious director positions, 480, is about equivalent to the size of the senior class at a middle-size high school. It seems a small number in a nation of 270 million. Moreover, the wealth, power, and prestige of corporate board membership are not distributed as much among the women as they are among the men who populate the director ranks

As mentioned, at least seventy-two Fortune 500 companies, or 14.4 percent, have *no* women directors. Approximately 228, or 45.6 percent, have only one woman director, surely evidence of tokenism. There are 143 Fortune 500 companies with two directors (28.6 percent), which still seems evidence of tokenism when one considers that many of these boards have eleven, thirteen, fifteen, or sixteen directors in total.

Forty-three companies (8.6 percent) seem to be making an effort, with three women on their boards.

The 2001 honor list (four or more women directors) includes only thirteen of five hundred companies. The leader is SBC Communications (14) with six women on a 21-person board. Next in absolute numbers (but with some being higher in percentage) are Wells Fargo Bank (62) (five of eighteen), Avon Products (310) (five of ten), and Golden West Financial (429) (five of nine). Significantly, both Avon and Golden West have women CEOs, Andrea Jung at Avon and Marion Sandler at Golden West Financial.

Rounding out the honor list are nine companies with four women directors. They include Bank of America (13) (four of seventeen); Aetna Insurance (63) (four of twelve); Walt Disney Company (67) (four of sixteen); Xerox Corp. (109) (four of fourteen); Eastman Kodak (141) (four of eleven); Principal Financial (215) (four of seventeen); and Hasbro Toy (438)(four of thirteen). A surprise was Boise Cascade, the forest products company. Ranked 241 in the 2001 Fortune 500, Boise has four women directors on its board of fourteen.

Worthy of note, too, is that Xerox is also one of the five Fortune 500 companies with a woman CEO, Anne Mulcahy. Three of the five companies with women CEOs in 2001 (Xerox, Avon, and Golden West) make the honor list of thirteen, reinforcing the conclusions of Catalyst and others that when women are at the very top there is a trickle-down effect, on the board at least.[7]

Sources of Female Directors

My purpose here is to examine routes to directorships and not necessarily the trophy-director phenomenon or the paucity of women directors and the tokenism on many boards of directors. Of women directors at

Fortune 500 companies, eighty-four (18.3 percent) come from positions as COOs, CFOs, vice-presidents, or CEOs of subsidiaries at other companies.

Holding second place is the university professor category, with seventy-nine women (17.2 percent) who hold one or more Fortune 500 board seats. Seventy-eight women directors (17 percent) are consultants of one sort or another (third-highest category). In the fourth-highest category, fifty-eight women directors (12.6 percent) come from the not-for-profit sector. Forty-eight women directors (10.4 percent) may be classified as independent businesswomen (fifth-highest category). Thirty-four women (7.4 percent) come to board seats from government service (sixth-highest category).

In the male director demography, CEOs of other corporations would be overwhelmingly the number one director category, holding over half of the board seats.[8] In marked contrast, only twenty-six of the 480 women (5.7 percent) holding board seats are CEOs of other, smaller corporations.[9]

Last of all, in the eighth category, twenty of the women directors (4.3 percent) are listed as practicing attorneys. This category barely surpasses the ninth category, women from Harvard, who have thirteen members but hold twenty-one board seats.

Implications

What can be made of these numbers?

First, the glass ceiling still seems firmly in place. There are so few women CEOs serving on other corporations' boards of directors because there are so few women CEOs. There are few women CEOs because, even at this late date, as they rise within organizations, women bump into a still existent glass ceiling. CEO suites are the second-lowest source of women directors, ranking only ahead of practicing attorneys.[10] In the larger world, CEO suites are by far the largest source of male directors. Executive recruiters who specialize in board placements note that "the typical search is for a chief executive [who almost by definition will be male] who manages a complex and global company."[11]

Second, glass walls, at least interfirm glass walls, are more permeable than glass ceilings. Chapter 6 related Sheila Wellington's observations that on an intrafirm basis, glass walls may prevent women managers from obtaining the line positions and experience needed to rise to the very top within a firm. Glass walls between firms are more porous.

The most common phenomenon for women in business seems to be the "sidestep." Women rise up the ladder in other organizations. They then sidestep through the more permeable interfirm glass wall onto the board of a prominent company.

Third, great sources of sidestepping women directors are the academic, not-for-profit, and governmental spheres. True, the single largest source of women directors is the CFO/COO/VP category, with 18.3 percent. If the academic, not-for-profit, and governmental sources of women on boards are combined, however, they account for 37.2 percent of women serving on Fortune 500 boards of directors.

Among male directors at Fortune 500 companies, one searches nearly in vain for directors who have sidestepped from a professorship onto the board of a major corporation. The picture in the not-for-profit sector is similar: few men move laterally onto board seats from the not-for profit world. Government service is different. Men move with frequency from government posts, especially at the cabinet or director level, to board seats in the private sphere.

The latter observation about women directors (37.2 percent from the academy, and so on) may show that in the academy and not-for-profit sectors, and to a lesser extent, in government, the glass ceiling is more permeable or does not exist at many institutions in those sectors.[12]

Inconsistencies and Contradictions

In all of this, contradictions surface. One is that the comparison between low numbers of women CEOs moving into board seats and the high number of academics has to be qualified. Of the seventy-nine women academics, twenty-seven are college or university presidents with CEOlike responsibilities. They range from presidents at more humble institutions (Jefferson Community College, Madison Area Technical College, Cuyahoga Community College) to presidencies at elite universities (Wellesley, Mount Holyoke, Penn, Brown, Smith, Cal Tech, University of Chicago, RPI). Between those extremes, women presidents of many middle-level and regional universities serve on Fortune 500 boards. They include presidents at the University of San Diego, Detroit Mercy, the University of Alabama–Birmingham, Kent State University, the University of California–Irvine, St. Mary's College (Maryland), and Appalachian State.

A similar contradiction surfaces in the not-for-profit sector. Many of the women serving on boards who sidestep from that sector have weighty bottom-line-type responsibilities, but in the not-for-profit world. At least five are United Way executives. Farah Walters, who serves on the boards of LTV Corporation (352), Kerr McGee Oil (405), and Poly One Corporation, is the CEO of University Hospitals of Cleveland, a major regional healthcare provider and research institution. Sarah Jewell, who serves on the board of Avista Corp. (239), a Spokane, Washington, energy company, is the CEO of REI, the outdoor clothing and equipment cooperative that began in a vacant Seattle gas station but is now a nationwide retailer. Bernadette Healy, who serves on the boards of National City Bank (210), Ashland Oil (234), MBNA (240), Medtronic (349), and Invarcare, is, or was until being deposed late in 2001, the CEO of the American Red Cross.

These contradictions tend to show two things. One is that whether examining women's or men's backgrounds, search firms, nominating committees or, in satrapies in which the CEO still controls board nominations, the nominators frequently look for a similar package. That package, which includes weighty bottom-line-type responsibilities, may be found in university presidents' offices or not-for-profit executive suites.

The second is that, in order to find that package in women candidates for directorships, search firms and nominating committees have to go outside of the corporate sector to find it. What better evidence, then, exists to demonstrate that in corporate America the glass ceiling still is firmly in place?

Nepotism and Celebrity Status

A few observations are in order here. Nepotism works—sometimes. Women directors Martha Ingram at Ingram Micro (49), Shari Redstone at Viacom (101), Abigail Wexner at The Limited (185), Charlotte Temple at Temple-Inland (390), and Linda Jacobs at Jacobs Engineering Group (476) all are related to a company founder or controlling shareholder.

Celebrity works, albeit slightly less often. One actress, Dina Merrill, is a Fortune 500 director, as is one opera diva, Beverly Sills Greenough. They are directors at Lehman Brothers (65) and American Express (74), respectively. The celebrity winner is "Judge Hatchett" of afternoon television fame. Glenda A. Hatchett sits on three Fortune 500 boards: HCA Health Care (119), GAP (147), and Service Master (300).

Sidestepping onto Corporate Boards of Directors

Examples of sidestepping women directors from academe include Laura D'Andrea Tyson, who is the dean of the University of California at Berkeley business school. From that position, she has moved onto boards at SBC Communications (14), Eastman Kodak (141), Fox Entertainment, Morgan Stanley (124), and Human Genome Sciences, Inc. Wendy Gramm, spouse of Senator Phil Gramm, professor at George Mason University, and director of the GMU's Regulatory Studies Program, sits on boards at Enron (then seventh but now essentially defunct), Iowa Beef Processors (117), State Farm Insurance (21), and Invesco Funds. Regina Herzlinger, a professor at the graduate school of business at Harvard, sits on boards at Cardinal Health (51), Deere & Co. (149), C. R. Bard, Inc., Noven Pharmaceuticals, Inc., and Schering-Plough Pharmaceuticals. Marina Whitman, a professor of business at the University of Michigan, sits on boards at J.P. Morgan Chase (12), Proctor & Gamble (31), Alcoa (77), and Unocal (207).

Sidesteps from high-level government positions are equally impressive. Gwendolyn King, who had been a commissioner of the Social Security Administration, sidestepped from there onto boards at Lockheed Martin (69), Pharmacia-Monsanto (113), and March & McLennon (183). Constance Horner held a variety of political appointments, including those of deputy director, Health and Human Services (1989–1991) and director of Presidential Personnel under President George Bush (1991–93). From those positions she did a "double side step," first to a not-for-profit (The Brookings Institute) and then onto boards at Pfizer (53), Ingersoll Rand (205), Foster Wheeler (420), and Prudential Insurance.

Women who are Democrats sidestep from government to corporate boards as well, but not usually to as many. Charlene Barshefsky, the very capable U.S. trade representative (1993–2001) in the Clinton administration, sits on boards at American Express (74) and Estee Lauder (389). Hazel O'Leary, Clinton's secretary of energy, sits on boards at United Airlines (UAL) (104) and AES (279).

One meets, as well, double sidesteps. Bonnie Hill jumped from the academy (dean, McIntyre School of Commerce, University of Virginia) to the not-for-profit sector (CEO, Times Mirror Foundation). Along the way she picked up board seats at Home Depot (23), AK Steel Holdings (372), Hershey Foods (398), and Niagra Mohawk Power (377).

Lynn Martin went from government (secretary of labor, 1991–1993) to the academy (professor, Kellogg School of Business, Northwestern University) to a number of corporate boards: SBC Communications (14), Procter & Gamble (31), Ryder Systems (333), Dreyfus Funds, Harcourt General, and TRW, Inc.

Bernadette Healy has covered all of the bases. She has been in government (Office of Science and Technology for the President in 1984–1985 and director, National Institutes of Health, 1991–1993). She has moved in and out of the academy (professor, Johns Hopkins University School of Medicine, 1977–1984, and dean, College of Medicine and Public Health, Ohio State University, 1995–1999). She has been in the not-for-profit sector (president, American Heart Association, 1988–1989, and president of the American Red Cross, 1999–2001). Wholly or in part though her triple (quadruple?) sidestep, she has picked up board seats at the five Fortune 500 corporations recounted earlier in this chapter.

Distributional Concerns

What one returns to over and over again while examining the data is just how little the wealth is spread around and how prevalent sexism (companies with no women directors) and tokenism (companies with one or two that should have many more) may be. On the "boo" or "hall of shame" list are, of course, the seventy-two companies with no women directors, which include General Dynamics, Bear Stearns, Apple Computer, American Standard, Micron Technology, Owens Illinois, Starwood Hotels, Avis Rent-a-Car, Ames Department Stores, Dillards Department Stores, Harrah's Entertainment, and others.

The entire airline industry (one woman per board except U.S. Airways, with two of twelve, and Southwest, with two of eleven) and the financial services sector (no women or one woman on most boards) have very poor records, especially given the number of women they employ in important positions.

It may be sexist to say so, but it seems that, even though they possess a varied portfolio of skills and characteristics that could be of service everywhere, women directors could be of great or special value on boards in the retail, grocery, consumer products, drug and home products, and home appliance sectors. Nonetheless, those industries by and large evince only tokenism when it comes to women on boards of directors.

In retail, Walmart has but one woman on a board of thirteen, Sears Roebuck two of ten, K Mart two of fourteen, Target two of eleven, J.C. Penny two of ten, Costco one of eleven, and Kohl's one of twelve. Women are asked to shop at Saks but out of Saks's seventeen directors, only one is a woman.

In grocery and food products, Kroger has two women of seventeen directors, Safeway one of nine, Sara Lee two of fifteen, Tyson Foods two of twelve, Kellogg two of eleven, and Quaker Oats two of nine. Special mention on the "boo list" might go to Campbells Soup, with two women of sixteen directors, and Hershey Foods, with one of eleven. Many a career parent feeds her child chicken soup or a chocolate bar. Enlightened self-interest, what management theorists denominate "market reciprocity," would seem to inform those companies in staffing their boards that if great numbers of women consume their products, then women should have significant, if not ample, representation on the board of directors.[13]

In drugs and home products, Procter & Gamble has two women of sixteen directors, Walgreens's one of ten, American Home Products one of ten, and Newell Rubbermaid two of eleven. Pepsi (three women) wins over Coca-Cola (two of thirteen) and Coca-Cola Enterprises (one of thirteen). Contrast Hasbro (toys) (four women of thirteen) to Mattel (one woman of eleven directors).

Especially short-sighted are Nike (one of eleven directors) and McDonald's (one of fifteen). Not only do those companies profess to being enlightened, but they also ask young parents to buy Nike shoes and apparel and McDonald's Happy Meals for both sons and daughters alike. Seemingly, they could do much better in staffing their boards of directors.

Meanwhile, returning to the theme broached in the introduction, we see that the numbers lag greatly behind the expectations long held for women and minorities in the CEO suite and the boardroom. The point has been that reality lags behind even the reported numbers. That double lag (numbers behind expectations, reality behind numbers) necessitates reexamination of the reasons advanced over the years for the one-step-forward, one-step-back nature of progress on diversity issues in corporate boardrooms.

8

The 2005 Proxy Data

Advocacy groups such as Catalyst, Inc., broadcast statistics about women's increased presence in business[1] that seem misleading, in at least two respects. One respect is that Catalyst, as well as journalists and others, report that 11.2 percent (in 1999–2000) or 13.6 percent (in 2004) of directors are women.[2] What the statistics really say is that women hold 11.2 or 13.6 percent of the board seats, not that 11.2 or 13.6 of the directors are women.

The second, and overlapping respect in which the statistics mislead explains the first. The number of female bodies on Fortune 500 boards may be significantly less, as chapter 7 explains. This trend continues, with the number of women among the ranks of trophy directors—those who hold seats on four, five, or even a greater number of corporate boards of directors—increasing. In 2001, 480 women had one or more of 5,821 directorships (8.3 percent) and, in 2005, 568 women held one or more of 5,161 positions (11 percent). Thus, although the number of women directors has increased over the last several years, the increase may not be as great as widely available statistics may lead one to believe.

Again, several law students undertook the basic research on women directors in the Fortune 500, finding the following trends.

- The number of women directors increased, from 480 in 2001 to 568 in 2005.
- Between those years boards downsized, from 5,821 to 5,161 directors in the Fortune 500. The reduced size of boards, as the good governance movement calls for, magnifies to an extent (falsely) the progress that women have made in the boardroom, at least when expressed in terms of percentages.
- The number of trophy directors among women increased dramatically, from approximately thirty in 2001 to seventy-nine in 2005.

- The top end (nine directorships held by the same woman) disappeared, replaced by a more modest eight directorships, held by Susan B. Bayh. Four women (Barbara Bowles, Bonnie Hill, Shirley Jackson, and Jackie Ward) tied for second place, with seven board seats each. A leader in 2001, former undersecretary of state Rozanne Ridgeway, with nine board memberships, sits on only five boards in 2005 (Boeing [25], Manpower, Inc. [140], Emerson Electric [134], Sara Lee Corp. [114], and 3-M, Inc. [105]).
- A new species has emerged, the academic trophy director. At least seventeen women with ties to higher education hold a total of ninety-seven board seats. The leader, Shirley Jackson of Rensselaer Polytechnic Institute, sits on seven boards (Marathon Oil [31], U.S. Steel Corp. [149], AT&T [56], Federal Express [78], Public Service Enterprise, Inc. (199), Medtronic (246), and the New York Stock Exchange).

The largest enlargement of the pathways by which women find their way to board seats came from the category of VP/COO/CFO or subsidiary CEO at other companies. The data reveals that 176 women directors came from this category, compared to eighty-four that could be identified in 2001.

However, the number of women rising to the board level at their own corporations remained small. Only eleven could be identified. Noteworthy was Publix Super Markets (117), which had four of eleven women directors, including two senior executives (Carol J. Barnett and Tina P. Johnson).

Overall, the data presents strong circumstantial evidence that one pool from which corporations may draw director nominees, the VP/COO/CFO pool, is enlarging. Unfortunately, what the data also reveals is a great expansion in the number of trophy directors, from thirty to seventy-nine, as well. Equally as likely, then, is that a given board of directors or corporation reaches into the existing director pool, adding a forth or fifth directorship to a particular woman's credentials rather than searching out the VP/COO/CFO talent pool.

Another sobering footnote, although one based upon a small sample, is that 50 percent of the women insider directors still come from staff executive positions while 95 percent of the men candidates have line positions with officer titles attached.[3]

With regard to the second point above, between 2001 and 2005 the number of director positions in the Fortune 500 decreased 11.34 percent. The number of female directors has risen as a percentage in part because the divisor is smaller and only in part because the actual number of females has increased.

Nine super-trophy women directors held six or more seats. The bulk of those (six) held seven seats:

1. Brenda Barnes (seven boards), former president and COO and now CEO of Sara Lee–Sears Roebuck (45), Sara Lee (114), Pepsi Cola Co. (61), Staples (146), Avon Products (278), Lucas Film Corp., and the New York Times.
2. Susan Bayh (eight boards), identified as an adjunct professor at Butler University—Wellpoint Health Networks (97), Anthem Insurance, Dendreon, Novavax, Curis, Inc., Ennis Communications Corp., Golden State Foods, and Dyax Corporation.
3. Barbara Bowles (seven boards), chairperson and CEO of the Kenwood Group–Georgia Pacific (109), Dollar General Stores (280), Black & Decker (359), Wisconsin Energy Corp. (471), Wisconsin Electric Power, Wisconsin Gas Co., and Hyde Park Bank.
4. Bonnie Hill (seven boards), who heads B. Hill Enterprises, LLC–Home Depot (13), Albertson's (35), Yum! Brands (244), AK Steel Holdings (376), Hershey Foods (436), ChoicePoint, Inc., and California Water Service, Inc.
5. Shirley Jackson (seven boards), a retired university president, sits the boards named in the bulleted list above.
6. Last, proxy data identifies Jackie Ward (seven boards), who also was among the two leaders in 2001 with nine board seats held, as sitting on boards at Bank of America (18), Wellpoint (97), Intel (50), Sysco (60), Flowers Industries, and Equifax.

The next layer of super–trophy director includes three women, who sit on six boards each:

- Penelope Hughes, a senior executive at Coca-Cola–GAP, Inc. (130), Trinity Mirror, Vodafone, PLC, Skandinaviska Enskilda Banken, Benlacers, and Reuters News Service, Inc.

- Lynn Martin, chair of the Deloitte & Touche Council on Advancement of Women–Procter & Gamble (26), SBC Communications (33), Ryder Systems (381), TRW, Constellation Energy, and Dreyfus Funds.
- Ann McLaughlin Korogolas, who tied Jackie Ward for the 2001 lead, with nine seats each—Microsoft (41), AMR (119), Kellogg (234), Host Marriott (486), Fannie Mae, and Harmon International.

Academic Trophy Directors

A surprise that emerges from the 2005 data is the number of female directors who hold four or more board seats. From a mere handful in 2001, the number has grown to at least seventeen academics in 2005. They include administrators who have weighty CEO-type responsibilities such as Donna Shalala, president of the University of Miami, or Judith Rodin, immediate past president of the University of Pennsylvania and now president of the Rockefeller Foundation, or Mary Metz, president emeritus of Mills College. All of these women sit on multiple boards of directors, in addition to carrying their weighty CEO-type responsibilities.

Academic trophy directors also include deans with responsibilities similar to those of presidents, such as Laura Tyson, dean of the University of London Business School (formerly dean, University of California School of Business), or Kristina Johnson, dean of the Pratt School of Engineering at Duke University. Rank-and-file faculty members who have also achieved trophy director status include Carolyn Woo, professor at the Mendoza School of Business at the University of Notre Dame, and Pastora San Juan Cafferty, professor at the University of Chicago.

Several trophy directors list their "day job" as being that of adjunct professor (usually a part-time position) at institutions of higher learning. They include Susan Bayh (eight directorships) at Butler University, Judith Hope (four directorships) at Georgetown University School of Law, Jill Kerr Conway (three directorships) at MIT, and Nancy DeParle (five directorships) at the Wharton School of Business, University of Pennsylvania.

A particularly promising route for female academics into the trophy directors' circle has been the health sciences, a field in which the number of directors with the requisite expertise might be scarce and the possibility of multiple directorships accordingly greater for a well qualified female academic. Thus, Mary Munding, dean of the School of Nursing at Columbia University, sits on boards at Health Corp. (40), Cell Therapeutics, Inc., Gentiva Health Services, and Welsh Allyn, Inc. Collen Conway-Welch, dean of the School of Nursing at Vanderbilt University, sits on boards at Caremark International (73), Pinnacle Bank, RehabCare Group, Inc., and Advent Health Services. Ann Reynolds, former president of the University of Alabama–Birmingham (primarily a health sciences campus) is on boards at Abbott Laboratories (100), Owens Corning (349), Humana (162), Maytag (410), and the Champaign-Urbana News Corp.

Why More Women Directors?

Growth of the health sciences has created director openings for qualified directors, many of whom are female. Two other reasons advanced are the July 2002 adoption of the Sarbanes-Oxley Act (SOA) and the increased unwillingness of CEOs (most of whom are male) to serve.

SOA requires that on every public company board a majority of directors must be independent.[4] Further, each corporation must have an audit committee of the board, and each audit committee must have at least one member who is a "financial expert."[5] The SEC has defined the term as requiring hands-on experience in auditing with at least one public company.[6]

In response, publicly held companies have outdone themselves. Many require two, or all, audit committee members to be financial experts. In addition, corporations are eager to add to boards of directors any candidates who are financially literate, even if they do not qualify as experts.[7] Catalyst reports that because of these requirements, requests for referrals for prospective women director candidates have doubled since Congress passed SOA, to about twenty per year. Overall, these requirements are seen as creating additional openings for female directors, many of whom come from financial or accounting backgrounds.[8]

The third cause of increased demand may be the withering up of a traditional source of directors. In 1999, CEOs of publicly held companies held an average of two directorships at publicly held companies other than their own. The executive search firm Spencer Stuart Associates reports that the figure had dropped quickly, to .9 in 2005. Many corporations (MCI Communications, for example) now forbid their CEOs from service on any other board, or limit them to service on one for-profit board of directors only.[9]

Some directors attribute the development to the Enron and WorldCom securities lawsuits, when as conditions of settlement plaintiffs insisted that independent directors pay $13 million and $18 million, respectively, out of their own pockets, a previously unheard of contribution. The prospect of paying damages from one's pocket, in addition to what Directors' and Officers' (D & O) insurance pays, deters CEOs, who are likely to be persons of affluence, from service as directors.

Others attribute the development to relativity. Michael Capellas, former CEO at Compaq Computer and then CEO at MCI Communications, reports that he might earn $50,000 yearly as an independent director of another public company but $3.8 million as CEO of MCI. Independent directors must work hard, reading reports and preparing for meetings. Mr. Capellas opines that he would rather utilize his time in being CEO than serving as an independent director, even if MCI were not to prohibit CEO service on other boards, which it does.

Overall Picture

Even though it is important to note that the number of women serving as directors has increased, the overall picture is far from bright. Fifty-nine corporations in the Fortune 500, or 12.27 percent, still do not have, as of 2005, any female directors. The largest category of corporations in the Fortune 500, 183 companies, or 38.9 percent, have only one woman serving on the board, the rest of which is comprised by men. Adding the categories reveals a startling fact: a clear majority, 51.2 percent, of United States major corporations have no women directors or engage only in apparent tokenism, with one director who is female.

While a single minority person, such as a woman, may be a token, a pair of women on a board or in any other similarly sized group may be in an even worse condition, as a member of a so-called skewed group. As chapter 9 discusses, sociologists have long analyzed the depredations and other treatments that a majority may visit upon tokens or members of a skewed group.

A subgroup of three, say, in a larger group of ten or eleven, stands a much increased chance of avoiding any negative treatments, subtle or otherwise, than would to a group of two. The presence of three or more women on a corporate board may thus be an important indicator. Eleven percent of corporations in the Fortune 500, or fifty-three, have three women sitting on their boards as directors.

The most honored position belongs, as it did in 2001, to SBC Communications (33), which has six women directors serving on a board of fourteen. Four large U.S. publicly held companies have five women directors. Those corporations are Albertson's (35) with five of ten; Wells Fargo (52) with five of fourteen; Wellpoint Systems (97) with five of seventeen; and Golden West Financial (435) with five of nine.

The study was able to find fourteen companies with four female directors. It may surprise the reader to learn that they are Johnson & Johnson (8), Cendant (107), Aetna (108), Sara Lee (114), Publix Super Markets (117), Washington Mutual (131), Office Max (159), General Mills (197), Pepsi Cola Bottling (202), Principle Financial (253), Avon Products (278), Estee Lauder (346), Pacific Life (396), and Omnicare (459).

Sources of Female Directors

The leading source (186 women, or 32.7 percent) was once again females who occupy VP/COO/CFO positions at other corporations. In a virtual tie for second were the categories of independent businesswoman (eighty-six, or 15.1 percent) and academics (university professors and administrators, active or retired) (eighty-four, or 14.9 percent). The fourth category consists of women who list their primary affiliation as being with a not-for-profit business. The total number was virtually the same as in 2001 (fifty-eight in 2001; sixty-two [10.9 percent] in 2005).

A growing source was CEOs of smaller companies. Sixty women (10.6 percent) identified themselves as such, and that category placed in the fifth position. The number of women who labeled themselves as attorneys, a very clear indicator, rose from last place, or ninth, with twenty in 2001, to sixth, with forty-eight (8.5 percent) in 2005.

The number of women listing themselves as consultants seems to have fallen dramatically, from seventy-eight to forty, and from fourth to seventh. Seemingly, some women who listed themselves as "Consultant" in 2001 list themselves as "Partner, Little Consulting" in 2005. In that way, some women directors may have migrated from the consultant to the independent business woman category.

The last category, government, fell dramatically, with the number of women listing themselves as being in or coming immediately from government service declining from thirty-four to eighteen. A possible explanation is that in 2001 many directors continued to list their prior affiliation with the Clinton administration in proxy materials. No similar change in administrations preceded the 2005 proxy season in the United States Women directors who once were in the Clinton administration have moved on to other affiliations.

In 2005, the number listing themselves as faculty from Harvard fell from thirteen to six and from twenty-one to fourteen board seats, principally as corporations fell out of the Fortune 500. The University of Chicago took second place, with four women sitting on eleven boards. Four universities tied for third, each having three women serving as directors of publicly held companies: the University of Cincinnati, MIT, New York University, and the University of Pennsylvania. As usual, the other institutions varied widely in the prestige each enjoys, from California Institute of Technology, Stanford, and Yale to Appalachian State, Bennett College (two), Florida Southern University, Hood College, and St. Mary's College (Maryland).

Nepotism and Celebrity Status

Glenna Hatchett, the television judge, remains on the board at HCA (80). Meredith Brokaw, who lists her occupation as author, and who is the spouse of former nightly news anchorperson Tom Brokaw, sits on the board of directors at Gannett (283). The leader in terms of status, or derived status, is Susan Bayh, forty-six, married to Birch "Evan" Bayh, the U.S. senator from Indiana. Bayh sits on eight boards of directors.

Madison Murphy sits on the board of Murphy Oil Co. (255). Penny Pritzker of the fabled and wealthy Chicago Pritzker family sits on the boards of William Wrigley Co. (416) and of the family-owned Hyatt Hotel Co. Abagail Wexner sits on the board of The Limited (240), a company founded and controlled by the Wexner family. Barbara Tyson sits on the board of directors of Tyson Foods (72). Martha Ingram is the board chairperson at Ingram Micro (76). Charlotte Temple remains on the board of directors at Temple-Island (405).

Sidesteps

Other routes from government service have opened. Particularly fruitful have been sidesteps by women commissioners of the U.S. Securities and Exchange Commission (SEC). Laura Unger journeyed from her term as commissioner to directorships at MBNA (171), Ambac Financial, and Borland Software, Inc. Commissioner Aulana Peters did even better, sidestepping to a major law firm (Gibson, Dunn, & Crutcher) and corporate boards at Merrill Lynch (53), Northrup-Grumman (58), 3-M Corp. (105), and John Deere & Co. (106). Commissioner Mary L. Shapiro became the director of enforcement for the National Association of Securities Dealers (NASD). She also sits on the board of directors at Cinergy (412).

Former ambassador Carla Hills, whose husband chaired the SEC and who has been U.S. trade representative under President George Bush and Housing and Urban Development secretary under President Ford, sits on boards at Chevron-Texaco (6), AIG (9), Time-Warner (32), and Lucent Technologies (247). Christine Whitman did a double sidestep, not always willingly, from the New Jersey governorship to head of the U.S. Environmental Protection Agency (EPA) to corporate boards at United Technologies (39), Texas Instruments (166), S.C. Johnson Co., and Millennium Challenge Corp.

Zoe Baird represents a double to triple sidestep or, more accurately, rebound. She went from a position as general counsel to a large publicly held insurance company (Aetna) to nominee for attorney general of the United States in the Clinton administration. When it was discovered that she had failed to withhold taxes and FICA on a maid/caregiver from Central America, the administration withdrew the nomination. Baird now sits on boards of directors at IBM Corp. (10), Chubb Insurance (161), Convergys, and Brookings.

Katherine Ortega, former treasurer of the United States, sidestepped therefrom to corporate boards at State Farm Insurance (19), Kroger (21), and Rayonier, Inc. Joan Spero served as under secretary of state for economic affairs. From that post, she sidestepped to the not-for-profit world, as president, Doris Duke Foundation, and to membership on corporate boards, at IBM (10), Delta Airlines (138), and First Data Corp.

Aside from Ortega, other's who have sidestepped to corporate boards from the not-for-profit world abound. They include presidents of regional United Way organizations, president of a PBS television station, advisor to the Brookings Institution, president of the Bill and Melinda Gates Foundation, chief economist at the Conference Board, trustee of the Nature Conservatory, president of the World Wildlife Federation, president at the American Museum of Natural History, COO of the Smithsonian Institution, president of the Los Angeles County Art Museum, director of the Breast Cancer Foundation, heads of the National Geographic Society and of the Cowbell Foundation, and executive vice-president of the Blue Cross Blue Shield of Northern California, among others.

An impressive sidestep is that of Phyllis Campbell, president of the Seattle Foundation. From that position, she has gone on to corporate boards at Safeco Insurance (285), Nordstrom (294), Puget Sound Energy, and Alaska Air Group, Inc. She has thus been able to obtain seats in the boardrooms of a number of impressive regional and national corporations.

Inconsistencies and Contradictions

The worst industry in its treatment of women is the computer industry (software and hardware). Nine corporations have six women directors out of seventy-night, as follows: Dell Computer (28)(one of ten); Microsoft Corp. (41)(one of nine); Cisco (91)(two of twelve); Sun Microsystems (194)(one of nine); Oracle (220)(one of eleven); Apple Computer (263)(zero of seven); Micron Technology (439)(zero of seven); Affiliated Computer Services (460)(zero of seven); and Gateway Computer (495)(zero of seven). Four large publicly held corporations in the consumer business have no women directors at all. Apple Computer and Steven Jobs sell iPods and computers for purchase by women and mothers but, in this day and age, have no women on their board.

Almost equally as bad is the retail drug industry, which is in the business of large-box (or medium-box) retailing, in which many items (not just drugs) are sold and a majority of the shoppers are women. Walgreen's (38), CVS (55), Rite Aid (128), and Long's (421) all have a single woman director out of nine or ten, with the exception of CVS, which has two. Eckerd's is owned by J.C. Penny (74), which has two women among ten directors. Rite Aid is particularly mystifying as the corporation has as female CEO (Mary Sammons).

Although much faded, the airline industry retains a presence in the Fortune 500. Even as a consumer-oriented industry with a large female employee group, airlines have a poor record of women membership on their boards of directors. AMR (119), UAL (129), Northwest (190), and Continental (232) all have but a single female director on boards ranging from eleven to fifteen. Delta Airlines (232) and U.S. Airways (295) have two. Only Southwest (318), the most dynamic and progressive of the group, has three women on its board.

Media corporations are terrible. Rupert Murdoch's News Corp. (98) and Liberty Broadcasting (253) have no women on their boards while Cox Communications (322) has only one.

The financial services industry is improved from 2001 but has room for improvement. Citicorp (8) and Merrill Lynch (53) do well, with three women directors out of eighteen and ten, respectively. J.P. Morgan Chase (20) and Morgan Stanley (36) do poorly, with one woman director out of sixteen and eleven, respectively. Goldman Sachs (59) and Lehman Brothers (94) are in between, with two female directors each.

Given expectations that they would find women board members valuable, grocery store chains do somewhat poorly. Winn Dixie Stores (182) has one woman director of ten, Kroger (21) has two of fourteen, and Whole Foods (479) has only two. Publix Super Markets (117), with four of eleven, and Albertson's (35), with five of ten, are bright spots.

Retailers generally continue to disappoint. Among fourteen retail merchandising corporations, only twenty-three of 145 directors are women. The worst corporations are Dillards (274), with none of eleven, and B.J.'s Wholesale Clubs (284), with none of eight. Seemingly as bad is Walmart (1), our nation's largest corporation in terms of revenues. Walmart has one woman among thirteen directors. K Mart (113), Kohl's (184), and Family Dollar Stores (373) are the same. Household names in retailing, such as Costco (29), Sears Roebuck (45), Federated Department Stores (133), and Saks Fifth Avenue (320), all have only two women on boards ranging in size from ten (Federated) to fifteen (Saks). Target Stores (27)(three of eleven), May Department Stores (147)(three of ten), and Nordstrom's (294)(three of seven) top the list in this group.

Specialty retailers fare about the same, with women holding twelve of sixty-six seats. Worst is Radio Shack (399), with one woman among fourteen directors. Surprisingly bad are "new age" retailers Amazon (303) and Starbucks (372), with two of eight and two of eleven women directors. Home Depot (13) and Best Buy (77) have only two as well. Only Circuit City Stores (231) has three directors who are female.

The 2005 survey identified seventeen corporations in the Fortune 500 that manufacture consumer products and that, accordingly, design, manufacture, and market products to consumer groups comprised largely of women. The worst seem to be those corporations who have two women directors but who seemingly should have more, because of the ubiquity of those products and of their need to appeal to female consumers. Corporations in that category include Procter & Gamble (26)(two of sixteen), Coca-Cola (92)(two of fourteen), Nike (173)(two of eleven), Whirlpool (160)(two of ten), Gillette (215)(two of twelve), Kellogg (234)(two of twelve), Campbell's Soup (247)(two of sixteen), and Mattel Toy (383)(two of eleven). In real terms, the worst are food companies— Smithfield Farms (222)(one of eight) and Dole Foods (369)(one of ten)— plus Clorox (445)(one of ten) and Reebok (483)(one of six). The absolute worst is somewhat of a surprise: Levis Strauss (464)(zero of six).

The best are the Pepsi Cola corporations. Pepsi Bottling (202) has four women among eleven directors. Pepsico (61) has three women among eleven directors. Colgate Palmolive (210) and H.J. Heinz (259) have three women on boards of nine each.

The most surprising statistic from an analysis of 2005 proxy filings? Five years into the twenty first-century, a clear majority (51.2 percent) of large publicly held U.S. corporations have *no* women directors, or have only a token, a single director who is female.

There has been progress, from 8.3 to 11 percent, in the proportion of directors who are women. And there has been backsliding. The number of trophy directors (four to seven seats) among women has increased, even though the super–trophy directors have all but disappeared. While women do not advance to board seats at their own companies, there has been an increase of women who achieve in business (versus not-for-profit, governmental, and academic spheres) and then sidestep from a VP/COO/CFO position at one corporation to a director's seat at another large company.

Overall, the conclusion is that the glass ceiling is still in place. Evidence of this fact is seen in the increased need of corporations to add women who thus become trophy directors and in the overall picture (51.2 percent with no women or a single woman director), among other things. An analysis of the data contained in the 2005 SEC proxy data reveals that the proposition with which this book began remains as true today as it was five, ten, or even fifteen years ago. The reality concerning women's presence on corporate boards of directors lags badly behind expectations. And the actual numbers lag even further behind yet.

9

Women and Minorities
in Organizations
The Legacy of Tokenism

Tokens and Skewed Groups

In the management ranks, women cannot be satisfied with incremental improvements. They, and their numbers in those positions, must make quantum leaps, achieving substantial presences. Social justice issues aside, a principal reason why this increase is necessary has to do with what sociologists and organizational psychologists teach us about how organizations function. Within an organization, members will treat a single minority group member as a token. She may have to bear the brunt of jokes at her expense. She will suffer from application of stereotypes by coworkers or others in her job classification or work group. Even with an incremental breakthrough (from one to two, from two to three), the token may no longer be a token but is still a minority in a skewed group. The dynamics often change for the worse. The dominants in the group will perceive that a threat exists. Practical jokes become crueler. Coworkers invoke stereotypes with a vengeance.

Undoubtedly, a woman or other minority director would not encounter these behaviors at the board of directors level in a major publicly held company, even on boards with token minority members. At that rarefied level, proper board decorum is paramount. Dominant-group board members would make it a matter of the highest priority to make someone different (a token women, a black) comfortable in the board's surroundings and with its work. Harvard Business School professor Rakesh Khurana confirms this:

The sense of internal cohesion on a corporate board . . . is reinforced . . . by the existence of group norms. . . . There is a strong emphasis on politeness and courtesy, and an avoidance of direct conflict and confrontation. [B]oardroom decorum seeks to avoid the emergence of prestige groups of any kind within the group. . . . Making a big fuss over some individual accomplishment [or attribute] is considered brash and rude. In its own particular way, each board is a gentlemen's club, in both the best and worst senses of the term.[1]

Impact on the Pool from Which Directors May Be Chosen

The legacy of tokenism and skewed groups is that further down in corporate organizations those phenomena cause women and other minorities to rise no higher than an intermediate management level. A result is a disproportionately small presence for women in the senior executive ranks from which nominating committees and full boards are likely to choose directors. Business executive Gail Evans takes a slightly different view but reaches the same conclusion:

The best you can say is that we've seen a kind of creeping incrementalism. Large numbers of women dot the current workplace, but like trees on a mountain, you'll see fewer and fewer of them as you climb higher in the executive landscape, until you reach kind of a timber line where you'll find about as many women as you'll find magnolias.[2]

The classical work by Georg Simmel analyzed the significance of numbers that constitute less than a critical mass. He concluded that numerical shifts (token to skewed group to critical mass, or the reverse, critical mass to skewed group or to token) transform social interaction within groups and organizations.[3]

A token is a solo, one of a kind (woman, black, Hispanic) in a smaller work group, job classification, or organization. In a larger group, one may be one of two, or even three, who are different, and still be a token. Two women in a group of twenty-five to thirty are tokens.

Skewed groups are those in which there is a significant preponderance of one type (the dominants) within the group, prevailing over the next most represented type by a ratio of up to 85 to 15. In skewed groups, the dominants control the group and its culture. They set the tone.

Heightened Visibility (Notoriety)

Tokens draw attention from other group members, much more so than any of the dominants. Partly as a result of their visibility, they will have applied to them by the dominants many of the stereotypes associated with their type (for women, emotional, intuitive, not rational). Dominant group members more readily stereotype tokens than other categories of persons found in greater numbers. As the token's type increases in number, her visibility may decrease "because each individual becomes less surprising, unique or noteworthy."[4]

A second perceptual phenomenon is that, among themselves, the dominants become more aware of their common characteristics (outdoorsmen, like sports, talk about cars and women) and their difference from the token (the dominant males are rational while the woman is not; the men are unemotional while the woman is emotional). To preserve their commonality, the dominants keep the token outside the dominant group. They offer a boundary to themselves, as dominants, within which their commonality flourishes.

The Taylor-Fiske empirical study utilized

[e]ither an otherwise all-white male group with one black man (the "token" condition) or a mixed black-white male group. In the token condition, disproportionate attention was paid to the token, his prominence in the group was overemphasized, and his attributes were exaggerated. . . . [T]he token was perceived as playing out special roles, often highly stereotypical ones. By contrast, in "integrated" groups, subjects recalled no more about blacks than whites, and their attributes were evaluated about the same.[5]

In her study of Industrial Supply Corp. (Indsco), Professor Rosabeth Kanter observed that token women in the sales force were the subject of inordinate gossip and constant scrutiny. Throughout a division of the company, men knew the women's assignments while no one typically knew those of the men. Men would bring up the women's names at meetings, often using them as examples. "Travelers to locations with women in [them] would bring back news of the latest about the women, along with other gossip."[6]

Women who rose in the organization but were still tokens became public figures. Anything they did on their job or at a social function would attract notice. The men highlighted the women's mistakes. Women's intimate relationships might be known. Many higher level women executives felt that their visibility limited their freedom of action. They would have preferred the men to notice them less.

Men accorded actions by tokens, especially higher placed ones, symbolic consequence—that is, significance beyond their ordinary meaning for the organization (subsidiary, division, work group, company as a whole). One such consequence was that the men would take such action as good, or even conclusive, evidence of how women perform. Dominants perceived problems on the basis of category membership (woman) rather than on the basis of situation (increased competition, product obsolescence).

Title VII Cases

A plurality of the plaintiffs alleging sex-based discrimination under the Civil Rights Act of 1964 were tokens in their work group or job classifications. Moreover, their male coworkers played up and then acted upon the woman's status as the token. In many instances, the males engaged in specific acts of sexual harassment, or created a hostile environment, or both.

As the only woman in a work group of twelve, Lisa Ocheltree was highly visible. In the early stages of her employment at Scollon Productions, a maker of theatrical costumes, the banter about her token status was "fun" and "friendly." Soon, however, "coarse sexual talk and sexual antics by several of the men began to occur with increasing frequency." Male coworkers would engage in simulated sex with mannequins. When Ocheltree told them "this needed to stop" her coworkers exaggerated their behavior, making "hand gestures at their private parts" and "constantly discussing their sexual exploits." The court of appeals opinion is quite graphic. The court affirmed an award of compensatory damages but reversed the award of punitive damages against the employer, a small company with fifty employees, that did have in place a policy against sexual harassment.[7]

Nancy Suders not only encountered a hostile environment but was the object of sexual harassment as well, all in a Pennsylvania State Police barracks. Again, she was the only woman, and the first woman, to work there. Every time Suders went to his office, the station commander would "bring up the subject of people having sex with animals." Wearing spandex exercise shorts, he would put his hands on his head and spread his legs apart in a chair facing Suder's desk. The station patrol corporal constantly grabbed his crotch, asking her to engage in lewd acts. Two other state policemen engaged in similar acts of harassment, contributing to the intolerable environment. Suder had given up ten years' long-term employment with a county sheriff's office in order to accept her position with the Pennsylvania State Police. But she "suffered mistreatment and sexual harassment so severe that she ultimately felt compelled to resign" after five months in the new position.[8]

Another solo was Lisa Petrosino, the only technician at a Bell Atlantic facility. Early on in her employment, she had to endure a physical attack from a coworker, who grabbed her from behind, groping and kissing her. Male coworkers made disparaging remarks about her "menstrual cycle, her weight, her eating habits," and her female anatomy. When she complained to a high-level manager, he told her she was "too thin skinned," casting these and other observations in "gender-wide terms, stating that women as a group were 'too simple,' 'too sensitive,' and 'too damned thin skinned.'"[9] The manager and coworkers acted as a sociologist would predict: they applied a stereotype, indeed an exaggerated stereotype, to the token woman in the workplace.

Many court cases, and very recent cases at that, feature women who, at least in part because of their token status and the high degree of visibility associated with it, became objects of sexual harassment or graphic locker room behavior that made continuation of their careers impossible.[10] In graphic, real-world terms, the court cases illustrate what the sociologists and organizational theorists describe in the textbooks. The cases also illustrate why in many corporate organizations women do not rise to the management level from which they will have a chance to springboard into upper management and director positions, or why they may have been sidetracked long before they came near to that level.

Performance Pressures

In meetings at Rosabeth Kanter's Indsco, male dominants would ask the token to provide the "woman's point of view." The men expected the woman to speak for all women, not just herself. A consequence was heightened self-consciousness on the part of the woman, about her presentation, personal appearance, and decisions. Insignificant or casual decisions about what to wear or where to sit at meetings or at lunch were no longer inconsequential.

Tokens face a number of other performance pressures that emanate from their status. One is that, for a solo woman (or other minority group member), the attributes the men associate with her token status will mask her actual achievements. "The token does not have to work hard to have her presence noticed, but she does have to work hard to have her achievements noticed," Professor Kanter concludes.[11] Aspects of her femininity eclipse actual job performance.

A second performance pressure born of token status is paradoxical. While a token woman may feel that she has to do better than anyone else to be noticed or win promotion, she cannot show up the dominants in her group. She will be regarded as aggressive, pushy, and overly ambitious. Because she is the token, it is difficult for her to keep her actual job performance a secret because, as the token, she has many eyes upon her. She may have to play down her accomplishments, or not speak of them at all. If she does not, she risks retaliation by the dominants.

In a group of ten middle managers Rosabeth Kanter observed, of whom two were women,

> [O]ne was well liked by her peers even though she had an outstanding record because she did not flaunt her successes and modestly waited her turn to be promoted. She did not trade on her visibility. Her long previous experience in technical work served to certify her . . . and her pleasant but plain appearance . . . minimized disruptive sexual attributes. . . . The other was seen differently [by the dominants]. The mention of her name as a "star performer" was accompanied by laughter. . . . [T]he publicity she has received for her successes created a negative climate around her. She was said to be aspiring too high, too soon, and refusing to play by the same rules the men had to use. . . . [12]

One form of retaliation is for the men to abandon the visible token the first time she encounters problems. Technical help, friendly advice, or cheerleading will evaporate. The men will predict that she will fail in her next assignment and be cut down to size. They may assist in that process.[13]

Australians term this the "tall poppy syndrome": one who rises too fast or becomes too visible too soon will be cut down to size. Another term is " High-and-Mighty." The later comeuppance the tall poppy or the High-and-Mighty faces may be due to personal performance and characteristics. It may also be due to her status as a token.

Tokens' Coping Strategies

Tokens may respond to performance pressures in several ways. A solo woman may overachieve but carefully construct a facade that minimizes peer concerns. She walks the tightrope between doing well, on the one hand, and generating peer resentment, on the other. As has been seen, she may a adopt a plain appearance. She will wait patiently in line to receive her share of kudos or a promotion, or, deferring to the dominants, stand near the end of the line when the bosses hand out praise, rewards, and promotions.

A second strategy is to revel in the notoriety of token status. The reveler may undercut possible new women hires and excessively criticize potential women peers. She enjoys or sees advantage in being the only woman so she intends to keep it that way, pulling the rope ladder up behind her. This is the Queen Bee syndrome the advice books describe.[14]

A third strategy tokens adopt is, as best they can, to make themselves socially invisible. Older generations of women workers pursued this strategy. They hid their sexuality as much as possible by, for example, adopting mannish forms of dress, from coveralls to mannish suits, and wearing little or no makeup. Many avoided public functions, whether meetings at work or social events surrounding work. They sat on the periphery of the meeting room or remained silent at meetings they did attend.

Observers of these coping strategies tend to think of the behaviors as gender linked but, Rosabeth Kanter feels, they "can be better understood as situational responses, true of any person in a token role."[15] Just as African-Americans and Jews did while trying to succeed in culturally alien environments, women may fear visibility because of retaliation costs and performance pressures token status creates for them. They play down any recognition of their presence.[16]

Title VII Cases

Again, the court cases bear witness to what the textbooks predict. An example is the case of Adrienne Corti, the only female Financial Services Manager (FSM) for StorageTek, a maker of data storage devices for computer networks. Corti was successful, winning a trip to Hawaii in a sales contest and also membership in StorageTek's "Master's Club" for her efforts. In 1995, Corti not only ranked first in her region but number one in the United States. Because of jealousy at her success, supervisors informed her that her position had been eliminated and offered her a demotion.

In truth, Corti's supervisor was smoothing the way for a regional FSM (male) whose higher level position StorageTek had eliminated. Rather than demote one of the two other males in the office, both of whom had consistently failed to meet sales quotas, the manager demoted the highly successful woman FSM, who had been too successful and had not adopted a coping strategy to compensate for her token status. Conti recovered $410,975 in damages from StorageTek.[17]

Retaliation against a token woman who had become too visible happens in larger organizations, which should know better, as well. Ann MacGregor was the senior female in marketing and the only female business segment director (BSD) for Mallinckrodt, Inc., a large publicly held producer of health care products (later acquired by the infamous Tyco International). When MacGregor's supervisor became national vice-president, he "reorganized his chain of command from seventeen direct reports, four of whom were female, to ten direct reports, none of whom were female." The new vice-president then promoted MacGregor's former peer, Stover, to be her supervisor. Stover would make comments such as "there are too many women at the table" in meetings—at which Mac-Gregor was the only woman in the room.

Stover determined to combine three BSD positions into a single director of marketing position. After announcing ground rules for filling the new position, Stover reopened the contest after it had neared completion so that the ultimate winner, a male from another facility who had no marketing experience, could enter the fray. Stover then offered MacGregor a new position, a demotion, with "no budgetary or supervisory responsibilities." After MacGregor balked over the salary Stover proposed, he filled the position with a less experienced male who received the very salary Stover had refused to give MacGregor. Thereafter, unbeknownst to

MacGregor, Stover sent a memo to all employees that MacGregor was leaving the company. She found out about her "consensual" departure by retrieving the memo from her mail box. The jury awarded Ann MacGregor $1 million in damages, which the court of appeals reduced to $700,000.[18]

These and other Title VII cases describe token women who have risen too high, or too fast, or are perceived by the male dominants as having done so, being cut down to size.[19] Gender-based tall-poppy syndromes live on in middle management ranks, highlighting the need tokens often have to be less visible or to adopt other coping strategies.

Boundary Heightening by the Dominants

If women as a group are ever to reach a meaningful level of participation in corporate governance, male superiors and women themselves must be aware of the obstacles they may face. For example, the presence of a woman may make the male dominants in a work group more aware of what they have in common. The males may also feel uncomfortable, or at least uncertain, in the presence of the token. The result may be that the majority group members take steps further to cement themselves together, emphasizing their sameness, and also to highlight more the token's difference. Sociologists call this process boundary heightening.

The dominants then exaggerate their culture. "Ironically, tokens, unlike people represented in greater proportions, are thus instruments for under-*lining* rather than under*mining* majority culture."[20] Among themselves the men increase camaraderie, which is based in part on tales of sexual adventure, sports talk, work prowess, and off-color jokes. The men act out, dramatizing the joke telling and the tales more when the token women are present than when they are not. In fact, when the token woman is not present, males' discussion reverts to more prosaic topics such as home repairs, child rearing issues, schooling, and household subjects.

The men isolate the women (or other token) further by reminding the token of the differences that the men deem to exist. Even if the men do so benevolently, out of a sincere wish to put the women at ease and to treat them appropriately ("let me get that for you," "that might not be safe for a woman"), the effect is the same. By its actions, the dominant group has demarcated even more clearly the boundary that exists between the token and the group.

The men may engage in creation of more formal boundaries by purposefully isolating the token. At Indsco, dominants whom Professor Kanter observed

> [m]oved the locus of some activities from public settings to which tokens had access to more private settings from which they could be excluded. [C]olleagues who rely on unspoken understandings may feel uncomfortable in the presence of "odd fellows" who cannot be trusted to interpret information in just the same way or to engage in the same relationships of trust and reciprocity. [T]he result was sometimes "quarantine"— keeping tokens away from some occasions. Informal pre-meeting meetings were sometimes held. Some topics of discussion seemed rarely raised by the men in the presence of their women peers. . . . [21]

Responses by Tokens to Boundary Heightening

Tokens may take extraordinary steps to demonstrate their loyalty to the group. They may also act out disloyalty to the minority group of which they are a part. A price of being one of the boys may be to be catty, to turn against women, even to backstab other women in the workplace. The token woman may also attempt to portray herself as exceptional to the male dominants who respond, "You're not a typical woman."

Humor may play a part. The token allows herself or her kind to be the object of the majority group members' humor, laughing with them as a way to signal acceptance of their dominant culture on their terms. In contrast, if the token objects to being the brunt of joke telling, the dominants deny any hostility, accusing the minority group member of lacking a sense of humor. The token may go drinking with the men, take part in conversations in which the men evaluate physical (sexual) attributes of other women, and otherwise become one of the boys.

In order to cope, the token may allow the males to encapsulate her in a role that represents a stereotype but one to which the majority is receptive. The token assimilates the characteristics associated with that stereotype. For example, the dominant males set the token woman up as the mother figure for the work group. The stereotype is that all women are sympathetic and good listeners. The males in the majority group seek her counsel and bring their troubles to her.

The downsides to role encapsulation as the mother figure are several. The group members value the token not for her independent job performance but for the counseling and other service she provides. The males expect her to be a noncritical, accepting mother figure. While her mother role gives her a place in the group as its emotional specialist, the role may come back to haunt her. As has been seen,[22] one of the stereotypical characteristics attributed to women, and one that may hold them back from promotion, is that women are regarded as excessively emotional.

As a coping strategy, a token may also permit the majority males to encapsulate her in the role of the group's pet. She is the mascot. The males expect her to be of constant good humor. She expresses appreciation of the males' displays and humor but does not enter into it herself. In turn, the males may compliment her but on the form rather than the substance. They may tell her "you talk so fluently" after she has given a presentation, whereas, after a presentation by a male, the commentary will be issue or content oriented.

Majority males may encapsulate token women in other roles as well, but by now the point is clear.[23] Tokens pay a price for pursuing a coping strategy, whether it involves becoming socially invisible or being encapsulated in a stereotypical role. The coping strategies tend to mask or diminish recognition by others in the organization of the productive activity the token has accomplished. Professor Kanter concludes that "[t]okens become encapsulated in limited roles that give them the security of a 'place' but constrain their areas of permissible or rewarded action" and delay or limit altogether their upward mobility in the organization.[24]

Token status forestalls recognition, and fewer women rise to the level at which they are potential entrants into the pool from which nominating committees and full boards choose directors for large publicly held corporations. Many of the dominant group behaviors, and the coping strategies as well, are distasteful to many women. They may leave the corporation altogether rather than put up with them. Thus, although we know that token and skewed-group status forestall's the entry of many women into corporate governance realms, that may only be the tip of the iceberg, as this phenomenon does not account for the numbers of tokens who leave the organization, never becoming players at all. We have known about and explored the legacy of token status for a long time, but we have never thought much about its ultimate effects on corporate governance.

Fallout from Boundary-Heightening Behaviors

The instances of boundary heightening when a token woman comes across the workplace threshold fairly leap out of many gender-based discrimination cases. The facts in the hostile environment cases constitute good samples of dominants emphasizing their commonality, isolating the token female.

Boundary-heightening behaviors also occur at higher levels within organizations, not distant from the glass ceiling. One such case was Reinee Hildebrandt's. Hildebrant had a Ph.D. in forestry. She was the only Ph.D., and the only female, among the four most senior program administrators in the Illinois Department of Forestry. Six years into her employment she had become the lowest paid administrator of the four. So she filed an equal pay complaint with the Department of Natural Resources' EEOC officer. Thereafter the state forester subjected Hildebrandt to quarterly evaluations while the men had only annual evaluations. Her working conditions had long varied greatly from those of the men:

> [U]nlike the men [she] was not allowed to communicate directly with forestry employees; she was required to submit monthly goal statements; she was denied adequate support staff; staff workers were disrespectful to her and were more friendly to the male administrators; she was provided fewer interns [and] denied computer equipment; and she was provided slower reimbursements [than the men for job-related expenses].[25]

Tidyman's, Inc., a mid-sized grocery chain in the Pacific Northwest, found itself with female barbarians at the [management] gates. Connie Hemmings had worked for the company for twenty-eight years, in 1987 rising to the level of controller from her beginnings as a store accounts payable clerk. Patty Lamphiear had fourteen years of service with the company, rising to the level of de facto customer prepaid inventory (CPI) manager and later assuming control of the Direct Store Delivery Department. She had begun her career as a part-time data entry clerk. These two experienced and capable women then learned that higher positions had become available. They applied for the positions: Hemmings for chief financial officer (CFO) and Lamphiear for a new position, grocery supervisor. That is when the males began heightening the boundaries.

Hemmings interviewed with an all-male committee, a first at the company. After the committee interview, the outgoing CFO told Hemmings that she did not get the job "because the board did not want to work with an emotional woman." When Hemmings filed an EEOC complaint, the new CEO began excluding her from conversations and intimidated and harassed her. She was "denied admission to meetings and excluded from the chain of command. . . . She no longer had power to hire and fire. [Her] salary was frozen from 1996 until 1999."

Lamphiear was told, "there is no way you could get the [management] position because the men in the company would run right over you." She, too, filed an EEOC complaint. Thereafter the CEO threatened her and the CFO insulted her. Her immediate supervisor engaged in nonstop verbal abuse. When Lamphiear would attempt to set up meetings to coordinate projects, the male managers would RSVP. "After confirming that they would attend, none of the men came to the meetings. Lamphiear felt undermined and increasingly insecure at work." The two women filed a court case and persevered through a trial, and appeal, ultimately recovering $1,930,000.[26]

The senior executives and other male managers at Tidyman's, including the CEO and the CFO, certainly circled the (male) wagons when two women seemed poised to enter the management ranks. There exist many other cases in which the males heighten the boundaries when a token female enters their midst, but few involving such senior positions.[27]

The Two-Token Situation

When a second token joins the team, the dominant males may attempt to play one token off against the other. The males may set up one woman as the superior performer and the other as the inferior performer. More overtly, the dominants may seek to insert a layer of hierarchy between two women who have started out at the same level, as for instance in making one the boss of the other.

As game theory (the prisoner's dilemma) teaches us, the appropriate response or coping strategy is for the two women or other tokens to develop a close alliance and refuse to be turned against each other.[28]

A slight shift in absolute numbers may relieve stresses for the first token but may also increase them. Two are few enough for the dominants easily to divide. Larger numbers may be necessary to relieve stresses and for supportive alliances to develop.

Skewed Groups

When the minority group numbers grow, say, four or five of thirty or so, minority status has moved beyond that of tokenism to that of a skewed group. In a skewed distribution, the mean (the average) is pulled to one side from the median (fiftieth percentile) whereas in a normal, or bell-curve, distribution the median and the mean are the same. Graphs of housing prices or executive salaries will be skewed because the presence of some very high prices or salaries will pull the mean to the right, away from the median.[29]

In the all-male group, the median and the mean are the same and there is no distribution around the median. If the situation were graphed as a bar chart, only one bar, a tall one, exists. If minority group members were inserted into the group, we would graphically represent the addition of four or so minority group members with a second, smaller bar off to one side. Were we to draw a line over the top of the bars we would have a representation (curve) similar to a skewed distribution.

Tokenism is hard on the solo or dual representative. As Professor Kanter portrays it, when a few additional minorities join the work group, the "temperature rises": "'X's' realize that circumstances are changing and they could be replaced by 'O's' competing for 'X' slots. A trickle of 'O's' can thus create backlash and a taste for discrimination to accompany the 'X' group's greater awareness of a threat to its dominance—to its monopoly over opportunity and power, its ability to define the culture and the values."[30]

Corporate Coping Strategies

In their response to token and skewed-group situations, organizations cope by a shifting to collaborative and team-production methods. Today many organizations organize tasks in project clusters that make people on the team aware of their interdependence. They provide training or facilitation to make teams work effectively. Periodically, when the team has completed a task or cluster of tasks, teams break. The necessity to adapt to a new team in order to complete a new project reemphasizes to the workers or managers just how dependent they may be on one another.

In organizations with old-fashioned hierarchies, the legacy of tokenism persists. If a free market ideology rules the roost, individuals "sink or swim based upon their ability to ferret out information and to make connections."[31] Males bond with males. Women may be crowded out in the quest to find a sponsor or mentor among the (male) higher-ups. Free market ideologies, which exist in many corporations, are the antithesis of the team building and collaborative ethics that, in turn, are effective antidotes to token and skewed-group situations.

For organizations, a second coping strategy is numerical. Executives redouble the organization's and their own personal efforts to move beyond tokens. They achieve a critical mass of women or other minority group members among entry-level management trainees, middle managers, and upper-level managers.

Senior executives, including President Lawrence Summers at Harvard University, believe that many traits and behaviors they have observed during their careers and within their organizations are gender linked.[32] Sociologists such as Rosabeth Kanter contend that it is not so. Many of those behaviors, including assimilation of stereotypical behaviors or entire stereotypes, are strategies lone representatives (tokens) adopt to cope with their status and the boundary heightening in which the dominant group members may be prone to engage. The situation may not ease with the addition of a second, or even a third, minority group member. In numerical terms, more than incremental breakthroughs are necessary in places in which the legacy of tokenism persists.

Boundary heightening and responsive coping strategies may well have caused women to deviate from maximizing their performance on the job, or to conceal their actual performance behind a role or stereotype they have assumed, or to leave corporate positions altogether. Those behaviors have limited many women's upward mobility, including their progress above middle managers' ranks. In that way, women have been disproportionately underrepresented in the pool of candidates from which directors of large publicly held corporations are likely to be chosen.

All may not be what it appears to be. Reality is subtler than perceptions of reality. Senior managers evaluate women as emotional because of the way in which they speak and act. Managers may associate behaviors with gender when the reality is that those behaviors are responses (coping strategies) to organizational settings in which women have found themselves and that have masked women's (or other minority group members') ability to achieve, be promoted, and rise to the top.

PART III

Corporate Governance and the Keeper of the Keys to the Boardroom

10

Corporate Governance in America

Another Glass Ceiling Story

For eighteen years, Jennifer Passantino had worked her way up through the Johnson & Johnson Consumer Products Division. She was poised to move from "high level 3" to a "high level 4" management position in which her income would jump over $200,000 per year. Her performance reviews were consistently outstanding. A supervisor had written, "Jennifer demonstrates very strong selling skills, organizational ability, good business judgment." She was "well qualified" and should be "strongly considered" for promotions.

The promotions, however, did not materialize. Jennifer thought that she was bumping up against the glass ceiling. She contacted the Johnson & Johnson Division EEOC (Equal Employment Opportunity Commission) officer. He counseled her that "she would have to live with the burden of coming forward" because filing a complaint "could have ramifications." He told her, falsely it turns out, that Johnson & Johnson had only promoted ahead of her males who had higher performance reviews. Passantino persisted. In June 1995, she filed her EEOC complaint.

Within Johnson & Johnson, retaliation began. "Job responsibilities (such as her training duties) were removed, accounts (including the European account) were transferred to other employees without notice, and she was no longer included in division managers' meetings." Senior managers told her that she would have "to take a step backward," that is, accept a demotion, "in order to advance."

Over four years of retaliatory behavior,

[s]he constantly worried, cried, and felt trapped and upset. She felt she was forced to spend less time with her family because she feared she

would lose her job. . . . She suffered stomach problems, rashes, and headaches which required medical attention. [S]he sought counseling. . . . [H]er advancement within the company was brought to a halt.

Johnson & Johnson is, of course, a Fortune 500 company, its shares are listed on the New York Stock Exchange, and it and its products are household names. In Passantino's case, however, the court found that Johnson & Johnson permitted "the worst kind of good old boy system that allowed discrimination and discouraged reasonable questions about the promotion process." The judge entered a judgment against Johnson & Johnson and in Passantino's favor for $3.98 million. On appeal, the judgment was upheld.[1]

A Perfect System

In the late 1990s, U.S. academics in law and in business who specialize in corporate governance hypothesized that they had, to paraphrase the cartoon character Pogo, "seen perfection and it is us." These academic elites divined perfection in U.S.-style corporate governance. In truth, the system has many defects.

The purpose of this book has been to explore one of them, namely, the lack of women at the top, in positions as members of boards of directors or, rarer still, at the very top, as chief executive officers (CEOs) of large U.S. public corporations. An associated question, but by and large one for another day, is the lack of African Americans (388 board seats) and Hispanics (eighty-six seats), who together hold only 4.1 percent of the 11,500 board seats in the Fortune 1000, even though the two groups combined constitute 25 percent of the U.S. population.[2] Jennifer Passantino's case is symbolic of a principal reason why the defect persists. The glass ceiling remains in place. Women, and persons of color, rise through the middle-management ranks higher than they once did, only to hit the ceiling. Few attain the senior positions from which they might enter the pool from which director and CEO candidates are chosen. Other reasons—the manner in which women speak and act, and implications drawn therefrom, the legacy of tokenism, women's status as those who bear and, for the most part, rear our children—help explain why women are underrepresented in the pool from which candidates for the board of directors are chosen.

Highlighting their view that the governance scheme had achieved perfection was the academics' global convergence hypothesis. That is to say, from a global inventory of best practices and governance structures in corporate governance, major corporations and their advisors around the world were selecting and installing the *best* practices. In that process, the governance of major corporations was converging on a single point, or locus of points, that represented best practices in corporate governance. Not surprisingly, that locus and the ideal governance structure were the perfect U.S. system of corporate governance, as it had evolved through the 1980s and 1990s.[3]

Governance Basics

The topic of corporate governance is the subject of how corporations, large or small, govern themselves. In the United States, even after federal inroads mandated by the post-Enron Sarbanes-Oxley Act of July 2002, state laws in large measure govern the subject. A central provision of every state's laws provides that corporate powers "shall be exercised by or under the authority of a board of directors" and that "the business and affairs of the corporation be managed under the direction of" a board of directors.[4] If corporate governance is a solar system, the board of directors is the sun and the highest ranked corporate officers, such as the chief executive officer, are the first circle of planets around that sun.

Corporate governance deals with how directors are nominated, elected (by the shareholders, usually in meetings), removed, sued by disgruntled shareholders, and indemnified or insured for any losses they may suffer by reason of holding office. The subject deals with how directors may act: informally, only at meetings, or through committees. A substantial overlay deals not with legal requirements but with what best practices are for boards of directors in staffing themselves, forming committees, evaluating senior executives, setting policy, doing strategic planning, creating succession plans for the office of CEO, and so on.

Both in the United States, and in most developed countries, for the last fifteen years or so corporate governance has become a headline topic. Continuing the planetary metaphor, the money, power and prestige involved in corporate governance is astronomical. The massive, systemic failures in 2002 and 2003, the years of our corporate governance discontent—Enron, Global Crossing, Tyco, Xerox, WorldCom, Adelphia Communications, and others—moved corporate governance issues even more into the headlines. Further scandals resulting from governance failures—HealthSouth, Marsh & McLennan, Hollinger International, and others—have followed.

Some U.S. academics, business people, and pundits believed that global convergence on the U.S. model would come about through foreign firms' stock exchange listings in the United States. As a condition to listing foreign corporations' shares, the New York Stock Exchange (NYSE) and the National Association of Securities Dealers Automatic Quotation System (NASDAQ) would require those foreign firms to observe U.S. corporate governance practices. These academics cited, for example, the number of Israeli high tech-firms that, in the 1990s, had come to U.S. markets seeking capital through a share offering and a stock exchange listing.[5]

The largest cluster of foreign listings on U.S. stock exchanges actually is of Canadian corporations, hardly robust evidence of a prospect of global convergence. Also, following a worldwide trend, stock exchanges in the United States may someday soon demutualize, that is, convert from member-owned institutions to shareholder-owned corporations whose shares trade like any others. Many other stock exchanges around the world, from Sydney and Hong Kong to London and Brussels, have already completed the process of demutualizion. With demutualization, profit maximization will become more the goal and the good governance movement, with stock exchanges as leaders of it, will assume a low priority.[6]

Following the Enron and WorldCom debacle, the U.S. Congress entered the corporate governance field for the first time, with the Sarbanes-Oxley Act of 2002. Sarbanes-Oxley (SOX or SOXA) establishes a number of corporate governance minimums about audit committees of the board of directors, loans to directors (which are now forbidden), composition of the board, certification of quarterly and annual financial results, and installation and certification of internal accounting controls. The legislation is expansive, making it difficult for even a knowledgeable person to get her arms around it, but one thing is clear: its provisions apply to foreign corporations that seek to have shares traded in the United States.

Estimates are that Sarbanes-Oxley imposes upon a foreign corporation whose shares trade in the United States extra costs ranging upward from $1,040,000 a year. The most recent evidence is that smaller numbers of foreign companies are delisting their shares, leaving the United States [7]

More importantly, the number of public companies coming to U.S. shares has slowed from 70–80 per year to nothing.

Recent events have laid firmly to rest any notion that corporate governance will improve, and will do so on a global basis, as the result of stock exchanges' regulations.

The End-of-History (Perfection) Hypothesis

A Harvard Law School professor, Reinier Kraakman, and a counterpart then at Yale Law School, Henry Hansmann, borrowed the title of Francis Fukuyama's celebrated books,[8] publishing an article they titled "The End of History." They posited a worldwide competition between economic systems and corporate governance practices. That competition, however, had ended. And the victor? U.S.-style corporate governance. The U.S. model had won the race, proving itself superior to any other system or set of practices.[9]

Not only had the U.S. model achieved superiority; it had also achieved perfection. Thus, the "end of history" for the evolution of new or differing corporate governance practices had arrived.[10] The student editors of the *Georgetown Law Journal* published "The End of History" in 2001, shortly before signs of Enron's implosion appeared in the headlines, raising serious questions about corporate governance in the United States.[11] Then, in 2002, Congress enacted and the president signed the Sarbanes-Oxley Act, evincing a belief that something was seriously wrong with corporate governance in the United States.

Defects remain in U.S. corporate governance.[12] The diversity question has long received attention from persons in fields other than corporate and business law or corporate governance. Most notably, in the social sciences, in 1973, professor of sociology Rosabeth Kanter of Harvard published "Men and Women of the Corporation," which dealt with the lack of power and opportunity and the effects of tokenism upon women at mythical Industrial Supply Corporation, modeled on a large company she had investigated. She published a revised edition of her classic in 1993.[13]

One of the earliest works in the field of corporate governance demographics was Canadian, published in 1985.[14] More recently, established legal scholars such as Donald Langevoort of Georgetown University and Marleen O'Connor of Stetson University School of Law have entered the field, layering the teachings of behavioral psychology over what law and management science contributes to the corporate governance field.[15] Law professor Kellye Testy has bemoaned the lack of demographic study in the field, a shortcoming this book remedies in part.[16] A few young scholars, the most notable of whom is Steven Ramirez, have begun to explore and to raise questions concerning the lack of diversity on boards and in CEO suites.[17]

The field of management science, concerned more with issues directly related to the bottom line, has contributed little to the subject of diversity, and particularly the lack of women, in the boardroom. An exception has been the journal *Women in Management Review* which has been published in the United Kingdom since 1992. The journal periodically publishes shorter works concerning diversity in the boardroom.[18]

The problem's dimensions extend beyond the top rungs of corporate hierarchies. Certain studies demonstrate that the more women there are in director positions, the greater the number of women in senior management positions.[19] That this trickle-down effect exists is without doubt, as its existence has been verified by clear and unambiguous findings. It provides additional evidence for the participation of more women on boards of directors and in senior management positions.

Tokenism at the Top

For a period of time in 1999, only a single female CEO, Jill Barad at Mattel Toy Co. (appointed January 1, 1997), served among the business elite, CEOs of Fortune 500 corporations. For a period of a few months in 2000, after the Mattel board had dismissed Barad in February, again only one female, Carleton Fiorina at Hewlett-Packard, served among CEOs in the Fortune 500. At each of these two moments in time, women constituted two-tenths of 1 percent of Fortune 500 CEOs.

The year 2001 saw a breakthrough. The number of women CEOs rose to four out of five hundred, and then in 2002 to five, or 1 percent. The current (2005) count is eight.

Boards of large publicly held corporations have eleven, thirteen, or even seventeen or nineteen directors but, in a majority of cases, only one of those directors will be a woman. A minority of boards, but still a significant number (14.4 percent of the 2001 Fortune 500; 12.3 percent in 2005) have no women members at all.

How can this be? Women have been graduating from the law and MBA schools in significant numbers since the early 1970s. By 2000, women earned 35 percent of the MBAs and over 42 percent of the law degrees awarded in the United States, compared with 1970, when women earned only 3.6 percent of the MBA degrees and 5.4 percent of the law degrees.[20] Today women fill out the ranks of middle and upper-middle management at most large corporations.

Academic writings in the law and business schools positing achievement of perfection in U.S. corporate governance perhaps provide a first response to the question, "How can this be?" If our leading corporate governance scholars detect an end of history because no further improvements need to be made, then surely complacency may be one reason for a lack of sustained progress in integrating women into corporate hierarchies and finally into boardrooms. Other reasons may be obvious, such as the failure to accord economic value to child bearing and child rearing. Or the reasons may be more subtle, such as the male proclivity to stereotype women on the basis of speech patterns and inflections, or the legacy of token status in a work group or job classification. The latter forces many women to adopt coping strategies that mask or retard achievements in their work, leading to underrepresentation in the senior management ranks from which director candidates are chosen.

As the introduction notes, this book attempts to tease out implicit male biases (including those resulting from complacency at and near the top of many corporate organizations) in the deep structure of corporate governance. The analysis sheds light on how patterns of male dominance in corporate governance replicate, from corporation to corporation. The book also has attempted to unpack those factors that may be important when women in business are on a climb that may lead to the boardroom or the CEO's suite. Now the analysis must move on from matters relating to women and their roles in corporate operations (speech patterns, tokenism, the price of motherhood, legal obstacles) to the system of corporate governance itself.

11

Women, Culture, and the U.S. Model of Corporate Governance

Governance and nominating committees, as well as CEOs and other male corporate higher-ups, deduce that the modern model of corporate governance ill suits, or suits not at all, the personality and the cultural background of women. The model's paradigm is a standup, ruggedly individualistic director (male) who will remove an underperforming CEO or file a lawsuit when he has to. Women may not have the right qualities, or may be perceived that way, in part because those qualities may not be as apparent in women as in men. For that reason, governance committees and corporations simply do not nominate women for directors' positions very often.

Boards of Directors circa 1960

Two patterns of board composition were common. One pattern, commonplace in the 1950s and 1960s, was the insider-dominated board on which the corporate president (today's CEO) placed family members, cronies, and subordinates executives, all of whom were probably beholden to him for their positions. Thus, a board of directors might consist of the corporation's president, the executive vice-president (equivalent today to the chief operating officer, or COO), treasurer (today chief financial officer, or CFO), a president or two of principal subsidiaries, a member of the corporation's founding family (if the family still had large shareholding), a crony or two, and two or so fellow CEOs from other publicly held companies. It is lonely at the top, for corporate presidents and CEOs as well as for ship captains. Fellow CEOs have always been the single largest source of corporate directors.[1]

The second pattern of board composition was the extremely large board, with as many as twenty-one, twenty-four, or twenty-six directors. Due to what are known as collective action problems, the outside directors would find it difficult to network among themselves. By default, an inner group of directors consisting of the president and the executives beholden to him controlled the agenda and decision making. Today, in the not-for-profit corporate sector, large boards predominate.[2]

Both patterns of board composition had similar characteristics. One was that, until the late 1960s, corporate boards of directors were made up of white Anglo Saxon Protestants (WASPs).[3] There were no Jews, Italians, Eastern Europeans; few Catholics; and no African Americans, Hispanics, or women.[4]

Second, board service was exceptionally long. Management (the corporate president) nominated and the shareholders elected the same individuals year after year. Twenty or more years' service on a board was not uncommon.

Third, directors were seldom, if ever, proactive. Save in the case of the corporate president's insanity or terminal disease, a situation necessitating planning for succession, directors sat back, listened, and rubber stamped decisions management had already made. Service on a board was like citizenship during the Vietnam War. You were either to "love it or leave it." Rocking the boat would result in a failure to renominate the director for the ensuing year and an end to board service.[5]

Fourth, many publicly held corporations used a device known as the executive committee to cement further in power the insider group the president headed. The executive committee of 3–4 members, authorized by the corporate law of most states, exercised the power of the full board between meetings, save for several key matters (declaration of dividends, reduction of capital, amendment of the corporate charter) that by law the board could not delegate to a committee. Use of an executive committee meant that the full board needed to meet less frequently, allowing the insiders to call even more shots.[6]

Fifth, a greater number of trophy directors, then almost all male, sat on five, six, eight, ten, or even twelve public company boards.[7]

Metaphors for board service abounded. In nineteen-century England, Lord Boothby's dictum was that "being a company director was akin to taking a nice warm bath."[8] There were "mushroom directors," who were kept in the dark, had a lot of manure piled upon them, and, if they grew too much in the job, would be "canned." One apocryphal story in presidential circles was that you fed your board a roast beef lunch, with ample quantities of mashed potatoes and good red wine, *before* the board convened for its quarterly meeting.

Long board service, with resulting low turnover, and the prevalence of male trophy directors, insured that in the 1950s and 1960s few openings existed for new blood—female, minority, or otherwise. Cronyism and political considerations (mainly consolidation of the CEO's power through nomination of loyal insiders) tended to insure that WASP males filled vacancies when they did occur.

Good Governance

Much of this has changed in the good governance movement, which dates from around 1980.[9] One leading blueprint for "good" corporate governance in the modern era is the American Law Institute's *Principles of Corporate Governance and Structure,* known in shorthand as the "ALI Corporate Governance Project," which was quite controversial at its inception in the early 1980s but which received little fanfare when it appeared in final form (in two volumes) in 1994.[10]

An early ALI recommendation was that law provide that all large publicly held corporations have a majority of directors who were independent of management. Because the proposal was controversial in 1980, the ALI drafters relegated it to only a suggestion of what good practice might be.[11] The independent director majority, or indeed supermajority, has now become standard, required by New York Stock Exchange and NASDAQ rules as well as the Sarbanes-Oxley Act. It is old hat.

The ALI also tried to transform and more narrowly focus the mission of a board of directors. From state corporate laws that mandating that "the business and affairs be managed by a board of directors" to later versions that commanding that the corporation's business and affairs be managed "under the direction of or under the supervision of a board of directors," the ALI drafts attempted to bring matters more into line with the reality of corporate operation. The ALI draft would have stated that the business and affairs of a corporation be "conducted by or under the supervision of [the] principal senior executives."[12]

In turn, the role of the now independent board would be to hire, monitor the performance of, and, if necessary, replace the senior executives, most particularly the chief executive officer.[13]

Another facet of the good governance movement was deemphasis, or elimination altogether, of the old-fashioned executive committee. Under best-practice standards, in its place corporations were to substitute three principal board committees. The audit committee (today mandatory under the Sarbanes-Oxley Act but in widespread use since the mid-1980s) would meet periodically with the corporation's outside and internal auditors, acting as a focal point for discussion of financial accounting and disclosure issues within the corporation. The audit committee's function was to act as a further filter for the financial information that went to the full board of directors and upon which it would evaluate performance of the senior executive officers.

The nominating committee, today often titled the "governance committee," had as its original, principal objective removal of the nomination of directors from the CEO's hands, in which it had traditionally been lodged. The committee was to be a device to insure that a critical mass of truly independent directors existed, if and when it became necessary for the board to replace the CEO or other senior executives. As a byproduct, the nominating committee might also be a force for increasing diversity on corporate boards.

A third principal board committee, the compensation committee, sets the cash and noncash compensation of the 4–5 most highly compensated executives. It may perform other functions, such as policy making with regard to stock option and deferred compensation plans (pension ad profit sharing).

The Modern Era

The ALI Corporate Governance Project continued for fifteen years, from 1979 to 1994. During that period of time, house counsel from major U.S. corporations joined the ALI in droves with the hope that they could influence the final product. On the floor of the ALI's annual meetings at Washington's Mayflower Hotel, house counsel caucused and took positions radically different from those proposed by the ALI reporters, authors of the drafts. While they railed against ALI positions on the floor of ALI meetings, corporate counsel returned to Atlanta, or New York, or St. Louis and told CEOs, boards of directors, and counsel at other corporations that they had seen the future direction corporate governance might take. On a voluntary basis, many large corporations implemented the governance structures and practices that had proven so controversial in the early 1980s, so much so today that they are the accepted wisdom of what minimally acceptable practices are.

Directors today very much focus on evaluation of chief executive officers. In the first half of the 1990s, 7 percent of Fortune 500 companies saw boards of directors confronting and forcibly removing underperforming or misbehaving CEOs. In 1992–1993 alone, twenty-two Fortune 500 CEOs resigned, forced from office.[14] Directors forced out CEOs at United Airlines (twice), General Motors (twice), IBM, Apple Computer (four times), American Express, Eastman Kodak (twice), Gillette, Mattel Toy, Lockheed Martin, Aetna Insurance, Westinghouse, and on and on. The trend accelerated in the late 1990s.[15]

Post-Enron, and post-WorldCom, the thinking has come full circle. The general consensus is that boards of directors and board committees, even though only part-time, should return more to the old model, in which boards had a broader, participatory focus. Instead of a sharpened focus on monitoring CEOs and other senior executives, boards should focus again on monitoring the business itself, as far flung and diversified as it may be, and as difficult as it may be for directors who meet four or five times per year.

Relational Investors and Blueprints for Good Governance

Good governance has become a rallying point for activist institutional investors such as public employee pension plans that have under management billions of dollars.[16] CALPERS, the California employee pension plan, under the leadership of Dale Hanson, each year promulgated a hit list of portfolio companies that were laggards in good governance. TIAA CREF, the Wisconsin Investment Board, and many labor union and public employee pension plans undertook similar activities. Those institutions had portfolio positions in individual companies so large that their managers felt exit by way of the market (selling shares) was not a viable alternative. They felt they had no choice but to become active players in corporate governance and in other affairs of portfolio companies.

Business Week magazine began publishing each year a list of the best and worst boards of directors in the United States.[17] Trade groups such as the Institutional Investors Responsibility Research Council began to play an active role in corporate governance initiatives.[18] Paid consultants such as Institutional Investors Services advise subscribers on breaking governance developments. They also recommend how to vote on public interest, governance, and similar proxy proposals shareholders have submitted at subscriber portfolio corporations.

As a byproduct of the successive removal of Roger Smith and then Robert Stempel as CEOs, the General Motors board published its "29 points," which became another influential yardstick for measuring good corporate governance.[19]

The phenomenon is not limited to the United States. In Canada, the Toronto Stock Exchange published "Where Were the Directors?"—a critique of the failure of governance systems and boards of directors to curb the financial excesses of the 1980s. In England, Sir Adrian Cadbury, of Cadbury Schweppes, chaired the first of several committees that dealt with suggestions for a code of best practices in corporate governance.[20] The London Stock Exchange requires listed companies to disclose which best practices companies have, or have not, installed.[21]

France has both the Vienot and Mazini reports on corporate governance.[22] In Australia, the Bosch Report and the Institute of Company Directors have proven influential.[23] Belgium and Italy have their own reports on corporate governance. In 2000, Korea became the first nation to enact into statutory law a corporate governance code for that country's publicly held companies.[24]

Culture versus Governance Model

What does the good governance movement portend for women as directors? Seemingly, with its disfavor of insider-dominated boards, overly long board service, cronyism, trophy directors, and so on, good governance should bode well for women and minorities in governance. But it has not. As Professor Rakesh Khurana observed, after extensive interaction with directors,

> Although not one director I met (including one woman and one African-American I interviewed) made reference to this obvious fact, board members are similar along a variety of observable demographic dimensions such as gender (they are almost all males), race (they are almost always white), age (they are in their fifties and sixties), occupation (most occupy or have occupied the highest administrative positions in organi-

zations), class (most are quite wealthy), and status (they are affiliated with high-prestige institutions and clubs, and almost all have a biographical sketch in Marquis's *Who's Who in America*).[25]

One explanation for the continuing deficit of women and minorities may be incongruities, indeed a clash, between culture and the governance model that results from the good governance movement.

The U.S. model portends more than a little dissonance between the model and women as potential directors, or gives support for those kinds of views in the eyes of the beholders, namely, the directors who will select likely candidates for board service. As has been suggested, the model's standup, ruggedly individualistic director paradigm may not suit the personality or cultural background of many women in business—or key decision makers may perceive such to be the case.

Corporate Governance and Post-Confucian Culture

Others have noted the dissonance between the U.S. model and Asian cultures, most notably post-Confucian culture. With 1.4 billion citizens, the People's Republic of China is the fastest growing and soon to be largest economy on earth. Good governance is a topic under constant examination there.

In addition, through the Chinese diaspora, an additional forty million Chinese have emigrated to other Asian nations, where they control large sectors of the economy.[26] They play significant roles in the economies of Taiwan, Singapore, Indonesia, the Philippines, Malaysia, and Thailand, among others. In the Philippines, overseas Chinese control forty-seven of the sixty-eight locally owned public companies; overseas Chinese account for 2.1 percent of the population but control 75 percent of the private domestic capital in Indonesia.[27]

Although Confucianism lacks both a deity and an organized church, Confucian values permeate the lives of Chinese peoples everywhere. From a very early age, as University of Hong Kong Professor of Law Gordon Redding describes it, "[i]n the school context, Confucianism is taught by the study of the main writings and the discussion of their implications. The child is encouraged to memorize the classics and to build relationships based upon Confucian principles."[28] Central to those relationships is a high degree of abnegation of self and tolerance or patience with others. "The Confucian ideal is that family, clan and head of state take precedence over the individual."[29] In the Confucian context, "the individual has a built-in sense of the legitimacy of the superior-subordinate relationship . . . [as] an extension of the natural order. The open challenge of formal authority is rare."[30]

Commentators have attributed the robust economic growth in the Asian "tiger" states and elsewhere to the pervasiveness of Confucian values in business.[31] Later commentators, positing a "global convergence" in corporate governance, have urged upon Asian governments and business communities the U.S. governance model reviewed earlier in this chapter.

Corporate Governance and Women Culture

One has to question how a corporate governance model that entails a degree of confrontation and a high degree of individualistic behavior (the U.S. model) fits with beliefs that "an individual must fit into and conform with the basic social ordering of his surrounding world." In that order, each individual regards herself "not only . . . as part of nature but also part of the natural order."[32]

Core values in economic behavior include a "concern for reconciliation, harmony and balance," coupled with "practicality as a central focus." It is doubtful whether Chinese and other post-Confucian societies, in which individuals learn from an early age that "the shiny nail is first to feel the sting of the hammer," will produce businesspeople who are prepared forcibly to remove underperforming CEOs, to step forward to voice their dissent when necessary, or to conform to other aspects of the U.S. governance model and its paradigm for who should be corporate directors.

In a similar way, women may also be not quite suited to the paradigm, or to the paradigm that key corporate decision makers have in their mind's eye. Women are problem solvers, not confrontationists. Women are task oriented—not-win-at-all-costs oriented. They are team players, not rugged individualists. Linguistics researchers, or some of them, find that women differ from men on subjects such as confrontation versus indirectness, interruption, silence versus volubility, topic raising, and adversariness or verbal conflict. "All of these strategies [predominantly of men] have been 'found' by researchers to express or create dominance or subordination."[33] Women express themselves in "a different register" than men.

More modern, or less simplistic research, such as that by Professor Deborah Tannen, has found that the "meaning of any of the identified linguistic strategies may vary depending upon the context," or may not be at all what it appears to be.[34] The perception of material differences endures in many quarters, however, subconsciously if not otherwise. The mismatch (or collision) between the U.S. governance paradigm and the characteristics of many very successful women resembles the collision of the governance model and culture seen with corporate governance and Chinese and overseas Chinese, who nonetheless, or because of cultural characteristics, have achieved stunning economic successes. Subconsciously, corporate CEOs and nominating committee members may be influenced by the governance-culture mismatch, deselecting women otherwise qualified for board service.

12

Women in Corporate Governance
The Numbers versus the Expectations

Eighty-four percent of Fortune 1000 companies, firms on the prestigious list of the largest corporations in the United States, have one director who is female. In 2001, seventy-two Fortune 500 companies, or 14.4 percent, had *no women* directors on their boards.[1] If one searches for boards with two female directors, the number falls to around 30 percent.[2] The number of corporations with three women directors is so small that few of the board composition studies tally the number.

For example, the Conference Board of the United States reports only whether public companies have a single female director. In 2003, the board reported that for 2002, out of 662 reporting small, medium, and large capitalization public companies, 36 percent of the manufacturing companies, 26 percent of the financial service companies, and 31 percent of the services companies had *no* women directors. Fifty-eight percent of the manufacturing companies, 49 percent of the financial services companies, and 52 percent of the services companies had no racial/ethnic minority representation on their boards. Moreover, the Conference Board reports the trends as flat. For example, the 2000 numbers for public companies with no female directors were 36 percent for manufacturing companies (35 percent in 2002); 25 percent in financial services (26 percent in 2002); and 33 percent in services (31 percent in 2002).[3]

Catalyst, Inc., the New York based–organization that advocates a greater role for women in governance, put a brighter face on the situation. Catalyst registers 13.6 percent of the board seats at Fortune 500 companies as being held by women, up from slightly over 11 percent in 2001.[4] In the Fortune 1000, according to another study, out of 11,681 board seats, 11.9 percent were held by women. In 1998, the percentage was 11.2 percent. "If this pace continues," remarked the author of the study, "women on top corporate boards won't equal the number of men until the year 2064."[5]

A more unbiased study, which factors in that many women at the top hold board seats at several corporations, shows that the number of real players is smaller. Statistical study shows that the numbers are bleaker, and the reality somewhat bleaker still, in U.S. corporate governance than Catalyst's numbers show.[6]

Board Size

The average (mean) board size of larger publicly held U.S. corporations is approximately eleven directors,[7] down from an average of thirteen a decade or so ago. Traditional board sizes range from eight or nine at investment banks such as Goldman Sachs, or even seven at Warren Buffet's Berkshire Hathaway, to eighteen directors at the Walt Disney Company, nineteen at Exxon and General Electric, twenty at Bank of America and Pfizer, or even twenty-one at Albertsons, the largest U.S. grocery chain.[8] In 2001, the largest board was at U.S. Bancorp, with twenty-six directors.

The subsequent trend has been toward the mean and median, with smaller boards expanding and overly large boards downsizing. This is relatively easy to accomplish for one of two reasons. First, in most corporations board size is fixed by a bylaw and it is the board of directors that has the power to amend the bylaws. Second, and in the alternative, many corporations have a variable-range board size authorized by statute and implemented by a bylaw.[9] Within that range, the sitting directors are free to expand or to downsize the board.

Berkshire Hathaway has expanded its board of directors to eleven members, in part as a reaction to criticism of Warren Buffett for his personal failure to institute good governance in the corporation he controls. On the other side of the median (or mean), for example, the Walt Disney Company, Albertsons, and SBC Communications have all downsized their boards in recent years, to thirteen, thirteen, and twenty-one directors, respectively.[10] Exxon-Mobil has downsized from nineteen to eleven directors, a sometimes seen development after a merger in which the boards combine and elect not to force any director off the combined board. Subsequently, board size atrophies through attrition.

On the typical U.S. board, nine directors are independent, that is, free of significant financial ties to the corporation or to its senior executives.

Two directors are nonindependent. The latter are usually the CEO and another insider, often a senior executive, although the latter could be replaced by a nonindependent outsider such as the corporation's outside counsel, its investment banker, or a commercial banker.

Following adoption of the Sarbanes-Oxley Act, in July 2002, both the New York Stock Exchange (NYSE) and the National Association of Securities Dealers Automatic Quotation (NASDAQ) trading organization adopted rules that corporations with securities listed must have a majority of directors who are independent.[11] A supermajority, that is, significantly more than merely 50 percent plus one (a simple majority), of publicly held corporations exceeded that standard—many by far—for a number of years before the exchanges adopted it.

Emphasis on Independent Directors

The most significant trend in corporate governance over the last fifteen years has been the insistence that a supermajority of directors of publicly held companies are independent. Board service by lawyers, investment bankers, and other economically dependent outsiders (termed "gray outsiders") has declined precipitously,[12] for a number of reasons. Their presence on the board might cloud their judgment when senior executives ask them for independent professional advice and counsel. In deciding whether or not to give deference to a decision made by a board of directors that has turned out badly, courts total the number, not of inside versus outside directors, but of independent directors versus nonindependent directors (whether formally inside or outside the corporation).

In the event of accounting or financial scandals at the corporation, aggrieved shareholders and their lawyers may sue lawyer or banker directors, and their law firm or bank. Given the astronomical costs and the adverse publicity, litigation may be especially unpleasant for the partners at the law firm or associates at the bank who may have received little direct benefit from their colleague's board service.

The 2005 settlements in the WorldCom and Enron cases may further deter persons with any significant net worth, which could include the lawyer or the commercial or investment banker, from board service as a director. In those cases, despite the existence of Director & Officer (D & O) liability insurance, and as a precondition to settlement, institutional investor plaintiffs insisted that independent directors disgorge 20 percent or more of their net worth (retirement plans, principal dwelling, and certain marital assets aside). In a settlement that unraveled but was later agreed to in similar form, ten WorldCom directors proposed to contribute $18 million to a $54 million settlement. Ten of seventeen Enron and ex-Enron directors contributed $10 million to a $168 million settlement, with insurance proceeds making up the remainder.[13] Those precedents will deter many suitable persons from service on boards of directors, including lawyers and bankers.[14]

It is too soon to tell what effect the WorldCom and Enron precedents and the threat of personal payments will have on women and other minorities' service as directors. If one assumes that, as a group, those categories of present and potential board members are more risk adverse than the larger pool of persons available for service, which may be a fair assumption, the negative effect of these widely publicized settlements on women and minority director candidates will be a more pronounced one.[15]

The Very Top: Women Chief Executive Officers

Women comprise slightly over half the U.S. population of 270 million. Sixty percent of women work, and they constitute 47 percent of the workforce.[16] Their presence on the boards of major corporations is thus disproportionately small, starkly so.

At the other end of the boardroom, in CEO offices, as of late 2005, only eight major U.S. corporations (Fortune 500 rankings in parentheses) have women chief executive officers (annual direct cash compensation in parentheses). They are

> Brenda C. Barnes, fifty-one, CEO of Sara Lee Corporation (114), Chicago, Illinois, the baking and food products company (cash compensation in 2005, $1.63 million);
> Mary Sammons, fifty-nine, CEO of Rite Aid (128), Camp Hill, Pennsylvania, the troubled drug store chain ($1,312,468 in 2004)($2.87 million in 2003);
> Anne Mulcahy, fifty-three, chairperson and CEO at Xerox (132), Stamford, Connecticut, the copier and information technology hardware company ($3,043,944 in 2004);

Patricia Russo, fifty-three, chairperson and CEO at Lucent Technologies (247), Murray Hill, New Jersey, a manufacturer of telecommunications hardware ($4,241,829 in 2004) ($9.04 million in 2003);

Andrea Jung, forty-six, chairperson and CEO at Avon Products, Inc. (278), New York, New York, the direct seller of cosmetics that has expanded into jewelry, accessories, apparel, decorative wares, home entertainment, and nutrition and health products ($3,718,157 in 2004) ($2.57 million in 2003);

S. Marce Fuller, forty-five, CEO of Mirant (424), Atlanta, Georgia, an owner of power plants and supplier of "merchant power" ($1,730,539 in 2004)($800,000 in 2003);

Marion Sandler, seventy-three, with her husband, co-CEO and cochair of Golden West Financial Corporation (435), the California-based holding company that operates savings and loans in California, Florida, Colorado, Texas, Arizona, New Jersey, Kansas, and Illinois ($1,449,313 in 2004);

Eileen Scott, fifty-two, CEO of Pathmark Stores (467), Carteret, New Jersey, Philadelphia, New Jersey, and New York supermarket chain ($649,000).[17]

In February 2005, as the next chapter recounts, the board of directors at Hewlett Packard Co., which is the eleventh largest company in the United States, removed from office CEO Carleton S. Fiorina (Carly), fifty, the most visible woman CEO in the Fortune 500. Fiorina had served H-P through six often turbulent years.[18]

In early fall 2001, the board of Xerox Corporation, the troubled copier company, awarded the CEO title to President Anne Mulcahy.[19] Prior to 2001, there were only two women CEOs in the select circle, Fiorina at Hewlett-Packard and Jung at Avon Products. With the entry, or reentry, of Golden West Financial into the Fortune 500, and the appointment at Spherion of Cynthia Hallman, who has since retired, the number jumped to four and the percentage to eight-tenths of 1 percent in 2001.[20] Finally, Mulcahy's elevation put the percentage at an even 1 percent, an apogee of sorts for women in U.S. CEO suites.

Upon Jill Barad's dismissal as CEO at Mattel Toy, in February 2000, a period ensued in which only *one woman chief executive officer,* Marion Sandler at Golden West Financial Corp., served at a large publicly held corporation in the United States. Because her career, and her dismissal, bears a strong resemblance to Carleton Fioria's dismissal, and teaches valuable lessons about women in corporate governance, the next chapter also recounts Jill Barad's tenure as a CEO.

In absolute numbers, the growth in women CEOs has come late, most of it occurring not until the twenty-first century, but has been significant: from none to two to four to five, then eight, and then seven in less than five years. In relative numbers, the population of women CEOs may still be said to be paltry: 1.6 percent.[21]

At the officer level, or among what are often termed the "bylaw officers," the numbers are hardly more encouraging. Women comprise less than 4 percent of the uppermost ranks, which at most companies include positions with titles such as president, executive vice-president, chief operating officer (COO), and chief financial officer (CFO). Women comprise less than 3 percent of the top wage earners in the corporate sphere.[22]

Importance of Women CEOs

Executive search firms such as Korn/Ferry International, Stuart Spencer & Associates, or Heidrick & Struggles, as well as corporate boards' nominating committees, compile lists of director candidates. A primary source of candidates is the roster of CEOs of publicly held companies.[23] If the number of women CEOs increases, so too might the number of women directors increase in even greater numbers, as a trickle-down effect takes hold.

The system of choosing chief executive officers, however, has today become a closed process of "Searching for a Corporate Savior," the title of a recent book by Professor Rakesh Khurana of the Harvard Business School.[24] Almost by definition, saviors, corporate or otherwise, are male. The nature of the CEO selection process itself excludes women:

> [T]he most recent studies of the social backgrounds of top executives reveal that they still are . . . male, white, native-born Protestants from socially and economically advantaged families. . . . [P]eter Temin has noted that while every study of the social composition of the executive class, ranging back over several decades, has found this same homogeneity, most have also predicted that this situation would not last. Researchers in the 1950s, 1960s, and 1970s, Temin says, "portray [the subjects of] their study as the last generation for which their observations would be

true. Conditions have been changing. . . . But the composition of the American business elite has not changed." . . . [It is a] closed type of system that the external CEO labor market most resembles—so much so that when a woman or an African-American becomes a CEO of a Fortune 500 company, it is worthy of a cover story in a business magazine.[25]

The "irony is that in America," where politicians, businessmen, and economists sing chorus after chorus in praise of free markets, "the process that determines who will lead [large corporate] organizations has been walled off, like the East Berlin Wall of old, from the tumultuous discipline of market forces."[26]

In the CEO selection process, corporate boards begin by forming a search committee comprised of from three to eight directors. Boards staff these committees with volunteers. Those who volunteer are the directors with the most free time, who tend to be retired from full-time endeavors and often are ex-CEOs. As the first order of business, the search committee then hires a prominent executive search firm (ESF) such as Korn/Ferry or Stuart Spencer to assist it.

The second order of search business is to draft a specification sheet for the CEO job. This is a curious priority. Seldom, if ever, do search committees first inventory the organization's needs. The "striking feature of these specification sheets is their emphasis on individual characteristics [consisting of] a collection of personal traits rather than a set of concrete skills or a discussion of the situational context of the search," Professor Khurana finds. The CEO should be "aggressive" and "able to balance risk with reward." The specification sheet names vague traits such as "change agent," "executive presence," "proven leader," "decisive," and "motivator."[27] Paramount among the "ill defined and contradictory" attributes listed on the specification sheet is "charisma," a term that originally meant "gift of grace" but now is a "creation of the social expectations vested in the candidate by the directors acting as a group."[28] Charisma, as in "charismatic CEO," has become trite, if not meaningless, but is the mantra du jour for the CEO selection process.

Board members themselves rather than ESFs are the greatest source of names for CEO searches, which means they tend to name their own kind—white, male CEOs or other experienced male senior executives who are "proven leaders" with "charisma." Surprisingly, ESFs tend to be the source of women and minority candidate names, if women or minorities appear as candidates at all. CEO searches are closed: unsolicited resumes do not appear. Thus the seventy-six CEO searches Professor Khurana examined contained not a single unsolicited resume, while in 411 searches for marketing vice-presidents the same ESFs received fifty-five hundred unsolicited resumes. The average CEO search collected thirty-one names at ESF "A" and forty-five names at ESF "B" while the comparable numbers for VP searches were 190 and 221.[29]

With a candidate list in hand, search committees begin a process of "social matching," "a filtering process that takes place when . . . organizational actors are confronted with choices that are difficult to select among because of limited information." The search committee members "seize upon one or more easily identifiable external characteristics of potential candidates to construct a narrowly defined candidate pool."[30]

One characteristic is the prestige associated with the company or position the candidate most recently held. Eighty percent of short-listed CEO candidates come from a firm or position the search committee members believe to be of equal or greater prestige than their own corporation. "[T]he notion that CEOs have a status that can be transferred from one company to another has become deeply ingrained in directors' new view of the CEO," but is viewed as misguided by Professor Khurana.[31]

The result of the method whereby directors chose CEOs is to create a closed CEO labor market in which serious candidates resemble one another and are younger clones of the white, male ex-CEO and similar directors who staff search committees. The "process that characterizes external CEO succession not only shed[s] light on the closed nature of the CEO market but also account[s], in particular, for the durable homogeneity we observe in the nation's CEO suite despite dramatic changes in the composition of the work force."[32] In short, the CEO selection process is a stacked deck, stacked against women executives and other minority candidates. In turn, the limited chances for greater numbers of female CEOs reduce the number of women in the pool from which corporate boards select director candidates.

Women on Boards of Directors: The Expectations

Back on the director side, in certain growth sectors, the statistics are even more bothersome. Among Internet companies in 2001, for example, according to advice book author Esther Wachs Book, only 2 percent of the board seats were held by women, as opposed to 11 percent in the Fortune 500 at the time. Thus one could scroll through the board rosters of six, seven, or eight companies in Silicon Valley or in Seattle before finding a single woman director.[33]

The scarcity of women in corporate governance roles is curious, because women have been entering the professional and managerial ranks in great numbers for nearly three decades now.

That entry may more easily be tracked, say, in the professions, where the professional associations have kept statistics. That is true, for example, of my profession, law, in which the American Bar Association and the Law School Admissions Council have keep statistics for a number of years now.

When I entered Northwestern University School of Law in Chicago in 1967, my class of matriculants included seventeen women, of 165 enrolling freshmen. The class that preceded my class, the class of 1969, included only one woman. The class about to graduate, the class of 1968, had two women. My law school class was thus the first breakthrough for women entering law school in numbers. The same was true at most other law schools, which either in that year, or within a few subsequent years, began receiving greatly increased numbers of applications from qualified women and admitting them.

The 1970s saw beginning entry in even greater numbers of women into MBA, law, and other professional schools. By the early 1970s, women comprised over 20 percent of the entering classes at the elite schools such as Harvard, Yale, Virginia, Michigan, and Stanford. Nationally, the percentages of women among all law graduates (who would have been admitted to law schools 3–4 years earlier) in the mid- to late 1970s were 19.1 percent in 1976; 22.8 percent in 1977; and 28.1 percent in 1979.[34] By 1987, women accounted for over 40 percent of the law degrees conferred, up from 37 percent in 1984, 38.3 percent in 1985, and 38.6 percent in 1986.

Throughout the late 1980s and 1990s, women as a percentage of law school graduates consistently hit in the mid- and high forties, ranging from 42.1 in 1990 to 42.6 in 1995 and climbing to 44.8 percent in 1999. In the new century, women students are now a majority of the students enrolled in U.S. law schools and accounted for 48.3 percent of the graduates in 2002 and 48.2 percent in 2003.[35]

In the MBA schools, the numbers have been good but not so robust as in the law schools. Throughout the 1980s and 1990s women comprised between 33 and 37.6 percent of those taking the Graduate Management Admissions Test.[36] In the early 1990s, however, the proportion of women test takers actually enrolling in MBA programs dropped from approximately 35–36 percent to the high 20s.[37] The phenomenon was pronounced enough that the Graduate Management Admissions Council commissioned a study that was completed in the late 1990s.[38]

Overall, MBA degrees conferred upon women were 11.6 percent of such degrees in 1976, rising to 19.2 percent in 1979.[39] The percentage reached 30 in 1984, ranging between 30 and 34 for the rest of the decade. There was an upswing in the 1990s to 36.9 percent of the MBA degrees conferred in 1995, 37.5 percent in 1996, and 38.9 percent in 1997. In 2000 and 2001, the latest years for which statistics are available, women received 39.8 percent and 40.7 percent of the MBA degrees conferred in the United States.

Thus women have been entering the professions and the managerial ranks of business in greater and greater numbers for between two and three decades now.

Reality versus Expectations

The statistics for beyond law school tell another story. By 1999, for example, women made up only 29 percent of the practicing profession. In law firms, women make up only 15.6 percent of the partners. At larger firms, where the money and the prestige is, the number is much lower, with women constituting only 7 percent of the equity partners (owners) at the United States'1,160 largest law firms.[40] Women make up only 13.7 percent of the general counsel at large corporations.[41] These numbers are paltry, given that the number of women being admitted to the bar has been in the 30, and then 40 percent range for over twenty-five years now.

But the statistics in law are not as surprising as are the statistics for the upper ranks of American business: CEOs and board memberships.

One inference from the board composition and other corporate governance statistics about American business is that, in many cases in which there are few women directors, women's presence in the boardroom or high managerial ranks is not particularly valued. So the inference that arises, and fairly so, is that CEOs and board members add women, and persons of color, to their ranks out of felt necessity rather than choice, in other words, for window dressing. The presence of *a woman,* or of two women, on a board may represent tokenism.

Whether or not the accusation of tokenism in U.S. corporate governance is a fair one is an important question for this book.

Director Compensation

A second question is, Are those women on boards and perhaps in CEO office suites golden tokens? What is in it (the climb to the top) for anyone, man or woman? Is the pearl worth the price?

A director at a major corporation will receive an annual retainer of, say, $15–20,000. The corporation also may pay her a meeting fee for each meeting attended. If the board meets every other month, a frequent arrangement, and has one or two special meetings, $2,500–3,000 meeting fees for full board meetings may total $20–24,000 annually.

In many corporations, one of those meetings may be a "fly away" meeting where directors go for a two- or three-day retreat at an exclusive resort or in a scenic city (San Francisco or London).

Corporations also compensate directors for service on board committees. If a director is on, say, the audit committee, exercising oversight regarding the corporation's inside and outside accountants and auditors, she may attend five, six, or seven additional meetings for which she is entitled to meeting fees. Directors on governance, compensation, or other committees would usually attend fewer committee meetings.

So, with her annual retainer ($15–20,000), her board-meeting fees ($20–24,000), and her committee-meeting fees ($12,500), our mythical director may receive total direct cash compensation of $47,500–56,500 for each year she serves.[42] Conference Board of the United States statistics confirm the guesstimates for our mythical director. For 2002 (the last year available), the board reported average director cash compensation for directors, by company category, as follows: (1) diversified financial services, $59,000; (2) petroleum companies, $55,500; (3) telecommunications, $ $54,500; (4) electric and gas, $48,500; and (5) industrial chemicals, $48,000.[43]

Stock options and other forms of indirect compensation are less rare today than they used to be, at least for rank-and-file directors, but when one finds stock option or restricted stock grants, the grants' amounts are usually small.[44] As of 1998, 50 percent of the S&P 500 offered options to nonemployee directors, up from 46.4 percent in 1997 and 42 percent in 1995.[45] Conference Board 2002 statistics for combined cash-stock compensation for directors, by company category, were (1) oil and gas field services, $96,028; (2) industrial chemicals, $76,805; (3) diversified financial services, $76,750; (4) food, beverage, and tobacco, $72,894; and (5) plastic and rubber products manufacture, $71,200.[46]

At the height of the 1998–1999 stock market bubble, directors of several high-tech enterprises set records for combined cash-stock compensation. For example, in 1999, directors at Sun Microsystems, Inc., received $409,500 and those at Compaq Computer Corp. received $363,448.[47]

Among the highest director compensations recently paid were the salaries received by Enron directors, who were paid approximately $350,000 per year, half in cash and half in unrestricted stock. In addition, many Enron directors had side consulting agreements with the company under which additional compensation of from a few thousand to over $100,000 was paid annually.[48] Today there is universal agreement that such side consulting agreements for directors, who are supposed to be independent, are per se improper. Similarly, corporate governance experts condemn compensation for directors that much exceeds what the mythical director reviewed above receives. Director independence implies directors who can and will assert themselves in proper circumstances and, if need be, walk away. A tendency not to rock the boat, and to be connected to one's director position by silver (if not golden) handcuffs, exists when companies pay their directors Enron-type compensation. Excessive compensation creates a moral hazard for directors who are tempted to turn a blind eye to tepid performance or even evidence of wrongdoing.

Most directors prepare for board meetings, reading feasibility studies and other reports, reviewing trial-balance and profit-and-loss statements, making telephone calls to corporate officers and managers, touring corporate facilities, and so on. Many directors say they spend on average a day and a half or two days preparing for each meeting. Our mythical director, with 10–12 meetings per year, and two days' preparation for each, would expend 30–36 days per year of her time for her $45–60,000 in compensation, a very fair bargain for an experienced and competent businesswoman.[49]

In fact she may spend more time. One survey of directors of large publicly held companies found that, on average, they expended forty days per year for each board on which they sat.

So a woman director may be a token of sorts on the board on which she sits, but so far she is not a golden token. Yet a number of the women directors discussed in ensuing chapters sit on four, five, or even six boards.

Trophy Directors

Although no precise definition exists, a director who sits on four or more corporation boards is generally considered, on the face of things at least, to be a trophy director. Thirty-five years ago it was not unheard of for a single person to sit on twelve boards of directors.

Today, and since the good governance movement began in the mid- to late 1980s, service on more than three or four boards is considered unacceptable. In the 1970s, former Supreme Court Justice Arthur Goldberg caused a stir when he simultaneously resigned from the eight boards on which he sat, pointedly stating that even with his talents he could not do an adequate job on so many boards of directors.[50]

If our mythical director sits on four or five boards, her direct cash compensation for board service may total between $180,000 and $270,000 per year. If she earns $200,000–300,000 as a partner in a law firm, as CFO or marketing director at another corporation, or even as a chaired professor in the business or law school of a prestigious university, the numbers begin to mount. In some of those capacities she may earn double or triple those sums.

And she has intangible benefits as well. Service as a director of a large publicly held corporation is a mark of great distinction in the legal and business worlds, both in the United States and around the world. Whether our mythical director approves of it or not, and whether it is deserved or not, the appellation "golden token" may be applied to her nonetheless.

CEO Compensation

In U.S. business, however, CEOs receive the greatest compensation. Large U.S. corporations compensate chief executive officers at an obscene level that exceeds CEO compensation anywhere else in the world.

In his 1991 book, *In Search of Excess,* compensation consultant Graef Crystal found that in the United States CEO compensation was 160 times that of the average shop floor or office worker; in Japan it was sixteen times; and in Germany it was twenty-one. By 2000, Crystal estimated for the *Washington Post,* the U.S. ratio of CEO to average worker compensation had climbed to over four hundred in the 1990s and was quickly climbing toward the five hundred level as we entered the new century.[51] Another estimate pegged 2000 CEO pay in the United States at 531 times the pay of the average worker.[52]

For individual companies, though, CEO compensation varies over a wide range. Among publicly held corporations, public utilities and banks historically have paid the least. For example, Allen Franklin, chairman, president, and CEO of Southern Company, the big Atlanta-based utility holding company, receives $1.9 million per year. William Osborne, the chairman and CEO of Northern Trust, the top-of-the-line Chicago-based bank holding company, makes $4.8 million.[53] In North Carolina, G. Kennedy Thompson, president and CEO of Wachovia, the large Charlotte-based bank, makes $5.8 million per year.

Among the few women CEOs, Patricia Russo at Lucent received $9.04 million in direct cash compensation in 2004, no doubt in part for her heroic efforts in being the turnaround leader at Lucent, which had been a troubled company. Carly Fiorina at Hewlett-Packard ($3.44 million), Ann Mulcahy at Xerox ($3.24 million), and Andrea Jung at Avon Products ($2.57 million) are in the same range.[54] Marion Sandler of Golden West Financial receives $1.39 million base compensation per year. Two of the newer women CEOs are paid less: Marce Fuller $800,000 at Mirant and Eileen Scott $654,000 at Pathmark Stores.

The king of CEO compensation had been Michael Eisner at the Walt Disney Company. For example, his 2000 compensation was $12.3 million directly in cash and $60.5 million from the exercise of stock options. His 1999 direct cash compensation was $23 million. In his best year, 1998, his annual compensation was $576 million, mostly from the exercise of stock options and sale of the Disney stock in the market.[55] From 1984, when he succeeded to the CEO title at Disney, until 1996, Eisner made an estimated $1.43 billion on exercise of stock options and over $300 million in cash compensation.

In 2002, Larry Ellison, the CEO of Oracle, the database management software producer, eclipsed Eisner. In that year, Ellison received $706.1

million, almost all of which represented proceeds of the sale of stock received pursuant to the exercise of stock options.[56]

Agog at these sums, in January 2006, the SEC rolled out proposed regulations that would treble the disclosures public corporations must make
about CEO and other senior executives' pay. Corporations will have to
narrate how the board of directors goes about setting pay levels, disclose
the long-term value of stock options, value executive perquisites, and
quantify severance and retirement pay to be received under existing provisions.[57] The SEC regulations are part of the growing dissatisfaction in
the Unite States about the inordinate growth and high levels of CEO
pay.[58]

At least on a financial basis, those are the compensation levels, and the
SEC response to them, both in the boardroom and in CEO suites, to
which some women may aspire and that some feel are being denied them,
along with the prestige and power that accompany such positions.

PART IV

Getting a Seat at the Boardroom Table

13

Paradigm Shifts
A Tale of Three Women

Paradigm One: The Tightrope

Women in business need not avoid altogether the behaviors that lead to the Bully Broad and Queen Bee stereotypes. At lower level management track positions, say, in sales or production, an aggressive approach may position the woman manager for the next promotion. Catalyst's Sheila Wellington finds that consistently not only meeting but exceeding quantifiable measures of performance is essential:

> Most smart capable women enter the workplace believing that their talent and hard work will carry them as far as they want to go. . . . Most people who succeed work hard. The women interviewed said that "consistently exceeding performance expectations" was more important than anything else they had done—more essential for women than for men.[1]

The line women must walk, however, is a tightrope. Too much aggressiveness and "[i]t's all the classical stuff: of a man they say 'He's hard-charging; he takes command,' but when a woman acts the same way, she's pushy."[2] "When a man applies the word *aggressive* to another man, he means that he's bold and forceful, that he has the strength and capabilities to achieve his goal. But when guys use the word to describe women. . . . [t]he woman becomes pushy, argumentative, domineering," businesswoman Gail Evans warns.[3]

On the other hand, sensitivity to the stereotypes derived from the way in which many women speak and act ("emotional," "not logical") also requires behavior modification. According to the former general counsel of Aetna, "[T]he single most important issue facing women at work is language; how people talk about women, the way they listen to women, and are they listened to."[4] Women are advised to lower the pitch of their voice. "[T]he most common terms describing male executives [are] 'quarterback,' 'absolute winner,' 'aggressive,' 'boastful,' 'desire to win,' 'holding power,' [and] 'tough skinned,' according to Evans.[5] Women managers might do well to mimic some of the traits those male paradigms suggest.

A common complaint is that men do not listen to women at meetings. Worse yet, men take what women say and rephrase it, taking credit for the idea. Women tend to be overly democratic, intent on everyone having their say. Women fear appearing too assertive. Wellington tells her readers that these timid behaviors do "nothing to establish you as a confident, competent person at a meeting table."[6]

Gail Evans frequently contrasts men's with women's mannerisms. "Men talk a lot. Women don't talk enough, even seasoned executives."[7] In meetings, take a seat at the table. "Women often take those peripheral chairs, because they think the table is for the boss and the key people. . . ."[8] "Men will tell you that women are too timid when they talk at the office, or too evasive, or too circuitous, or too unsure of themselves. [S]peaking forcefully isn't about speaking loudly or softly. It's about learning how to use your voice effectively."[9]

Without appearing pushy, women managers can still insist that male coworkers or supervisors not interrupt them. Advice books espouse as a tactic that a woman repeat what she has said, addressing her remarks directly to someone in the meeting that she believes to be receptive, if not an ally.

Should women adopt male behaviors? The advice is mixed but the theme that runs through the advice is to remain authentic, true to oneself. A danger is that superiors may perceive a woman as two persons: masculine and aggressive at work, more relaxed and feminine in informal settings, and thus, overall, somewhat duplicitous. Women should not play "the man's game" if it is uncomfortable. "If you enjoy sports, by all means learn to play golf," but it is not necessary.[10]

Do not get a chip on your shoulder. Take slights in your stride. Remember that it may be more difficult for women. Ginger Rogers danced all the same steps as Fred Astaire—but she did it backwards and in high heels.[11]

Paradigm Two

A close reading of the advice books demonstrates that at some point, say, after the second or third promotion, the paradigm shifts. As long ago as 1977, Margaret Henning noted the change:

> The skills you may need to get close to the executive level (and I'd be the first to admit that you may have to be relatively aggressive) may not serve you well once you get there. After you become a member of the "team," you need to learn to be a team player, and that requires a different set of behaviors. Indeed, managers—especially women, unfortunately—often antagonize others [by being] perceived as overly ambitious or a threat.[12]

At this point, aspiring women should begin to think in terms of four or five careers, and three or four paradigms, even within the same company. "Women have to shift their focus from how well they do their job to what job they have." They must become, and appear to have become, more diplomatic, more strategic: "[U]nderstand the big picture. Have a clear sense of what will work and what won't, given competing trends, demands and situations," social psychologist Carol Gallagher urges.[13] Wellington hints at the transformation with the advice:

> If your only strategy is working like a dog, you're likely to find the path to upper management blocked. So what's the missing ingredient? Something called style. The women who've reached executive levels today say their success depended on developing a style with which men felt comfortable working.[14]

A host of different axioms tends to crowd out some early rules to live by ("be aggressive") or to coexist with others of them (for example, Sheila Wellington's aphorisms such as "[t]he best isn't good enough. Deliver results on time or ahead of time. Deliver more than people expect").[15]

Some of those axioms that form the midcareer composite, or paradigm, are as follows:

> Develop areas in which you are an expert. Prove yourself continually by invoking you expertise. "Expertise impresses" (Wellington).[16]

"Find a style with which men will be comfortable. . . . Style matters. Style is the sum total of your self presentation. It consists of how you look and how you act. . . . [It] includes not only the sartorial . . . but also your carriage, your attitude, the way you do things. It is the way you speak, the subliminal messages you send, the way you manage your workload" (Wellington).[17]

At this middle stage, "you have to be approachable and generous with praise, gratitude, and your time in order to succeed. . . . Business is a very human interaction. . . . [T]he higher people rise in the corporate pyramid, the more their future promotions are based upon relationships with superiors, colleagues, and subordinates" (Gallagher).[18]

"No one is surprised to hear a man raise his voice, see him show his anger publicly. . . . [In contrast] [w]hen a woman does display anger, people are often uneasy, frightened; they perceive her as difficult, unladylike. . . . [M]en perceive a show of anger as something out of character for a woman, they judge it as a loss of control" (Evans).[19]

Sartorial advice: develop the right look. Spend money. Appear contemporary because that conveys a sense that you are well informed.

Develop "room radar." Make a practice of reading whatever room you enter, assessing the people there and the dynamics of their interaction. Act accordingly.

Learn the art of the humorous comeback. Radiate confidence. Carry things off with aplomb. Take slights with a grain of salt. Let negative comments slide. Keep things in perspective.

Be seen as a team player. "Most women really are team players. The difference is that [women] seldom draw attention to the work they have done. Women join a team, participate in the planning, get their assigned tasks, go off and do a bang-up job on them, and move on. Men on a team tend to talk about what they have to do, talk about what they're doing, and talk about what they've done" (Wellington).[20]

Paradigm Three

As a manager approaches the upper ranks of middle management, the paradigm shifts again. Some aggressive behavior creeps back in. As a team member, a woman must shift from being a team player to being a team leader:

> "Develop a reputation as someone who can provide sound advice but also solve problems; move the ball forward, work effectively with other people, manage projects, manage people, bring people together, facilitate the reconciliation of conflicting viewpoints" (Wellington).[21]

If you don't blow your own horn, nobody else will.

> "If you're a vice president, act like a vice president, talk like a vice president, do the work of a vice president. There are no relationship issues here. It's a board game issue. You are sitting at a certain level of the pyramid. Act accordingly" (Evans).[22]

The Fourth and Final Paradigm

At what one might consider the fourth stage, the mix of aggressive behavior with strategic and diplomatic behaviors has added to it progressively larger doses of self-promotion and the appearance of "executive presence."

> "Your organization wants to know that it can send you anywhere in the world on any assignment or to solve any problem, that you will project the right image anywhere, that you will never embarrass it."

Get media training. Do media interviews. Hire a personal public relations advisor. Visibility generally is good but by and large should be tied to your areas of expertise.

Take calculated risks. "Women have to be aggressive with everything, taking risks with tough jobs, big moves, and putting themselves out in front in [certain] situations. . . ."[23]

Judicious use of press coverage may be part of a success strategy. Good internal publicity within the company and visibility in the community become more important at this stage. Seek out public speaking opportunities. Spearhead discussion at staff workshops. Attend conferences. While there, be visible, and ask questions. Write letters to the editor. Host customer relations seminars and other events.

There is not *one* paradigm for women who wish to succeed in business, contrary to many of the advice books.[24] It is not one size fits all. The paradigm shifts as a woman moves upward through an organization. As they do so, women encounter greater numbers of men in ascendent positions, with the power to promote women, or assign additional responsibilities, who have seen through and do not apply the stereotypes. By contrast, on the way upward, through the lower and middle ranks, women must adopt coping strategies ("be aggressive," for instance). They must do so to deal with the perceptions middle managers and peers have about women in business, stereotypes based upon the way in which many women speak and act or upon women's roles in bearing and rearing children.

Even the how-to tomes that seem to recognize the evolution of behaviors thought necessary do not seem to recognize that toward the top the paradigm seems to come nearly full circle. Bully Broads, or Iron Maidens, come across too strong, too tough, and too pushy, usually at a point in mid-career. The reality or the perception then stalls or completely sidetracks their careers. If, however, they become suitably strategic, diplomatic, a team player, and so on, as managers, women will continue to progress.

But then at some further point, usually when on the cusp of senior management's ranks, women have to come on strong again, with behaviors that at an earlier stage would have been deemed overly pushy and might have doomed their hoped-for career progression. There is reversion of sorts.

But not quite. After this twisting and tortuous path they must follow, women should see that the circle does not close at the top. If they fail to discern that, and revert completely to behavior that might have won them their initial promotion or promotions, they may fall completely from grace, as the careers of Bernadette Healy, Jill Barad, and Carly Fiorina demonstrate. The principal lessons to be learned from those careers, along with lessons that may be discerned from a close reading of the advice books, are two in number: one is that the paradigm that will get women to the top shifts and changes, coming almost full circle, and the second is that, despite those paradigm shifts, the circle does not quite close at the top.

Woman and CEO Number One

In September 1999, Dr. Bernadette Healy succeeded Elizabeth Dole as the second female president of the American Red Cross since Clara Barton, its founder. Dr. Healy was a Harvard-trained physician who taught at Johns Hopkins University School of Medicine, headed the National Institutes of Health, and served as the dean of the School of Medicine at Ohio State University.

She was a blunt-speaking New Yorker who was raised in Queens. Her straightforward and direct manner was instrumental in some of her early career successes. Those manners also brought her highly publicized Red Cross presidency to an end after only twenty-five months.[25]

After the hijacked airliner crashed into the Pentagon on September 11, 2001, Red Cross disaster relief workers were nowhere to be found. At noon, Washington, D.C., Red Cross headquarters received a telephone call from the site: "Where in the hell are you guys?" The Pentagon requested food, water, cots, blankets, and the other relief items the Red Cross normally would supply.

Healy had a subordinate telephone the Red Cross Disaster Operations Center (DOC) from which disaster teams are dispatched. Later in the day Healy visited the scene of the breathtaking devastation at the Pentagon. She found only a four-person team from the Arlington, Virginia, Red Cross chapter. There was no water, food, or cots, and no Red Cross chaplain. Disaster teams had never been dispatched.

Healy made some calls, taking swift and decisive action. Soon thereafter the two women who operated the DOC, who together had sixty years' Red Cross experience, were dismissed.

Following September 11, Americans poured into Red Cross blood banks, donating blood in record numbers, much more than could be used. When questioned about the surplus, Healy was blunt: "People don't realize that red blood cells are a perishable commodity. They expire. It happens. Better to have too much than too little." This was accurate, but it was a public relations gaffe that might well have been caught had Healy vetted her remarks with her staff.

Earlier Healy had received reports of embezzlement by the long-serving director of a small Red Cross chapter in Hudson County, New Jersey. Healy ordered the director and the bookkeeper suspended without pay, and hired an accounting firm to do a forensic audit. When the auditors confirmed the embezzlement, Healy referred the matter to the local New Jersey prosecutor.

Within the Red Cross, whispering among staffers was that Healy had been "too fast and too tough." Many Red Cross lifers thought that Healy should have suspended the wrongdoers but *with pay*.

September 11 also resulted in an outpouring from wallets and purses. The Red Cross raised over $600 million. Traditionally, though, the Red Cross solicits funds as an all-purpose disaster relief organization. It never solicits funds for individual disasters.

Many post–September 11 donors felt that the Red Cross had betrayed them when they discovered that their dollars had made their way to the large, amorphous Red Cross "piggy bank." They had contributed to alleviate conditions in New York, and in New York alone. So, on her own, Healy directed that Red Cross staff create a stand-alone fund for New York City and the disaster relief there in the aftermath of the World Trade Center terrorist attacks. Within the Red Cross, staffers criticized Healy for her "go it alone" decision-making style.

The Red Cross has two principal lines of business. One is disaster relief. The other is operation of the nation's largest blood bank system, which supplies the nation with 45 percent of its whole blood supply.

The Red Cross has badly managed its blood bank system for years. After eight years of listening to the Red Cross promise reform, in the 1990s, the Food and Drug Administration obtained a federal court-supervised consent decree, in which the Red Cross agreed to clean up its act.

Healy had been in office only five months when FDA inspectors arrived at Red Cross headquarters. They stayed two months. They then delivered a 21-page list of deficiencies: inadequate tracking of inventories of blood and blood types; release for distribution of blood that the Red Cross was to have quarantined because of donors' medical histories; and errors in labeling, among others things.

Healy was "stunned." She importuned the Red Cross board to set aside $100 million to upgrade the blood business. She hired high-profile new executives to help fix the blood business.

Red Cross veterans did not see the need for action. They found the new hires threatening. They criticized Healy for her "hard-charging style." They questioned whether Healy was engineering the takeover of the Red Cross by "bloodless professionals."

While at the Red Cross, Bernadette Healy was an on-the-ground, decisive, purposeful, and entrepreneurial manager. When changed conditions necessitated it, she broke with Red Cross traditions. She also bought much needed reform to the Red Cross's blood bank and other operations.

The result? On October 23, 2001, the Red Cross Board of Governors removed her, six members voting for Healy, four abstaining, and twenty-seven voting to remove her as president.[26] Bernadette Healy failed to note that the circle is not a full circle. It does not close at the top. Thus, the assertive and decisive behaviors that brought her success earlier in her career were not quite suited for the very top.

Woman and CEO Number Two

Jill Barad of Mattel, Inc., the Los Angeles–based toy maker, was unconventional for a CEO, whether male or female, and she made a big splash on the U.S. corporate scene. She "looked and acted like a Hollywood star." She wore bright clothing, "often with accoutrements such as fur collars and cuffs," much like the Barbie doll line she nurtured on her way to the top at Mattel.[27] *Fortune* named her one of the fifty most powerful women in the United States, *People* one of the "Fifty Most Beautiful People." She reveled in the "puff publicity" she received from the likes of *People.*[28]

Appearances aside, her leadership style was unconventional as well. Coworkers described her as "of sharp tongue and combative nature." She had an aggressive, "hands on" style of management. Reportedly, she "obsessed over the slightest details of 'her' toys" at Mattel.[29]

Despite her high profile, in February 2000, in an 8-hour emergency meeting, the Mattel board of directors fired Jill Barad as CEO, after only two years in office.

After giving birth to her two sons, Jill Barad had reentered the workforce in 1981, as a $38,000-a-year product manager for Mattel. She had found the position through a headhunter. She showed up for her first day of work at Mattel wearing a purple mini-skirt and cowboy boots.[30]

Her first product at Mattel, something called a "Bad Case of Worms," was a flop from the beginning but Barad's homemade advertising campaign seemed to move some of the product. After the product flopped, Barad went straight to see CEO Tom Kalinske. She stormed into

Kalinske's office, asking "What the f——do I have to do to get a decent assignment around here?"

Barad became known as the "woman who saved Barbie." When Barad took charge of the Barbie product line, the average American girl had one Barbie. By the time Barad left the Barbie line, the average American girl had nine Barbies, plus countless clothing outfits and accessories. Barad caused her staff to market dolls and accessories to older, adult Barbie Doll collectors. She introduced a Barbie Doll gift voucher system for use during the holiday season. Barad successfully employed market segmentation and brand proliferation within the Barbie line to increase sales.[31]

By 1984, Barad had garnered a vice-presidency title. Barad's quick rise, her success, and her aggression did not sit well with many comanagers at Mattel. She recalls, "Many men hated me. I think it can be a tough thing for a man to lose to a woman."

In 1986, Mattel promoted Barad to executive vice-president in charge of the Barbie line. Her business prowess enabled Mattel to escape bankruptcy in 1987 when the wave it had been riding, action figure toys, suddenly crashed. The poor performance of Mattel's action figure collection, Masters of the Universe, was offset by another sterling Barbie line performance. In 1990, Barad became president of Mattel USA.

Despite her rise in the corporate organization, Barad remained obsessed with Barbie doll products. Mattel executives and employees gossiped about "her overweening attention to detail, monitoring doll designs down to minor details on their faces." In the eight years she had been involved with Barbie, sales of the line had gone from $235 million to $1.5 billion annually.

Within Mattel, Barad complemented her attention to detail with an aggressive approach. One colleague remembers that "[s]he was never afraid to go in and ask for a raise. She would just go in and tell people what she wanted and ask: 'What do I have to do to get it?'" In 1992, she entered Mattel CEO John Amerman's office. She threatened to leave Mattel if Amerman did not assure her that she would succeed him. Amerman would not make that promise. Barad then went so far as to procure the offer of a high-level position at Reebok International. Barad even told Mattel that she had been house hunting in Boston.

Amerman underwent a change of heart. He assured Barad that she would be his successor. In just twelve years, she had risen from an entry-level position to being the nation's second highest paid female executive, with the promise that she would succeed the incumbent as CEO. In 1996, Mattel paid her $6.17 million in annual compensation.[32]

The eventual succession of Barad to CEO took place on January 1, 1997. Journalists portrayed her as "arguably the most powerful business woman in the nation."[33]

It was not an auspicious time to assume the top position at Mattel. In July 1996 Mattel reported its first flat quarter of earnings since the 1980s. Mattel had also failed in its bid to acquire the second largest U.S. toy maker, Hasbro. Barad had been the lead executive on the 1996 attempt. Mattel had had to withdraw its $5.2 billion bid after the government raised antitrust objections. The failed Hasbro bid was seen as a "major public relations blow" to Mattel.

Throughout the quarters that followed, when Mattel had numerous earnings disappointments, Barad consistently promised good things to Wall Street. She publicized Mattel's goals of 10 percent annual increases in sales and 15 percent in profits.[34]

In March 1997, the Federal Trade Commission gave Mattel Hart-Scott-Rodino clearance for its proposed acquisition of Tyco, the third largest toy maker. Barad hailed the acquisition as an opportunity for Mattel-Tyco to "expand their business into 36 countries." But the $755 million acquisition, as well as other merger activity, would cause Mattel to take a one-time charge of $275 million against earnings for merger and consolidation expense. Barad then announced that Mattel-Tyco would eliminate two thousand seven hundred jobs, nearly 10 percent of their combined workforce, mainly by closing down "noncore" lines of business.[35] During the second quarter of 1998, Mattel's earning were 20 percent lower than the previous year. Barbie sales had fallen 15 percent during the second quarter when compared to the previous year. The shrinkage in Barbie sales appeared to be becoming permanent.

By September, the share price was down to $29.25. Toys "R" Us business would be off as much as $200 million in 1998. Mattel lowered its per share earnings estimate from $1.95 to $1.80.[36]

Then, in December, Mattel stunned Wall Street with drastic revisions. There had been an "unforeseen slowdown in shipments following Thanksgiving." For 1998, sales would fall $500 million below projections. The earnings forecast was revised downward again, to $1.20 per share.[37]

Seemingly trying to put some positive spin on things, on the same day in December 1998, Mattel and Barad announced that they would expend

$3.04 billion to acquire The Learning Company (TLC), maker of Carmen San Diego (Where in the U.S. is Carmen San Diego? Where in the world is Carmen San Diego?), software for highly popular interactive computer games. Almost immediately, speculation began that Mattel had overpaid drastically for TLC.

Wall Street was losing faith in Barad. Several top executives left Mattel. In April, Mattel announced that it would again cut its workforce by 10 percent, costing two thousand five hundred employees their jobs.[38]

Then TLC began to loom large. In July, Mattel announced that TLC would produce an "expected loss" for the year. At Mattel, sales of Barbie, Disney, and Sesame Street merchandise were all falling. Barad discovered that TLC had not informed her or others at Mattel of revenue shortfalls that would now cause a $50 million to $100 million loss at the TLC unit.[39]

Early in 2000 the stock reached an all-time low of $10.88. There had been a botched acquisition (Tyco) and a bad acquisition (TLC). There had been numerous failures to realize on glowing projections. Wall Street had lost faith in the company and its CEO. Executives were departing.

In her February 3, 2000, press conference, Barad stood tall. "The board of directors and I view the performance of The Learning Company, and its effects on our results, as unacceptable. Therefore, the board and I have agreed that I resign effective today."[40]

As CEO of Mattel, Jill Barad certainly encountered a parade of horrors: bad acquisitions, large layoffs, product recalls, earnings disappointments, and a falling stock price, to name a few. In nearly every month of her short tenure she, and the company, faced yet another material adverse development that had to be announced to the world. It is difficult to imagine a more unfortunate sequence of events.

Of course, other CEOs have weathered protracted spates of adverse developments, but they usually did so by keeping a low profile. Barad never lowered her head. Even when bad news hit she did not shy away. She continued to make forecasts of sales growth, albeit more moderate ones. One analyst summed up feelings in the analyst community: "People feel they were lied to. . . . I asked [Mattel executives] hundreds of times . . . and now I am finding that the numbers are not so good. I don't know what to expect from this company."

Psychoanalysts categorize leaders such as Jill Barad as "productive narcissists," who can accomplish a great deal in some settings but prove disasters when matters do not go quite as they should.[41]

Did sexism play a role in Wall Street's and Mattel's evaluation of Jill Barad's performance and her demise as CEO? Privately, due to her flamboyance and her "puff publicity," there were many who were rooting for her to fail. Jim Collins's study of highly successful businesses would have lent support to Barad's detractors. Collins finds that "[1]arger-than-life celebrity leaders . . . are *negatively* correlated with taking a company from good to great."[42] A corporation does better with a "ploughhorse" rather than a "showhorse" in the CEO suite, according to Collins's empirical studies.

Why do CEOs make "big dumb acquisitions" as Barad did? Often the dumb acquisition follows on the heels of a failed one. The failure, as with Mattel's failure to acquire Hasbro, perhaps made Barad the CEO want to prove her mettle even more.

We also live in an age of deal makers. Pulling off a large acquisition builds a CEO's reputation as a deal maker, prized in the business community. The splash an acquisition makes puts the CEO on the front business page, or in the *Wall Street Journal,* adding to her celebrity aura. Last of all, acquisitions, whether in the form of one large acquisition or in the form of a series, can screen from view deterioration in a portion of the existing business, thus prolonging the inevitable. The latter was undoubtedly true at Mattel and of Jill Barad, as a female CEO, as well.

Woman and CEO Number Three

Another female CEO who never shied away and never put her head down even when she should have was Carleton Fiorina, the CEO of Hewlett Packard from 1999 to early 2005. Fiorina reveled in stories about the "Carly Machine" and "All Carly All of the Time." She worked 100-hour weeks crisscrossing the globe in her Gulfstream corporate jet.[43] She never stopped issuing rosy earnings forecasts even though H-P's share price fell 50 percent during her tenure.[44]

The deposed Carly Fiorina's acquisition moves parallel those of Barad at Mattel to a tee. Early in her career at Hewlett-Packard, Fiorina failed in an attempt at an upscale acquisition, offering $17.5 billion for accounting firm Price Waterhouse's consulting business, which IBM eventually acquired. H-P investors and employees laid the failure at Fiorina's feet, due to her ill-considered attempts to renegotiate the purchase price at the eleventh hour.

On the rebound, so to speak, and over vociferous objections of H-P employees and dissident director Walter Hewlett, Fiorina caused H-P to make an even larger, but downscale acquisition. Fiorina waged an 8-month fight, warding off a proxy challenge and then a lawsuit by the son of founder William Hewlett, H-P director Walter Hewlett, who resigned after his defeats. H-P then acquired Compaq Computer, which has been mired in the junkyard end of the business spectrum, personal computer manufacture, in which operating margins can be 1 percent or less and no one has succeeded in competing with Dell Computer. The failure of the Compaq acquisition to meet even modest profit projections for it caused it to be a principal contributing factor in the downfall of Fiorina, "America's most powerful business woman."[45]

Fiorina, the daughter of a California State court judge, withdrew from UCLA law school after only one year. She climbed the corporate ladder instead, becoming a top-performing sales person at AT&T and then spearheading the IPO at Lucent Technologies, where H-P found her. Her jet-setting ways, designer suits, and forceful personality turned out not to be what H-P's board determined it wanted. Creating a buzz around the company, as Fiorina did, ultimately did not mask the reality that most of H-P's profits (75 percent in fact) came from one line of business, its printer division. "It had become increasingly clear that H-P's need for a nuts-and-bolts operations whiz far outweighed the benefits of a high-profile CEO."[46] Yet Fiorina stubbornly refused even to hire a chief operating officer as a subordinate. The H-P board of directors asked her to step aside after a 5.5-year tenure.

At Mattel, Jill Barad made a big dumb acquisition. So, too, did Fiorina at H-P. Both women also had talents—especially marketing and sales brilliance. Neither Barad's nor Fiorina's nor Healy's aggressiveness, however, ever seemed to subside. At the very top of a large public organizations, they all reverted to the same take-charge or even manic behaviors that won them their early promotions. They never learned to put their heads down while the shrapnel was flying through the air.

Male CEOs, or some of them, make these same types of mistakes. They are overly aggressive, imitators of "Chainsaw Al" Dunlap (he also reveled in being called "Rambo in Pinstripes") who ran Sunbeam Corp. into the ground. But more than a majority of male CEOs keep a low profile, achieve success over the long haul, and, again, are what author Jim Collins deems "ploughhorses" rather than "showhorses." What is troubling is that all of the female CEOs (Fiorina, Barad, Healy), and not just some of them, have been "show horses," whose nonrelenting aggression did them in in the end.

They, too, never came to realize that what had gotten them there would not keep them there. The paradigm shifts. But the circle never quite closes, even at the top.[47]

There are at least four paradigms that may, and probably will, apply to women as they move upward toward the pool of women executives from which nominating committees and boards are likely to choose CEOs and directors. By contrast, men who make it to the top seem effortlessly to move from a more energetic, aggressive stance to a more diplomatic or strategic one, and that is it. Why the difference? It may be that, unlike men, women must cope with stereotypes as well as build up a reservoir of tangible successes as they advance. The careers of the three women (the sample is still very small) who have made it to the very top and then fallen from grace demonstrate a second point, or set of points. One is that the same behavior that propelled them upward thorough the lower and middle ranks will not keep them at the top. The second is, again, the related metaphorical point: the paradigm shifts and comes almost full circle but, for women especially, the circle never quite closes at the top.

14

Prescriptions

What benefits are women directors supposed to bring to boardrooms once they get there? The obvious candidate would be profits. Corporations' managers tend very much to focus on the bottom line. If advocates can convince CEOs and incumbent directors of a likelihood that the presence of women will add to profits, those decision makers will take steps to put additional female directors in place. But, alas, the evidence for that proposition does not exist. Indeed, the best evidence is that no correlation exists between profitability and board composition. And, the notion that boards should be staffed with profitability in mind misconceives the role boards of directors have.

The studies abound, with contradictory conclusions.[1] Catalyst, Inc., is among the organizations that promulgates and promotes studies finding a correlation between the ample presence of women managers and directors and profitability or firm value.[2] Most knowledgeable scholars, those who do business and corporate finance rather than race and gender subjects, deny (and many lament their finding) that any correlation exists. The most widely cited empirical work on the subject conclusively finds that no correlation can be found between the composition of boards of directors and the value or profitability of publicly held corporations.[3]

The discussion, which is considerable, misconceives the role of a board of directors. As the metaphor Australian Henry Bosch is fond of stating says, "a board of directors is much like the fog lights on an automobile. You don't need them often but you are glad to have them there when you do." That is because the modern board's highest and best calling is not to induce profitability. It is to monitor the senior managers and avert catastrophe when it looms large or, hopefully, even when catastrophe first appears on the horizon.

Over the decades, corporate business and legal schematics have steadily pointed more and more to such a role, or indeed exclusive role, for the board. State corporate law statutes went from the imperative phrasing of the 1950s ("The business and affairs of the corporation shall be managed by a board of directors" and "Thou Shalt Manage") to less imperative stances ("the business and affairs of the corporation shall be managed under the direction of, or the supervision of, a board of directors"). As has been seen,[4] the American Law Institute went so far as to provide that the senior managers should manage the corporation's business. In turn, according to the ALI, the board's role was to select, monitor, and, if necessary, replace the senior managers, most particularly the chief executive officer, should managers underperform.

The Enron and WorldCom scandals reveal how little the public and even regulators know about these developments and about modern large corporations. These groups want directors to manage and to supervise, making scant allowance for the part-time positions directors occupy. The wisdom of current events, however, is fodder for another book. What is important to note is that, under either model, a central if not exclusive role of the board is to oversee and, if necessary, replace the managers.

Diversity

Today diversity is still lacking. Less than 11 percent of directors are women, even though women began obtaining law and business degrees in great numbers almost thirty-five years ago and for twenty years or more have constituted a near majority of those receiving Juris Doctor and MBA degrees. Women in business who take any time off beyond minimal maternity leaves find themselves earning 60 percent of what male peers earn at age forty, regardless of talent or achievements. As a result, they become disillusioned, pursue other lifestyles and careers, and never reach the pool from which corporate directors and senior managers are chosen. Men in business still get away with consigning women to lesser roles on the basis of notions that stereotypes exist and that stereotypical behaviors indicate more than just a manner of speaking or a different way of acting.

More importantly, diversity of viewpoints, which results from a diversity of race and gender backgrounds, is essential to the task of monitoring senior managers' behavior. Diversity is necessary to avoid the perils of "groupthink" in appointing a CEO or a CFO, and in strategic planning.

Irving Janis is one of the leading writers to have explored the perils of groupthink and how they led to Pearl Harbor, the Bay of Pigs, U.S. involvement in the Vietnam War, and the Watergate coverup, among other bedacles.[5] Professor Marleen O'Connor has applied Janis's work to the modern corporate board of directors.[6]

A prime determinant of groupthink is cohesiveness among members of the group. The "we-feeling" and clubbiness that infects most boards, and other collegial groups as well, is a starter for groupthink, causing the board to avoid hard questions or otherwise rock the boat. Boards tend to be "good ole boys' clubs" and "elite private clubs with a rubber stamp."[7]

Groupthink may lead to "(1) a sense of invincibility, (2) belief in [the] inherent morality of goals, (3) collective rationalization, (4) stereotyping of out-groups, (5) appearance of unanimity, (6) self-censorship, (7) pressure on dissenters, and (8) self appoint[ment as] mind guards," all traits boards of directors should wish to minimize or eliminate.[8] In Enron, the "perfect storm" of corporate governance, most or all of those perils of groupthink were present. They contributed to the board's failure to accomplish its mission, to avert the catastrophe Enron eventually encountered.

The point is not that the presence of women or minorities will always enable boards to avoid groupthink. After all, a woman, economist Wendy Gramm, who is an Asian American, served as a director at Enron, as did an Asian American man, a Hispanic man, and an African American man.[9] The point is that groupthink is less likely in the presence of diversity and with diversity as an avowed goal.

Women and other minority members' presence on boards of directors and beyond token status bring other benefits:

Stereotype negation at the top and throughout the organization.
Monitoring for junior managers and aspiring minority group members.
Accountability for minority group members as well as for others.
Cooperation among races and sexes.[10]

These trickle-down benefits resulting from the presence of women directors on the board and as senior managers are tangible ends that modern organizations must achieve.

Diversity will enhance small-group decision making and diminish the isolation of corporate boards. Many boards are men's clubs, in which members dress the same, have attended the same schools, and represent a single social class. Directors and the boards on which they sit tend to be isolated from what goes on in the society that surrounds them.[11]

By contrast, well functioning boards are made up of a selection of differing backgrounds and talents. One talent that one or more members should possess is that of mediator.[12] The directors on a board most capable of mediating between factions or between board members and the CEO may well be women.

Then there is the matter of social justice and avoidance of hypocrisy. For thirty years, corporate organizations have told women that places at the top exist for those women willing to build up the necessary educational and occupational experience. The numbers in this book alone show the untruth of what has been said. As of 2000, only a single Fortune 500 corporation had a CEO who was female. Even today, nearly forty years after women began to enter higher echelons in business, only 1.6 percent of corporations in the Fortune 500 and 1.3 percent in the Fortune 1000 have female CEOs. It is time to speak straight and to set matters right.

How (Mechanically) Directors Are Elected

Once upon a time, the corporation's CEO staffed the board. The CEO's spouse, the joke goes, played a leading part as to who his golfing partners were. To remove the specter of CEO involvement from the process, governance engineers invented the nomination committee.[13] Supposedly comprised of directors independent of senior management, the committee is supposed to identify candidates for the board of directors and recommend their election. It may identify candidates for senior management positions as well, but the original conception was to remove the directorial nomination process from the CEO and possibly to increase diversity at the board level.

The nomination committee has worked tolerably well. Many corporations have broadened its functions, renaming it the "Governance and Nominating Committee," or the "Governance Committee." Boards of directors adopt, periodically update, and publish in annual proxy statements committee charters. The SEC requires publicly held companies to disclose the process they use to identify, nominate, and cause the election of candidates for the board.[14]

The device works only "tolerably well" because many CEOs figure out how to keep their fingers in the pie. They know where the power lies, namely, in the ability to control nomination and election to the board of directors. Some, such as Bernie Ebbers at WorldCom, insist on membership on the committee, prevailing wisdom be damned. Other CEOs cause the appointment of a fellow CEO (present or retired) to the committee. The incumbent CEO uses the appointed one as a backchannel to follow the committee's deliberation or, more affirmatively, to direct the committee.

Professor Rakesh Khurana comments on the manner in which directors are chosen.[15] Search consultants urge adoption of specifications that barely rise above the level of platitudes. The candidate should have public company experience, the ability for strategic thought, line experience, attendance at one of a list of schools, and so on. These all-things-to-all-people specification sheets cause the committee to lose sight, or obscure altogether, more simply stated ambitions, such as increasing board diversity or finding a qualified woman or minority candidate.

Aspiring Women: Private Roles

The prevailing advice is to "be patient but not passive," working one's way up through the ranks of organizations. Women should have mentors, several of them. They should strive to obtain the line experience (male) higher-ups purport to find so essential.

Today at least the prevailing advice may be ill advised. The best route to the top may be more indirect. Education is important. Obtain a doctorate, teach, and then sidestep onto corporate boards of directors. Seek out positions of authority in the not-for-profit sphere, in which the amounts at stake are large but women more easily garner line experience and reach other goals. A plurality of directors who are women, almost a majority, have risen through the ranks of the academic, not-for-profit, and governmental spheres, contrary to the advice given by those who purport to know.

Know, too, that the advice books are wrong on another score as well. There is no one paradigm for advancement of women. The paradigm mutates as a woman's career advances, much more so than a man's. An aspiring woman manager may have to be aggressive early in her career, be more strategic in her behavior later on, then morph into a statesperson, and finally become somewhat aggressive again, in her climb up the ladder to a leadership position.

Aspiring Women: Public Roles

Among women, according to author Ann Crittenden, "There is a pervasive fear of alienating men, and a 'rich white woman syndrome.' . . . The big women's organizations don't want to be involved in anything that could be interpreted as women against men. . . ."[16]

Catalyst, Inc., the organization whose goal is to add females to corporate boards of directors, is a prime example of what Crittenden discusses. Catalyst obtains its funding from corporate America, including large corporations with poor records on promoting women and minorities up through the ranks or to boards of directors.[17] These companies become the named sponsors of Catalyst programs. They supply Catalyst with most of the funds for a budget that includes funds for operation of offices in New York, Toronto, and San Jose, California.

Despite ample evidence that corporate America's record is a very poor one, and little progress has been made, Catalyst only has praise for corporations and their efforts, perhaps because corporations fund many of the organization's programs. Catalyst's studies are also questionable: they claim that 11.2 or 13.6 percent of directors are women when the reality is that those percentages represent the number of board seats held. The actual number of women is less, perhaps far less.

Corporations

Every publicly held corporation could put a woman on the Governance and Nominating Committee. Some (many?) of those women directors would take it as part of their mission to increase the diversity of the board and would be especially likely to seek out female candidates.

Another prescription is that corporations should rid themselves of trophy directors, male as well as female. Experts, analysts, and others all agree that few human beings can be effective directors sitting on more than three boards. A Susan Bayh, who sits on eight boards, should see her employment for what in part it is–an attempt to curry influence with her spouse, a U.S. senator.

Elimination of trophy directors altogether will open the process to, among other things, aspiring women board candidates. Some trophy directors (men and especially women) could even make their resignation contingent on the nomination of a woman as successor.

Some things corporations must do to allow women to move toward the top are more difficult. Today most, if not all, organizations have eliminated blatant forms of sex discrimination. Whether because regulations require it, because courts hold them or their peers liable for it, or because it was the right thing to do, companies have forbidden sexual harassment by superiors and coworkers. They have put in place mechanisms that tend to insure that the workplace does not become a hostile environment in which women or minorities have difficulty doing their jobs.

What remains, and is infinitesimally more difficult to eliminate, Professor Susan Sturm has termed "second generation employment discrimination."[18] This form of discrimination consists of acts and practices that, while facially neutral, in practice have a much more deleterious effect on women than on men. These types of practices have a "disparate impact," often one that is difficult to discern. They play out only "over time." Intention, upon which first-generation laws and court decisions place so much emphasis, appears to be lacking, or is difficult to trace.

An organization that facilitates managers in their proclivity to hold late-day or Saturday-morning meetings seems to be doing nothing more than supporting managers and workers who are going the extra mile. In reality, the timing of those meeting discriminates against women, who have significantly greater responsibilities in rearing children. Consequently, as a group, women have much reduced or no availability late in the day or on a Saturday.

A large law firm may pride itself upon and aggressively recruit new female lawyers. Over time, however, the firm finds that it promotes women far less frequently. Analysis only follows a number of disparate complaints by women that vary much in their tone and content. No bad apple or apples are discernible to those who examine the matter. This is a form second-generation employment discrimination may well take.[19]

One recommended start is for corporations to appoint diversity officers. Senior managers task diversity officers with analyzing acts and practices within the corporation and cataloging how they might constitute of more subtle forms of discrimination. They then recommend how the company, and its managers, might rearrange the conduct of business to eliminate forms of second-generation discrimination.

An old, often used, and tried-and-true epigram prevalent in business circles is "you manage what you measure."[20] Senior managers who preach about their own and the corporation's zero tolerance for discrimination may do just that—preach. Managers who benchmark the organization's progress in terms of results, and react accordingly, do more than preach. Managers who record and analyze not only results but also the organization's progress in implementation of the programs and devices that management installs send a louder message through the organization. In several instances large organizations, such as Deloitte & Touche, Ernst & Young, and Eli Lily Company, found that measurement of progress led to the large breakthroughs they had been looking for in the employment of women.[21]

A Nutshell

Appointment of diversity officers, second-generation sex discrimination, managing what one measures, and other recommendations all may be helpful in enlarging the pool from which women are likely to aspire to and be nominated for directorships. They are difficult, though, to keep in mind, at least all at one time.

At a cocktail party the CEO of a large corporation approached me. We talked about my work in corporate governance and then about this book. He then asked, in the manner of CEOs everywhere, "I have two hundred women in my organization, many of whom occupy middle and senior management positions. What should I tell them, and the organization, about what my company's policies will be on this important issue?"

I thought about it, and still think about it. This is what I come up with. "Tell everyone that the organization will bend over backwards to treat them fairly and equally." All employees will receive equal pay for equal work, equal benefits, equal opportunities afforded for expanded responsibilities and promotions. Not only will disparate impacts and hostile environments be eradicated: the corporation constantly will revisit those issues to insure fair and equal treatment for all.

With one exception. Equality gives way when there exists a universal and defined biological trait that requires equality to assume a secondary role. And there is only one such trait—child bearing, which by definition is exclusively the females' role. Any woman who goes on the "mommy track" for any reason (more lengthy maternity leave, part-time when children are entering school, Fridays off when the children are young) for up to X or Y (as individual corporations decide) amount of time nonetheless is entitled to equal treatment. No adverse inferences are to be drawn. No negative or neutral ("damning by faint praise") evaluation practices will be tolerated. The exception, as well as the rule, is to become part of the organization's very fabric.

Time and time again corporate America is short sighted, even irrational. Child bearing replenishes the genetic stock essential for perpetuation of the economic and social systems upon which we all depend. To relegate a woman to a secondary role, or to 60 percent of the pay a comparable male earns, because, overall, she took two years out to help rear a family, when that woman may have a 35-year career with the organization, is irrational.

The furor has still not died down. In January 2005, Lawrence Summers, a Ph.D. in economics, former cabinet secretary, and former World Bank president, spoke at a meeting of Harvard faculty. Because Summers was then the president of Harvard, the leading U.S. institution of higher learning, those present hung on his every word.

Addressing the question of why women had such a poor record of tenure and promotion in mathematics and the sciences at Harvard, Summers wondered if there were not "innate" and "biological" differences between men and women and whether these innate differences accounted for tenure and promotion rates. He questioned women faculty's ability and desire to work the late nights and weekends necessary to do the research and to write the articles that bring tenure and promotion. In a bit of melodrama, one Harvard professor of women's studies termed herself so ill that she had to leave the room while Summers held the floor.[22]

Leading business publications, as well as Summers himself, wondered what the furor had been about.[23] They believe it to be demonstrable that women do not compare to men in visiospatial skills and in interests in the core content of fields that go into the makeup of modern mathematics and science.

What the furor had been, and remains, about is that the moment persons in authority begin to think, let alone talk and act, in the manner in which Summers did, progress ceases. There may be differences between men and women, but by and large they are small and overrated. In the workplace or on the job ladder, we must strive to ignore those differences, except when they are absolutely undeniable and inescapable. Then we embrace them. Only when such an attitude is the most widely held one will corporate America remove many of the obstacles that now forestall the advancement of women. The further result will be to enlarge the number of women in the pool from which directors and senior executives are chosen, and that, ultimately, will result in a greater number of women being seated at the boardroom table.

Appendix A

Fortune 500 Corporations
with No Women Directors

2005 Rank	Board Seats	Name
75	13	Honeywell International, Inc.
96	7	Plains All American Pipeline, L.P.
98	14	News Corp.
115	12	General Dynamics Corp.
142	8	Computer Services Corp.
177	8	Tesoro Petroleum Corp.
179	10	The Directv Group, Inc.
188	9	PACCAR, Inc.
193	8	TransMontaigne
198	17	CHS, Inc.
243	11	Devon Energy Corp.
248	6	International Steel Group, Inc.
254	5	Liberty Media Corp.
258	12	Bear Stearns Companies
260	6	Enterprise Products Partners
261	13	Fidelity National Financial, Inc.
271	5	Kinder Morgan Management, LLC
272	9	Sonic Automotive, Inc.
274	12	Dillards
306	9	Danaher Corp.
314	12	El Paso Corp.
324	8	Jabil Circuit
329	10	Autoliv
351	8	World Fuel Services Corp.
361	7	Group One Auto
362	11	Allied Waste Industries, Inc.
374	11	AGCO Corp.
404	10	Commercial Metals, Inc.
406	7	EMCOR Group, Inc.
431	9	W.R. Berkley Corp.
432	8	York International Corp.
437	10	Hughes Supply, Inc.
438	7	Smith International, Inc.
439	7	Micron Technology, Inc.
444	9	NVR, Inc.
446	7	NTL, Inc.
456	6	Engelhard Corp.

Fortune 500 Corporations with No Women Directors (Cont.)

2005 Rank	Board Seats	Name
457	9	Hovnanian Enterprises
460	7	Affiliated Computer Services, Inc.
464	8	Levi Strauss & Co.
466	7	MDC Holdings, Inc.
472	8	American Financial Group
474	13	Collins & Aikman Corp.
477	11	Toll Brothers, Inc.
491	12	Level 3 Communications, Inc.
495	7	Gateway, Inc.
499	8	Kindred Healthcare, Inc.

Appendix B
Fortune 500 Corporations with a Single Woman Director

2005 Rank	Board Seats	Name
1	13	Wal-Mart Stores, Inc.
6	11	Chevron Texaco Corp.
12	11	Berkshire Hathaway
14	11	Verizon Communications
16	13	Cardinal Health, Inc.
17	12	Altria Group, Inc.
20	16	J.P. Morgan Chase & Co.
22	9	Valero Energy Corp.
23	10	AmerisourceBergen Corp.
28	10	Dell, Inc.
31	11	Marathon Oil Corp.
36	11	Morgan Stanley
38	10	Walgreen Company
41	9	Microsoft Corp.
43	11	Long's Companies, Inc.
44	9	Archer-Daniels-Midland Co.
48	9	Medco Health Solutions, Inc.
57	14	Caterpillar, Inc.
58	10	Northrup Grumman Corp.
63	12	Delphi Corp.
64	11	Prudential Financial, Inc.
69	14	Viacom International, Inc.
70	9	International Paper Company
71	12	Johnson Controls, Inc.
88	11	Hartford Financial Services Group
90	9	MCI, Inc.
95	10	Electronic Data Systems
102	12	Comcast Corp.
110	8	Tech Data Corp.
112	8	AutoNation, Inc.
113	10	Sears Holdings Corp.
121	13	ConAgra Foods, Inc.
123	15	Coca-Cola Enterprises
124	11	Northwestern Mutual Life Ins.
127	11	Lear Corp.
128	10	Rite Aid Corp.
129	12	UAL Corp. (United Airlines)

Fortune 500 Corporations with a Single Woman Director (Cont.)

2005 Rank	Board Seats	Name
132	9	Xerox Corp.
134	14	Emerson Electric Co.
136	11	Premcor, Inc.
137	11	Express Scripts
144	11	Loews Corp.
148	11	American Electric Power
149	10	United States Steel
150	13	Countrywide Financial Corp.
151	13	Dominion Resources
154	11	Qwest Communications
155	11	Progressive Corp.
156	9	Solectron Corp.
162	7	Humana, Inc.
166	10	Texas Instruments
168	8	Waste Management, Inc.
174	11	Union Pacific Corp.
175	8	Sanmina-SCI Corp.
178	8	TRW Automotive Holdings Corp.
180	10	Southern Company
181	11	Polte Homes
182	10	Winn-Dixie Stores, Inc.
183	9	Illinois Tool Works, Inc.
184	10	Kohl's Corp.
185	11	Health Net, Inc.
186	11	Occidental Petroleum Corp.
187	11	Edison International
189	8	Nucor Corp.
190	15	Northwest Airlines Corp.
194	9	Sun Microsystems, Inc.
195	10	TXV Corp.
200	11	Burlington Northern Sante Fe
203	7	D.R. Horton, Inc.
204	10	Centex Corp.
205	14	Dean Foods Company
206	9	Capital One Financial Corp.
209	11	Centerpoint Energy
211	11	National City Corp.
212	13	Amgen, Inc.
213	12	FPL Group, Inc.
214	9	Lennar Corp.
216	12	Textron, Inc.
219	11	Aramark Corp.
220	11	Oracle Corp.
222	8	Smithfield Foods, Inc.
225	11	United Auto Group, Inc.
227	10	Eaton Corp.
232	11	Continental Airlines, Inc.
233	11	Navistar International Corp.
238	7	American Standard Companies
239	7	Clear Channel Communications
247	9	Lucent Technology, Inc.
250	6	Reliant Energy, Inc.
262	9	Smurfit-Stone Container

Fortune 500 Corporations with a Single Woman Director (Cont.)

2005 Rank	Board Seats	Name
265	11	ALLTEL Communications
266	8	EMC Corp.
268	10	Unocal Corp.
269	9	CSX Corp.
270	9	Applied Materials, Inc.
275	10	R.R. Donnelly & Sons Company
277	10	Automatic Data Processing
284	8	B.J. Wholesale Club, Inc.
286	10	Norfolk Southern Corp.
290	9	Agilent Technologies, Inc.
291	9	Echostar Communications
291	8	Owens-Illinois, Inc.
292	14	Bank of New York Co.
299	11	Phelps Dodge Corp.
307	10	Yellow Roadway Corp.
311	11	NiSource
313	12	American Family Insurance
315	9	Prexair, Inc.
316	10	Eastman Chemical Company
317	15	Fifth Third Bankcorp.
319	16	Thrivent Investment Management
322	7	Cox Communications, Inc.
326	8	Federal-Mogul Corp.
328	6	Performance Food Group
330	11	Baker Hughes
331	11	Sherman-Williams Company
332	10	Interpublic Group of Companies
333	10	Anadarko Petroleum Corp.
337	9	NCR Corp.
338	13	Lyondell Chemical Company
339	10	CNF, Inc.
340	10	Mohawk Industries Inc.
343	11	Unisys Corp.
345	6	SPX Corp.
350	8	Auto Zone, Inc.
353	15	Burlington Resources, Inc.
356	11	CMS Energy Corp.
358	11	Ashbury Automotive Group, Inc.
359	9	Black & Decker Corp.
360	11	Ball Corp.
364	13	Pilgrim's Pack Corp.
366	11	Avery Denison Corp.
367	13	Apache Corp.
368	10	Harley-Davidson, Inc.
369	11	Dole Food Company, Inc.
370	12	Lexmark International, Inc.
371	10	Coventry Health Care, Inc.
373	9	Family Dollar Stores, Inc.
377	11	Brunswick Corp.
382	10	Quest Diagnostics Incorporated
384	10	Leggett & Platt, Inc.
385	11	WW Grainger, Inc.
387	10	Advanced Micro Devices, Inc.

Fortune 500 Corporations with a Single Woman Director (Cont.)

2005 Rank	Board Seats	Name
390	9	Charter Communications
391	16	Mellon Financial Corp.
392	11	Pitney Bowes, Inc.
394	15	Cablevision Systems Corp.
396	10	Harrah's Entertainment, Inc.
399	14	RadioShack Corp.
400	13	Energy East Corp.
401	11	Caesar's Entertainment, Inc.
408	11	Goodrich Corp.
409	11	The Brink's Company
412	9	Cinergy Corp.
414	11	Fisher Scientific International
415	11	Ikon Office Solutions, Inc.
417	9	Terex Corp.
419	9	Laidlaw International, Inc.
421	9	Long's Drug Stores Corp.
422	11	Car Max
423	12	Jacobs Engineering Group
424	8	Mirant
427	12	Owens & Minor, Inc.
430	9	Timken Company
440	9	Starwood Hotels & Resorts
441	9	Big Lots Stores, Inc.
442	7	C.H. Robinson Worldwide
443	7	Conseco, Inc.
444	9	NVR, Inc.
445	12	The Clorox Company
448	7	Enbridge Energy Partners
449	17	MGM Mirage, Inc.
450	7	Stryker Corp.
452	8	Ross Stores, Inc.
454	10	H & R Block, Inc.
455	13	Ecolab, Inc.
458	7	Universal Health Services
461	9	Jefferson-Pilot Corp.
463	8	Mutual of Omaha
465	13	Henry Schein, Inc.
467	9	Pathmark Stores, Inc.
468	8	United Stationers, Inc.
469	11	Ryland Group, Inc.
470	9	Cooper Tire and Rubber Co.
471	9	Wisconsin Energy Corp.
478	11	SCANA Corp.
480	13	Corning Incorporated
481	8	Sealed Air Corp.
482	6	Maxtor Corp.
483	6	Reebok International Ltd.
484	9	UGI Corp.
487	10	Advanced Auto Parts, Inc.
489	9	WESCO International, Inc.
492	10	Brinker International
494	10	Western & Southern Financial
500	13	Cincinnati Financial Corp.

Notes

Notes to the Introduction

1. Joan Biskupic, *Sandra Day O'Connor* (New York, Harper Collins, 2005) at 99.

2. Kathy Sawyer, "Women's Ranks Are Growing in Many Job Areas; Women's Ranks Growing in Many Traditional Male Organizations," *Washington Post,* August 24, 1981.

3. The terminology ("tease out" and "unpack") forms part of a framework that feminist scholars have utilized in examining issues related to the "economic subordination" of women in our society. *See* Martha Chamallas, *Introduction to Feminist Legal Theory* (New York, Aspen Law and Business, 2000) at 172–73.

Notes to Chapter 1

1. Gail Evans, *Play like a Man, Win like a Woman* (New York, Broadway Books, 2000) at 7.

2. *Zahorik v. Cornell University,* 729 F.2d 85 (2d Cir. 1984).

3. *Margolis v. Tektronix, Inc.,* 2000 U.S. App. LEXIS 16296 (9th Cir. 2002).

4. *See, e.g.,* Anthony Stith, *Breaking the Glass Ceiling: Sexism and Racism in Corporate America: The Myths, the Realities, and the Solutions* (Toronto, Warwick Publishers, 1998); Pat Heim & Susan K. Golant, *Smashing the Glass Ceiling* (New York, Simon & Schuster [Fireside Books], 1995); and Ann Morrison, Ellen Van Velsor, & Randall P. White, *Breaking the Glass Ceiling* (Cambridge, MA, Perseus Publishing, 1992).

5. Betsy Morris, "How Corporate America Is Betraying Women," Fortune, January 10, 2005, 64, at 70 (recounting settlements by Merrill Lynch and by Mitsubishi as well as those in the text).

6. *Id.;* Kate Kelly & Colleen DeBaise, "Morgan Stanley Settles Bias Suit for $54 Million," *Wall Street Journal,* July 13, 2004, at A-1.

7. Martha Chamallas, *Introduction to Feminist Legal Theory* at 184 (New York, Aspen Law and Business, 2000).

8. Joann Lublin, "The Serial CEO," Wall St, J., Sept. 19, 2005, at B-1 (sitting or former CEOs are often the safe choice but also "highlight a shortage of in-house talent and weak succession planning at many companies").

9. Federal Glass Ceiling Commission, "Good for Business: Making Full Use of the Nation's Human Capital," Fact Finding Report, BNA Daily Labor Report, March 17, 1995, at 634–37.

10. Catalyst, Inc., "Women in Corporate Leadership: Progress and Prospects," at 136 (1996).

11. *See* Rene Denfeld, *The New Victorians: A Woman's Challenge to the Old Feminist Order* (New York, Warner Books, 1995) at 250; Laura Ingraham, "Enter Women," *New York Times,* April 19, 1995, at A17.

12. *See, e.g.,* Nadja Zalokar, "Male-Female Differences in Occupational Choice and the Demand for General and Occupation-Specific Human Capital," 26 Econ. Inquiry 59, 71 (1988); Solomon W. Polacheck, "Occupational Self-Selection," 63 Rev. Economics & Statistics 60 (1981).

13. A leading work espousing this view is Richard Epstein, *Forbidden Grounds: The Case against Employment Discrimination Law* (Cambridge, MA, Harvard University Press, 1992) at 41–42 & 102. *See also* Richard Posner, "An Economic Analysis of Sex Discrimination Laws," 56 U. Chi. L. Rev. 1311 (1989).

14. *See generally* Richard Delgado, "Rodrigo's Roadmap: Is the Marketplace Theory for Eradicating Discrimination a Blind Alley?" 93 Northwestern U. L. Rev. 215, 219 (1998).

15. *See* Beth Corbin, "Women Go Center Stage in Affirmative Action Debate," *National NOW Times,* May-June, 1995, 1, at 3.

16. Quoted in Morris, *supra.*

17. *See, e.g.,* Pamela Winnick & Stephanie Franken, "Trapped under a Glass Ceiling?" *Pittsburgh Post-Gazette,* June 2, 2002, at F-1 (25,194 gender discrimination cases filed in 2000, up from 21,796 in 1992).

18. *See* Kevin M. Claremont & Theodore Eisenberg, "Plaintiffphobia in the Appellate Courts: Civil Rights Really Do Differ from Negotiable Instruments," 2002 University of Illinois Law Review 947, 957–58 (analysis of seven thousand four hundred federal civil appeals decided between 1988 and 1997).

19. Deborah L. Rhode, *Speaking of Sex: The Denial of Gender Equality* (Cambridge, MA, Harvard University Press, 1999) at 157.

20. *See* Kristin Bumiller, *The Civil Rights Society: The Social Construction of Victims* (Baltimore, MD, Johns Hopkins University Press, 1988); Rhode, *supra,* at 162 & n. 58.

21. *See, e.g.,* Chamallas, *supra,* at 207–10.

22. Jonathan Liu & Doirean Wilson, "The Unchanging Perception of Women as Managers," 16 Women in Management 163, 168 (2001).

23. Morris, *supra*, at 66.

24. Joan Williams, *Unbending Gender* (New York, Oxford University Press, 2000) at 28, reviewing Ellen Israel Rosen's study, *Bitter Choices: Blue Collar Women in and out of Work* (Chicago, University of Chicago Press, 1987).

25. Rhode, *supra*, at 146. Because of the subjective nature of the process toward the top, and the difficulty of evaluating it, courts have shied away from Title VII cases involving senior executive positions. *See generally* Tracy Anbinder Baron, "Keeping Women out of the Executive Suite: The Courts' Failure to Apply Title VII Scrutiny to Upper-Level Jobs," 143 U. Pa. L. Rev. 267 (1994).

26. Rosabeth Moss Kanter, *Men and Women of the Corporation* (New York, Basic Books, 1977, rev. ed., 1993) at 52.

27. *Id.* at 53.

28. *See, e.g.*, David Charny & G. Mitu Gulati, "Efficiency-Wages, Tournaments, and Discrimination: A Theory of Employment Discrimination Law for 'High-Level' Jobs," 33 Harvard C.R.-C.L. L. Rev. 57, 77–83 (1998)(may be more efficient to sort out employees, retaining those with common traits to work together); Donald Langevoort, "Overcoming Resistance to Diversity in the Executive Suite: Grease, Grit and the Corporate Promotion Job Tournament," 61 Wash. & Lee L. Rev. 1615, 1630 (2004)(suggesting that in tournaments grease may win out over grit). *See also* Edward P. Lazear & Sherwin Rosen, "Rank-Order Tournaments as Efficient Labor Contracts," 89 J. Pol. Econ. 841 (1981).

29. *See, e.g.*, Jack Welch & John A. Byrne, *Jack: Straight from the Gut* (New York, Warner Books, 2001) at 158.

30. *See, e.g.*, Marleen O'Connor, "The Enron Board: The Perils of Groupthink," 71 U. Cinn. L. Rev. 1233, 1313–14 (2003).

31. For documentation that men are less risk averse that women, *see, e.g,,* Brad M. Barber & Terrence Odean, "Boys Will Be Boys: Gender, Overconfidence, and Common Stock Investment," 116 Q.J. Econ. 261 (2001); Ammon Jianakoplos & Alexandra Bernasek, "Are Women More Risk Averse?" 36 Econ. Inquiry 620 (1998).

32. Behavioralists term this the Machiavellian or "High Mach" personality, which they purport to find to be more prevalent among men. *See* Martin Kilduff & David V. Day, "Do Chameleons Get Ahead? The Effects of Self-Monitoring on Managerial Careers," 37 Acad. Management 1047 (1994); Langevoort, *supra*, at 1629–31 ("a bias toward overconfidence, risk-taking, and ethical plasticity").

33. The leading piece is Susan Sturm, "Second Generation Employment Discrimination: A Structural Approach," 101 Columb. L. Rev. 458 (2001).

34. The English case in which water got loose from a mineshaft, flooding

plaintiff's land, is the leading precedent. *See Rylands v. Fletcher,* 3 [1868] H.L. 330.

35. These are the facts of the seminal case, *Meritor Savings Bank v. Vinson,* 477 U.S. 57 (1986).

36. *Burlington Industries, Inc. v. Ellerth,* 524 U.S. 742 (1998), and *Faragher v. City of Boca Raton,* 524 U.S. 775 (1999).

37. *Faragher, supra,* at 808.

38. Indeed, in the *Meridor* and the *Burlington Industries* cases, plaintiff women had received one or more promotions. Thus, they had an uphill struggle, at best, to make out any claim of an adverse "tangible employment action" that had harmed them in any way.

39. Demonstrating that the employer had done those things would be the best way, although strictly speaking not the only way, for a corporation to establish its affirmative defense and thereby avoid liability. Rather, in *Faragher* at 807, Mr. Justice Souter held that "[t]he defense comprises two elements: (a) that the employer exercised reasonable care to prevent and correct promptly any sexually harassing behavior, and (b) that the plaintiff employee had unreasonably failed to take advantage of any preventive or corrective harm provided by the employer or to avoid harm otherwise." In *Burlington Industries,* Mr. Justice Kennedy said very much the same thing. *Burlington* at 765.

NOTES TO CHAPTER 2

1. *Passantino v. Johnson and Johnson Consumer Products, Inc.,* 212 F.3rd 439 (9th Cir. 2000).

2. Richard A. Oppel, Jr., "Retaliation Lawsuits: A Treacherous Slope," *New York Times,* Sept. 29, 1999, at C-8 (women have a 57 percent chance of prevailing, compared to 55 percent on the sex-discrimination claim, 47 percent in age-discrimination claims, and 44 percent in race-discrimination cases). *Cf.* the findings of Kevin Claremont and Theodore Eisenberg, "Plaintiffphobia in the Appellate Courts: Civil Rights Really Do Differ from Negotiable Instruments," 2002 University of Illinois Law Review 947, 957–58, on appeals from those claims.

3. *Bergene v. Salt River Project,* 272 F.3rd 1136 (9th Cir. 2001).

4. *Smith v. Kentucky State University,* 2004 U.S. App. LEXIS 6973 (6th Cir. 2004). Another retaliation case is *Hemmings v. Tidyman's, Inc.,* 285 F.3rd 1174 (9th Cir. 2002)(new CEO and other executives harassed and intimidated women managers who had filed EEOC demand letter, stating to one they "would sooner pay $5 million to fight a lawsuit than to pay her a penny").

5. *See* the discussion of tokens, skewed groups, and boundary heightening in chapter 9 *infra.*

6. *Abeita v. Transamerica Mailings, Inc.,* 159 F.3rd 246 (6th Cir. 1998).

7. *Black v. Zaring Homes, Inc.*, 104 F.3rd 822 (6ᵗʰ Cir. 1997).

8. *Quinn v. Consolidated Freightways, Inc.*, 283 F.3rd 572 (3ʳᵈ Cir. 2002).

9. 42 U.S.C. § 2000e-2(a)(1).

10. Pat Heim & Susan K. Golant, *Smashing the Glass Ceiling* (New York, Simon & Schuster [Fireside Books], 1995) at 13.

11. *Id.* at 14.

12. *Luciano v. The Olsten Corporation*, 110 F.3rd 210 (2d Cir. 1997).

13. *Bellaver v. Quanex Corp.*, 200 F.3rd 485 (7ᵗʰ Cir. 2000).

14. Other mini-RIF cases include *Corti v. Storage Technology Corp.*, 304 F.3rd 336 (4ᵗʰ Cir. 2002)(number of financial services managers in Federal Division reduced from three to two: woman manager terminated even though she would have been one of the most profitable managers that year on a company-wide basis); *Wood v. Wick Communications Co.*, 2002 U.S. App. LEXIS 4703 (9ᵗʰ Cir. 2002)(RIF found to be pretext to eliminate magazine advertising director because supervisor thought that "a young woman" should not be in the position); and *Franulic v. Bozell Worldwide*, 2001 U.S. App. LEXIS 27310 (6ᵗʰ Cir. 2001)(RIF of sixteen account managing partners at large advertising agency, allegedly based upon profitability, eliminated only woman partner, retained male partner with no track record of profitability, and promoted another male with poor record the day before RIF announced).

15. *Zimmerman v. Associates First Capital Corporation*, 251 F.3rd 376 (2d Cir. 2001).

16. The number of new boss cases is surprisingly large, including *McGregor v. Mallinckrodt, Inc.*, 373 F.3rd 923 (8ᵗʰ Cir. 2004)(only female in marketing demoted and then terminated after male peer promoted to become her new supervisor); *Smith v. Kentucky State University*, 2004 U.S. App. LEXIS 6973 (6ᵗʰ Cir. 2004)(retaliation against only woman professor intensified after new dean appointed in business school); *Hemmings v. Tidyman's, Inc.*, 285 F.3rd 1174 (9ᵗʰ Cir. 2001)(intimidation and harassment began after new CEO took office); *Dumnway v. International Brotherhood of Teamsters, Inc.*, 2002 U.S. App. LEXIS 23702 (D.C. App. 2002)(new boss was peer over whom plaintiff had been promoted years earlier: gave her first negative evaluation in twenty-two years and then attempted to force her to resign); *Quinn v. Consolidated Freightways, Inc.*, 283 F.3rd 572 (3ʳᵈ Cir. 2002)(sexual harassment of only female sales manager began after new boss took over); *Franulic v. Bozell Worldwide, Inc.*, 2001 U.S. App. LEXIS 27310 (6ᵗʰ Cir. 2001)(only female account managing partner of sixteen such partners RIFed by new managing partner of group); *Bergene v. Salt River Project*, 273 F.3rd 1136 (9ᵗʰ Cir. 2001)(new superintendent of engineering began scheme to deny only woman technician a promotion); *Beard v. Southern Flying J, Inc.*, 266 F.3rd 792 (8ᵗʰ Cir. 2001)(pattern of harassment began with appointment of new general manager); and *Cifra v. Lockheed Martin Co.*, 252 F.3rd 205 (2d Cir. 2001)(only

female senior industrial hygienist faced performance improvement plan and other discriminatory actions leading to termination after merger of departments and new boss took over).

17. *Ezold v. Wolf, Block, Schorr & Solis-Cohen,* 983 F.3d 509 (3rd Cir. 1992), *cert. denied,* 114 S. Ct. 88 (1993).

18. *Ann B. Hopkins v. Price Waterhouse,* 920 F.2d 967 (D.C. Cir. 1990), on remand from 490 U.S. 228 (1989).

19. At one of the other "big four" international accounting firms, Deloitte Touche, the number of women partners increased from 6.5 percent in 1993 to 17 percent in 2003, partly as a result of a formal effort by the firm. Email from Kathryn D. Wood, Senior Manager, Institute for the Advancement of Women, Flexibility & Choice, Deloitte & Touche, Oct. 28, 2003, reported in Joan Williams, Cynthia Thomas Calvert, & Holly Green Cooper, "Better on Balance? The Corporate Counsel Retention Project: Final Report," reproduced in 10 Wm. & Mary J. Women & Law 367, 382 (2004). Deloitte has been on *Fortune* magazine's list of best places to work for over six years. *Id.* Another firm, Ernst & Young, has been on the lists both at *Fortune* and at *Working Mother.* See also Ernst & Young, "Getting to Equity: Creating a Level Playing Field for Women at Ernst & Young" (Oct. 2003).

Notes to Chapter 3

1. Department of Labor, "Bureau of Labor Statistics Chart Book" (1993). By 2000, the number of women in the workplace had peaked and then fallen, to 57.5 percent of women, holding 46.7 percent of the jobs available. United States Census 2000, at Chart QT-P24. Ten years earlier, 53 percent of women worked, holding 45.7 percent of the jobs. United States Census 1990, at Table 233.

2. Catherine Ross, "The Division of Labor at Home," 65 Social Forces 816 (March 1997).

3. Sue Shellenbarger, "Pregnant Pause: Deciding When to Tell a New Boss You Are Expecting a Baby," *Wall Street Journal,* October 14, 2004, at D-1.

4. Lisa Belkin, "The Opt-Out Revolution," *New York Times Sunday Magazine,* October 23, 2003, at 42.

5. *See* David Brooks, "Empty Nests, and Hearts," *New York Times,* Jan. 15, 2005, at A-15.

6. The phrase was coined by Felice N. Schwartz, the founder and first president of Catalyst, Inc. *See* Ann Crittenden, *The Price of Motherhood* (New York, Metropolitan Books, 2001) at 44.

7. Reported in Crittenden, *supra,* at 35.

8. Piper Fogg, "Female Professors Assail Remarks by Harvard's President, Who Says It's All a Misunderstanding," *Chronicle of Higher Education,* Jan. 19, 2005, at 3, also discussed in the conclusion, *infra.*

9. Crittenden, *supra,* at 2.

10. *Id.* at 5.

11. *See, e.g.,* Joan Williams, Cynthia Thomas Calvert, & Holly Green Cooper, "Better on Balance? The Corporate Counsel Retention Project: Final Report," reproduced in 10 Wm. & Mary J. Women & Law 367, 377 (2004).

12. *Id.* at 417–18.

13. Joan Williams, *Unbending Gender* (New York, Oxford University Press) at 17, quoting Deborah Fallows, *A Mother's Work* (New York, Houghton Mifflin, 1985) at 11.

14. Beverly Sills & Lawrence Linderman, *Beverly: An Autobiography* (New York, Bantam Books, 1987) at 117.

15. Belkin, *supra,* at 44 (citing U.S. census data).

16. *Id.* at 45.

17. Reported in Belkin, *supra,* at 44.

18. Crittenden, *supra,* at 13.

19. Council of Economic Advisers, "Families and the Labor Market, 1969–1999: Analyzing the 'Time Crunch,'" at 4 (1999).

20. Candy Saigon, "Dinner Time," *Washington Post,* Mar. 3, 1999.

21. Crittenden, *supra,* at 26–27.

22. Belkin, *supra,* at 47.

23. *Id.*

24. *Id.* at 29.

25. Claudia Goldin, "Career and Family: College Women Look to the Past," National Bureau of Economic Research Working Paper No. 5188 (1995).

26. Judith P. Walker & Deborah J. Swiss, *Women and the Work/Family Dilemma* (New York, Wiley, 1993).

27. Reported by Crittenden, *supra,* at 36.

28. Thereafter Deloitte devoted specific resources to the hiring and advancement of women with its Initiative for the Advancement of Women/Flexibility & Choice, described in Williams et al., *supra,* at 450–52.

29. Williams et al., *supra,* at 392–94 describe practices such as late-day and weekend meetings and 24-hour availability ("on call") as emanating from tradition and from perceptions that the work requires face time ("People walk down the hall and ask questions and invite us to meetings. We need to be here."). A female in-house attorney states that "I am expected to check my email on weekends so that I can give my client a quick response, and to have my cell phone on at all times."

30. Reported in Catharine MacKinnon & Reva P. Siegel, *Directions in Sexual Harassment Law* (New Haven, CT, Yale University Press, 2003) at 1092.

31. *See* Gary S. Becker, *Human Capital* (Chicago, University of Chicago Press, 3rd ed., 1994); Gary S. Becker & Nigel Tomes, "Human Capital and the Rises and Fall of Families," J. Labor Economics 43 (July 1986).

32. 42 U.S. Code § 2000e(k).

33. *Zimmerman v. Direct Federal Credit Union,* 262 F.2d 70 (1st Cir. 2001).

34. *Laxton v. GAP, Inc.,* 333 F.3rd 572 (5th Cir. 2003).

35. *See, e.g., Palmer v. Pioneer Inn Associates, Inc.,* 338 F.3rd 981 (9th Cir. 2003)(experienced pregnant woman hired, first as waitress and then as a supervisor, unhired before first day of work by boss's boss who stated he would not allow her to "work there being pregnant"); *Gorski v. New Hampshire Dept. of Corrections,* 290 F.3rd 466 (1st Cir. 2002)(female police sergeant subjected to derogatory comments about her pregnancy by both her direct and ultimate supervisor; hostile work environment based upon her pregnancy); and *Golson v. Green Tree Financial Corp.,* 2002 U.S. App. LEXIS 472 (4th Cir. 2002)(pregnant loan collection agent who missed twelve days of work for pregnancy-related illness that included three days' hospitalization terminated for failure to meet performance goals, despite evidence that employees with other nonpregnancy illnesses had regularly been excused from performance goals in periods in which they were ill).

36. Quoted in Belkin, *supra,* at 58.

37. Williams et al., *supra,* at 414.

38. Rosabeth Moss Kanter, *Men and Women of the Corporation* (New York, Basic Books, 1977, rev. ed., 1993) at 305.

39. Crittenden, *supra,* at 95.

40. U.S. Bureau of the Census, "Current Population Reports: Money Income in the U.S.," at 46–49 (2000).

41. Robert G. Wood, Mary E. Corcoran, & Paul N. Courant, "Pay Differences among the Highly Paid: The Male-Female Earnings Gap in Lawyer's Salaries," 11 J. Labor Economics 417 (1993).

42. Reported in Crittenden, *supra,* at 96.

43. Catalyst, Inc., "Women and the MBA: Gateway to Opportunity" (2000).

44. *Id.* at 107.

45. Today birth rates only match death rates in many industrialized nations, meaning that certain genetic stocks may not be replenishing themselves at all. For example, in 2005, the birth rate is only 8.8 per 1000 population and the rate of population growth is zero in Germany. The birth rate is 10.1 and the rate of population growth is zero (.15 percent) for all practical purposes in Spain. The same is true for the European Union overall, with population growth at a very small percentage of one percent (.15 percent). CIA, The World Factbook (2005), available online at http://www.cia.gov/cia/publications/factbook/geos (last visited Oct. 7, 2005). The 2000 birth rate is 14.4 per 1000 and the rate of population growth is .92 percent in the United States.

46. The phrase comes from a landmark U.S. Supreme Court discrimination case, *Griggs v. Duke Power Co.,* 401 U.S. 424, 432 (1971).

47. Crittenden, *supra,* at 256–74 ("How to Bring Children Up without Putting Women Down").
48. Williams et al., *supra,* at 422–32. Professor Williams and her coauthors go on to set out an equally detailed set of recommendations for implementation of their ideas. *See id.* at 432–45 ("best practices for implementation").
49. Williams et al., *supra,* at 432. *See also* Edward S. Adams, "Using Evaluations to Break Down the Male Corporate Hierarchy: A Full Circle Approach," 73 U. Colo. L. Rev. 117 (2002).

NOTES TO CHAPTER 4

1. John M. Conley, William M. O'Barr, & E. Allen Lind, "The Power of Language: Presentation Style in the Courtroom," 1978 Duke L. J. 1375.
2. Deborah Tannen, *Gender and Discourse* (New York, Oxford University Press, 1994) at 31.
3. *Hemmings v. Tidyman's, Inc.,* 285 F.3rd 1174, 1179 (9th Cir. 2002).
4. *See, e.g.,* Sheila Wellington, *Be Your Own Mentor* (New York, Random House, 2001) at 92; Gail Evans, *Play like a Man, Win like a Woman* (New York, Broadway Books, 2000) at 31 ("Women must learn that we are playing in a world where our opponents have been taught to hide their emotions.").
5. The observation is empirically proven in Erving Goffman, *Gender Advertisements* (New York, Harper & Row, 1979).
6. Tannen, *supra,* at 217.
7. Robin T. Lakoff, *Language and Woman's Place* (New York, Harper Trade, 1975).
8. In a number of tribal languages, the linguistic usages of male and female speakers differ dramatically. Men and women actually speak distinct variants of the same language. *See, e.g.,* Edward Sapir, *Selected Writings of Edward Sapir in Language, Culture, and Personality* (Berkeley, University of California Press, 1949); *Language, Gender, and Sex in Comparative Perspective* (Susan Phillips et al., eds.)(New York, Cambridge University Press, 1987).
In English, the speaker's gender does not require the use of contrasting grammatical forms. Rather, with English and the languages of other industrialized nations, certain syntactic and other characteristics may be disproportionately distributed according to gender.
9. Deborah Tannen, *You Just Don't Understand* (New York, William Morrow, 1990).
10. *See, e.g.,* Tannen, *Gender and Discourse,* at 31–37, 65–60 & 195 et seq.
11. *See, e.g.,* David Graddol & Joan Swann, *Gender Voices* (Malden, MA, Blackwell, 1989).
12. *See, e.g., The Sociology of the Languages of American Women* (Betty L. DuBois & Isabel Crouch, eds.)(New York and Berlin, De Gruyter, 2d ed.,

1979). *See also* Bent Preisler, *Linguistic Sex Roles in Conversation: Social Variation in the Expression of Tentativeness in English* (New York and Berlin, De Gruyter, 1986); *Women in Their Speech Communities* (Jennifer Coates & Deborah Cameron, eds.)(White Plains, NY, Longman, 1989); Jennifer Coates, *Language and Gender: A Reader* (Malden, MA, Blackwell, 1997).

13. *See* William O'Barr, *Linguistic Evidence: Language, Power, and Strategy in the Courtroom* (London, Elsevier Science & Technology, 1982).

14. Janet E. Ainsworth, "In a Different Register: The Pragmatics of Powerlessness in Police Interrogation," 103 Yale Law Journal 259 (1993).

15. *Id.* at 274.

16. *See, e.g.,* Tannen, *supra* note 9, at 53–83 ("Chapter Two: Interpreting Interruption in Conversation").

17. Lakoff, *supra,* at 18.

18. Tannen, *supra* note 9, at 34.

19. Mary R. Key, *Male/Female Language* (Lanham, MD, Scarecrow Press, 1975) at 75–76.

20. Ainsworth, *supra,* at 280.

21. *See* Ainsworth, *supra,* at 276.

22. Evans, *supra,* at 147 (2000).

23. Lakoff, *supra,* at 53–54.

24. Ainsworth, *supra,* at 282–83.

25. Lakoff, *supra,* at 17.

26. *See, e.g.,* Ruth M. Bend, "Male-Female Intonation Patterns in American English," in *Language and Sex: Difference and Dominance* (Barrie Thorns & Nancy Henley, eds.)(London, Stationery Office, 1975).

27. Wellington, *supra,* at 85. *See also id.* at 92: "Lower the pitch of your voice. A lower voice commands more attention and respect."

28. Ainsworth, *supra,* at 283.

29. Lakoff, *supra,* at 205.

30. Tannen, *supra* note9, at 40.

31. Stephanie Coontz, *The Social Origins of Private Life* (New York, Norton,1988) at 85, *quoted in* Joan Williams, *Unbending Gender* (New York, Oxford University Press, 2000) at 23.

32. Jean Hollands, *Same Game, Different Rules: How to Get Ahead without Being a Bully Broad, Ice Queen, or " Understood"* (New York, McGraw-Hill, 2002).

33. *See* Debra E. Meyerson & Joyce K. Fletcher, "A Modest Manifesto for Shattering the Glass Ceiling," 78 Harvard Bus. Rev. 127, 133 (Jan.-Feb. 2000).

34. *See, e.g.,* Martha Chamallas, *Introduction to Feminist Legal Theory* (New York, Aspen Law & Business, 2000) at 188.

35. *See* Barbara F. Reskin & Patricia Roos, *Job Queues, Gender Queues: Explaining Women's Inroads into Male-Dominated Occupations* (Philadelphia, PA, Temple University Press, 1990) at 11–15; Deborah Rhode, "Occupational Inequality," 1988 Duke Law Journal 1207, 1228–29.

36. Williams, *supra,* at 1.

NOTES TO CHAPTER 5

1. *See* Jean Hollands, *Same Game, Different Rules: How to Get Ahead without Being a Bully Broad, an Ice Queen or "Ms. Misunderstood"* (New York, McGraw Hill, 2002) at 163.

2. *Id.* at 164.

3. The nuances associated with tokenism are complex and still present in the workplace and management ranks of many corporations. For that reason, this book devotes an entire chapter to the subject. *See* "Women and Minorities in Organizations: The Legacy of Tokenism," chapter 9, *supra.*

4. Rosabeth Moss Kanter, *Men and Women of the Corporation* (New York, Basic Books, 1977, rev. ed., 1993) at 236.

5. Carol Gallagher, *Going to the Top* (New York, Penguin Group, 2000) at 109.

6. *Id.* at 108.

7. Hollands, *supra,* at 5 & 19.

8. Hollands, *supra,* at 202.

9. *See, e.g.,* Gallagher, *supra,* at 108–9 ("Bride of Dracula syndrome"); Hollands, *supra,* at 226–27 ("the Sounding Off Tyrant," "the Selectively Quiet Type," " Sarcastic-Aggressive," and the "Silent Judge").

10. *Id.* at 101.

11. *Id.* at xix.

12. *See* chapter 1 *supra.*

13. Kanter, *supra,* at 52–53.

14. Hollands, *supra,* at 49 (Rule 6).

15. *See, e.g.,* Sheila Wellington, *Be Your Own Mentor* (New York, Random House, 2001) at 55, quoting Avon Products CEO Andrea Jung: "I developed good listening skills, to learn and to understand. Developing listening skills is part of credibility."

16. Hollands, *supra,* at 31 (Rule 4).

17. *Id.* at 83 (Rule 10).

18. Gallagher, *supra,* at 94–95.

19. Hollands, *supra,* at 107 (Rule 13).

20. Gallagher, *supra,* at 29–31.

21. Hollands, *supra,* at 147 (Rule 17).

22. Hollands, *supra,* at 171 (Rule 20).

23. The study is summarized in Stanley A. Hetzler, "Variations in Role-Playing Patterns among Different Echelons of Bureaucratic Leaders," 20 American Sociological Review 700 (1955).

24. Kanter, *supra,* at 191. In her work, Professor Kanter summarizes many of the previous explorations of this phenomenon.

25. *See, e.g.,* Melville Dalton, *Men Who Manage* (New York, Wiley, 1959) at 247 (relatively powerless supervisors "hesitate to act without consulting superiors and take refuge in clearly formulated rules").

26. Kanter, *supra,* at 199.

27. Garda Bowman & N. Beatrice Worthy, "Are Women Executives People?" 43 *Harvard Bus. Rev.* 14 (July/Aug. 1965).

28. Donald Laird & Eleanor Laird, *The Psychology of Supervising the Working Woman* (New York, McGraw Hill, 1942) at 175–79.

29. Kanter, *supra,* at 202 (italics in original).

NOTES TO CHAPTER 6

1. As recounted in the introduction, the uncomplimentary "Bully Broad" appellation comes from a recent book by a Silicon Valley organizational psychologist, Jean Hollands. *See* Jean Hollands, *Same Game, Different Rules: How To Get Ahead without Being a Bully Broad, Ice Queen, or "Ms. Misunderstood"* (New York, McGraw-Hill, 2002).

2. *See* chapters 5 *supra* & 12 *infra.*

3. Toddi Gunther, "Three Simple Steps to the Top," *Business Week,* Oct. 9, 2000, at 206 (interview with Pamela Thomas-Graham).

4. Patricia Sellers, Ann Harrington, & Alynda Wheat, "America's Most Powerful Businesswomen: Patient but Not Passive," *Fortune,* Oct. 15, 2001, at 188.

5. Andrea Jung, president and CEO, Avon, quoted in Sheila Wellington, *Find a Mentor* (New York, Random House, 2001) at 157.

6. Wellington was succeeded as CEO of Catalyst by Irene Lang, CEO of Individual.Com, Inc., in August 2003. Catalyst, Inc., press release, dated August 14, 2003.

7. Rosabeth Moss Kanter, *Men and Women of the Corporation* (New York, Basic Books, 1977, rev. ed., 1993) at 183.

8. Wellington, *supra,* at 110–11.

9. *See, e.g.,* Kanter, *supra,* at 206–42. *See also* the extended discussion of the legacy of tokenism and skewed distributions of minorities in chapter 9 *infra.*

10. Wellington, *supra,* at 114.

11. Carol Gallagher, *Going to the Top* (New York, Penguin Books, 2000) at 67–68.

12. *See, e.g., id.* at 72–82.

13. Wellington, *supra,* at 122.

14. Wellington, *supra,* at 179 & 190.

15. Catalyst, Inc., "Women in Corporate Leadership" (undated brochure).

16. Catalyst, Inc., "Catalyst Study Finds Women Need Experience in the Business of Businesses to Claim Top Leadership Roles," press release dated June 3, 2003 (study funded by General Motors, Inc.).

17. *See, e.g.,* Debra E. Meyerson & Joyce K. Fletcher, "A Modest Manifesto for Shattering the Glass Ceiling," 78 Harvard Bus. Rev. 127, 133 (Jan.-Feb. 2000).

18. Kanter, *supra,* at 132.

19. Wellington, *supra,* at 185.

20. Wellington, *supra,* at 178.

21. G. E. Clements, F. J. Lunding, & D. S. Perkins, "Everyone Who Makes It Has a 'Mentor,'" Harvard Bus. Rev. 89 (July-August 1978).

22. Marie Knowles, quoted in Wellington, *supra,* at 157.

23. Wellington, *supra,* at 3.

24. Kanter, *supra,* at 188.

25. *Id.* at 182–83.

26. *Id.* at 184.

27. Joan Winn, "Entrepreneurship: Not An Easy Path to Top Management for Women," 19 Women in Management Rev. 143, 144 (2004).

28. *Id.* at 150.

NOTES TO CHAPTER 7

1. *Cf.* Deborah D. Zelechowski & Diana Bilimoria, "The Experience of Women Corporate Inside Directors at Fortune 1000 Firms," 18 Women in Management 376, 377 (2003)(preliminary finding of thirty-six firms with female inside directors but able to verify only eight through responses to interview requests).

2. *See* the discussion of the modern governance model in chapter 11 *infra*. As related in chapter 9, New York Stock Exchange (NYSE) and NASDAQ rules now require that a majority of directors be independent.

3. *Chronicle of Higher Education,* Annual President's Salary Survey, available at Chronicle.com/colloquy, Facts and Figures. See also *Los Angeles Times,* November 26, 2000, at B-2 (Rodin ranked second after L. Jay Oliva, president of New York University); Tamar Levin, "Survey Shows 27 Presidents of Colleges Top $500,000," *New York Times,* Nov. 17, 2002, at 22 (Judith Rodin at the University of Pennsylvania earned $808,021, ranking second again).

4. Obtaining information on mutual (member-owned) organizations such as Northwest Mutual Life Insurance (116), United Services Automobile Association (USAA)(224), or Mutual of Omaha (394) was more difficult, because mutual organizations do not file annual proxy statements with the SEC. Informa-

tion about those organizations' boards was obtained from their web sites, via email, or by telephone. The only Fortune 500 organization abut which no data could be obtained was the Aid Association for Lutherans, which ranked 477 on the *Fortune* list (2001).

5. The American Bar Association's Revised Model Business Corporation Act (1985) provides in section 8.03(c);

> The articles of incorporation or bylaws may establish a variable range for the size of the board of directors by fixing a minimum and maximum number of directors. If a variable range is established, the number of directors may be fixed from time to time, within the minimum and maximum, by the shareholders or the board of directors.

6. In 1996, Ann McLaughlin, a former secretary of labor, sat on eleven boards of directors and was classified by the *New York Times* as a trophy director. At that time the *Times* estimated that she made $352,250 annually in directors' fees. Another woman trophy director, Lilyan Affinito, a retired executive of Maxxam Group, Inc., sat on six boards, making $397,000 per year. *See* Judith H. Dobrzynski, "When Directors Play Musical Chairs," *New York Times,* Money and Business section, November 17, 1996.

7. Professors Devon Carbado and Mitu Gulati tend toward the opposite conclusion for persons of color. "[T]here is reason to believe that the racial minorities at the top of the corporate hierarchy neither racially reform the corporation, nor engage in door-opening activities, for the minorities on the bottom." Carbado & Gulati, "Race to the Top of the Corporate Ladder: What Minorities Do When They Get There," 61 Wash. & Lee L. Rev. 1645, 1692 (2004).

8. *See, e.g.,* Deborah D. Zelechowski & Diana Bilimoia, *supra,* at 378.

9. There are thirty-one CEOs listed in the data but the number includes the five women CEOs in the Fortune 500 in 2001.

10. It also has much to do with the method by which boards of directors conduct searches for CEOs. *See generally* Rakesh Khurana, *Searching for the Corporate Savior* (Princeton, NJ, Princeton University Press, 2002).

11. Dobrzynski, *supra,* quoting Dennis C. Carey, codirector of board services for Stuart Spencer & Associates, Inc.

12. Nineteen percent of college and university presidents are women, compared to 1.6 percent of corporate CEOs. Twenty percent of U.S. university and college full professors are women, compared to 11.6 percent of corporate directors. *See* Rachel Smolkin, "Barriers Confront Working Women," *Pittsburgh Post Gazette,* June 3, 2001, at A-14. *Cf.* comments of University of Pennsylvania president Judith Rodin: "Clearly, there's still a glass ceiling in academia, although not in department chairman so much as there used to be," quoted in Sheila Wellington, *Be Your Own Mentor* (New York, Random House, 2001) at 14.

13. Carolyn Kay Brancato & D. Jeanne Paterson, "Board Diversity in U.S. Corporations: Best Practices for Broadening the Profile of Corporate Boards" at 8 (1999), cited in Marleen O'Connor, "The Enron Board: The Perils of Group Think," 71 U. Cinn. L. Rev. 133, 1308 & n. 436 (2003).

NOTES ON CHAPTER 8

1. "Women in the Fortune 500," Catalyst, Inc., press release, February 1, 2005, at available http://www.catalystwomen.org (visited Sept. 2, 2005). *See also* "Alliance for Board Diversity Factsheet," Catalyst, Inc., press release, May 11, 2005.

2. *See, e.g.,* "Make Way for Madame Director," *Business Week,* December 22, 2003, at 57 (women held 11.2 percent of board seats in 1999 and 13.6 percent in 2003).

3. Deborah D. Zelechowski & Diana Bilimoria, "Characteristics of Women and Men Corporate Inside Directors in the U.S.," 18 Women in Management 337, 340 (table 4)(2004).

4. Sarbanes-Oxley Act § 303(m)(3) (2002) (hereinafter SOA). *See also* SOA §§ 406–7.

5. SOA §§ 103 & 497(b).

6. The SEC implemented the authority SOA creates for it, defining "expert" in SEC Release No. 33–8177 (Jan. 23, 2003, effective March 3, 2003).

7. The New York Stock Exchange regulation requires that each audit committee member be "financially literate" and that at least one "have accounting or related financial management expertise" (NYSE Rule 303A.07). The NASDAQ requires that each audit committee member "be able to read and understand basic financial statements" and has a more detailed list of qualifications that a person must have in order to be the one financial expert SOA requires. NASD Rule 4350(d)(2)(A).

8. *See* "Make Way for Madame Director," *supra,* at 57.

9. Avita Raghhavan, "Many CEOs Say 'No Thanks' to Board Seats," *Wall Street Journal,* January 28, 2005, at B-1.

NOTES ON CHAPTER 9

1. Rakesh Khurana, *Searching for the Corporate Savior* (Princeton, NJ, Princeton University Press, 2002) at 84–85.

2. Gail Evans, *Play like a Man, Win like a Woman* (New York, Broadway Books, 2000) at 10.

3. *See* Kurt Wolff, *The Sociology of Georg Simmel* (New York, Wiley, 1950).

4. Rosabeth Moss Kanter, *Men and Women of the Corporation* (New York,

Basic Books, 1977, rev. ed., 1993) at 210. This chapter draws heavily on Professor Kanter's chapter 8, "Numbers: Minorities and Majorities."

5. Shelley Taylor & Susan Fiske, "The Token in the Small Group: Research Findings and Theoretical Implications," in *Psychology and Politics* (J. Sweeney, ed.)(New York, Holt, Rhinehart, 1976).

6. Kanter, *supra*, at 212.

7. *Ocheltree v. Scollon Productions Incorporated*, 335 F.3rd 325 (4th Cir. 2003)(en banc).

8. *Suders v. Easton*, 325 F.3rd 432 (3rd Cir. 2003).

9. *Petrosino v. Bell Atlantic*, 385 F.3rd 210 (2d Cir. 2004).

10. *See, e.g., Lauer v. The Schewel Furniture Co.*, 2004 U.S. App. LEXIS 53 (4th Cir. 2004)(only woman of twenty-seven employees suffered abuse "on a daily basis"); *White v. Burlington Northern & Sante Fe Railway Co.*, 364 F.3rd 789 (6th Cir. 2004)(en banc)(only woman subjected to "general anti-woman feeling" and demoted from preferential position on grounds that it ought to be filled by a "more senior man"); *Costa v. Desert Palace, Inc.*, 299 F.3rd 838 (9th Cir. 2002)(en banc)(sole woman "penalized for her failure to conform to [female] sexual stereotypes"; branded as "confrontational" and "bossy"; suspended for behaviors routinely engaged in by male coworkers and tolerated by employer).

11. Kanter, *supra*, at 216.

12. *Id.* at 218.

13. *See, e.g.,* the discussion of sand bagging by male coworkers in chapter 2, *supra*.

14. *See, e.g.,* Carol Gallagher, *Going to the Top* (New York, Viking Penguin, 2000) at 109; the discussion in chapter 5 *supra*.

15. Kanter, *supra*, at 221.

16. *See* Seymour Sarason, "Jewishness, Blackness, and the Nature-Nurture Controversy," 28 American Psychologist 962 (1973).

17. *Conti v. Storage Technology Corporation*, 304 F.3rd 336 (4th Cir. 2002).

18. *MacGregor v. Mallinckrodt, Inc.*, 373 F.3rd 923 (8th Cir. 2004).

19. *See, e.g., Smith v. Kentucky State University*, 2004 U.S. App. LEXUS 6973 (6th Cir. 2004)(highly successful only woman faculty member in business school treated with extreme hostility by dean after she requested pay equal to that of male peers).

20. Kanter, *supra*, at 223.

21. *Id.* at 226.

22. *See* "In a Different Register," chapter 4, *supra*.

23. Professor Kanter identifies other encapsulations, such as the "woman's slot" in a work group, or "women's jobs," such as those in benefits administration or human resources (which others term "pink collar jobs"), or the mock "seductress." Kanter, *supra*, at 232–35.

24. *Id.* at 231.

25. *Hildebrandt v. Illinois Department of Natural Resources,* 347 F.3rd 1014 (7th Cir. 2003)(affirming decision awarding $115,052 in damages).

26. *Hemmings v. Tidyman's, Inc.,* 285 F.3rd 1174 (9th Cir. 2002)(en banc).

27. *Cf. Cifra v. General Electric Company,* 252 F.3rd 205 (2d Cir. 2001), which represents the opposite of boundary heightening. When the plaintiff, the only female industrial hygienist in her department, came under duress and criticism by a new boss, who later caused her termination, a male coworker came forward to testify that he viewed "her work was at least as good as, and probably better than, his own," and that the new boss did not send to the male coworkers memoranda as "harsh in tone and in content" as he sent to the token woman.

28. *See, e.g.,* Robert Axelrod, "Effective Choices in the Prisoners' Dilemma," 24 Journal of Conflict Resolution 379 (1980); Robert Harris, "Note on Optimal Policies for the Prisoners' Dilemma," 76 Psychology Review 375 (1969). *See generally* Robert Axelrod, *The Evolution of Cooperation* (New York, Basic Books, 1984).

29. *See, e.g.,* David Cope, *Fundamentals of Statistical Analysis* (New York, Foundation Press, 2005) at 15–16.

30. Kanter, *supra,* at 316.

31. *Id.* at 318.

32. Also recounted in chapter 14 *infra.*

Notes on Chapter 10

1. *Passantino v. Johnson & Johnson Consumer Products, Inc.,* 212 F.3rd 493 (9th Cir. 2000), also discussed in chapter 2 *supra.*

2. *See* Steven A. Ramirez, "A Flaw in the Sarbanes-Oxley Reform: Can Diversity in the Boardroom Quell Corporate Corruption?" 77 St. John's L. Rev. 837, 838 (2003).

3. Described in more detail in chapter 2 *supra.*

4. The language may be found in Delaware General Corporation Act § 141(a) and in the American Bar Association Model Business Corporation Act § 8.30. The Model Act is the corporations law (with modification) in thirty-nine U.S. jurisdictions.

5. *See, e.g.,* John C. Coffee, Jr., "The Future as History: The Prospects for Global Convergence in Corporate Governance and Its Implications," 93 Northwestern University Law Review 641 (1999).

6. *See, e.g.,* Roberta Karmel, "Turning Seats into Shares: Causes and Implications of Demutualization of Stock and Futures Exchanges," 53 Hastings L. J. 367 (2002).

7. *See., e.g.,* Sylvia Ascarelli, "Foreign Companies Flee U.S. Exchanges," *Wall*

Street Journal, Sept. 20, 2004, at C-1 (estimates of 500,000 Euro savings if no Sarbanes-Oxley and of 800,000 Euros overall if no U.S. stock exchange listing).

8. The principal work is Francis Fukuyama, *The End of History and the Last Man* (New York, Simon & Schuster [Free Press], 1992).

9. *See, e.g.,* Reinier Kraakman & Henry Hansmann, "The End of History for Corporate Law," 89 Georgetown Law Journal 439, 443 (2000), positing that "at the beginning of the twenty-first century we are witnessing rapid convergence on the standard shareholder-oriented [U.S.] model as the normative view of corporate structure and governance. We should expect this normative convergence to produce substantial convergence in the practices of corporate governance and in corporate law."

Globally, then, we will witness the dominance of the U.S. model, with the "appointment of larger numbers of independent directors to boards of directors, reduction in overall board size, development of powerful board committees dominated by outsiders (such as audit committees, compensation committees, and nominating committees), closer links between management compensation and the value of the firm's equity securities, and strong communications between board members and institutional shareholders." *Id.* at 455.

10. Kraakman & Hansmann conclude that "[o]ver time, then, the standard [U.S.] model is likely to win the competitive struggle" and that "no important competitors to the standard model of corporate governance remain persuasive today." *Id.* at 451 & 454.

11. Kraakman & Hannsman, *supra,* at 439.

12. *See, e.g.,* Douglas M. Branson, "The Very Uncertain Prospect of 'Global' Convergence in Corporate Governance," 34 Cornell Journal of International Law 321 (2001).

13. The best previous work may have been C. Wright Mills, *The American Business Elite: A Collective Portrait* (New York, Oxford University Press, 1963), which describes the history and content of white collar work in the United States. Although Mills noted the paucity of women in the white collar ranks, he did little analysis to account for their absence.

14. Kathleen A. Lahey & Sarah M. Salter, "Corporate Law in Legal Theory and Legal Scholarship: From Classicism to Feminism," 23 Osgoode Hall L. J. 543 (1985).

15. *See, e.g.,* Donald C. Langevoort, "Overcoming Resistance to Diversity in the Executive Suite: Grease, Grit, and the Corporate Promotion Tournament," 61 Wash. & Lee L. Rev. 1615 (2004); Marleen O'Connor, "The Enron Board: The Perils of Group Think," 71 U. Cinn. L. Rev. 1233 (2003). *See also* Langevoort, "The Behavioral Economics of Compliance with Corporate Law," 2002 Columb. Bus. L. Rev. 71.

16. Kellye Testy, "Capitalism and Freedom—For Whom? Feminist Legal

Theory and Corporate Law," 67 Law & Contemp. Problems 87, 96 (2004) ("[w]hat is most striking . . . is how sparse the literature remains").

17. *See, e.g.,* Steven A. Ramirez, "Games CEOs Play and Interest Convergence Theory: Why Diversity Lags in America's Boardrooms and What to Do about It?" 61 Wash. & Lee L. Rev. 1 (2004); Ramirez, *supra* note 2.

18. *See, e.g.,* Jonathan Liu & Doirean Wilson, "The Unchanging Perception of Women as Managers," 16 Women in Management 163 (2001); Joan Winn, "Entrepreneurship: Not an Easy Path to Top Management for Women," 19 Women in Management 143 (2004); and Deborah D. Zelechowski & Diana Bilimoria, "The Experience of Women Corporate Inside Directors on the Boards of Fortune 1000 Firms," 18 Women in Management 376 (2003). MCB University Press of Bradford, England, publishes the journal (available online at Emeraldinsight.com).

19. *See* Sheila Wellington, *Be Your Own Men*tor (New York, Random House, 2001) at 37. Until August 2003, Wellington was chief executive officers of Catalyst, a New York based not-for-profit corporation founded in 1962 to promote greater roles for women in senior management and on the boards of directors of U.S. corporations. Presently, Wellington is an adjunct professor at New York University's Stern School of Business.

20. *See, e.g.,* Carol Gallagher, *Going to the Top* (New York, Penguin Books, 2000) at 5.

Notes to Chapter 11

1. *See, e.g.,* Ralph D. Ward, *The 21ˢᵗ-Century Corporate Board* (New York, Wiley, 1997) at 46 ("Then, as now, active CEOs of other firms were the most prized board candidates, especially if they brought the proper social connections, family lineage, or school backgrounds").

2. An example is the American Red Cross, whose board of governors has fifty members. *See* Deborah Sontag, "Who Brought Bernadette Healy Down? The Red Cross: A Disaster Story without Any Heroes," *New York Times Magazine,* Dec. 23, 2001, at 32.

Critics have laid at the feet of its large board size the dysfunctional nature of the American Red Cross. *See* Stephanie Strom, "Senators Press Red Cross for a Full Accounting: Questions Are Raised about Governance," *New York Times,* Dec. 30, 2005, at A12. Nevertheless, the University of Pittsburgh Medical Center Board, for example, has sixty-one trustee members. *See* Christopher Snowbeck, "UPMC Moves to Provide More Board Information," *Pittsburgh Post-Gazette,* Jan. 25, 2005, at A-1. Not-for-profit corporations usually have legitimate reasons for large board sizes, namely, the difficulty of mustering quorums in that sphere, whether it be at the director level, or the member level in membership not-for-profit corporations, and also the multiple ties to potential donors a substantial number of directors bring.

3. *See, e.g.,* Rakesh Khurana, *Searching for the Corporate Savior* (Princeton, NJ, Princeton University Press, 2002) at 84 (directors were "almost all males . . . almost always white . . . in their fifties and sixties. . . .").

4. The monolithic nature of board composition was noted at the time in works such as David Riesman, *The Lonely Crowd: A Study of the Changing American Character* (New Haven, CT, Yale University Press, 1961); C. Wright Mills, *The Power Elite* (New York, Oxford University Press, 1956); and William H. Whyte, *The Organization Man* (New York, Simon & Schuster, 1956). Board members were white male Republicans who shared a common bureaucratic background and culture and who viewed business as having reached a detente with government and labor. Mills noted that the homogeneity eased role-taking and identification with other board members and with the collectivity. Michael Unseem, *The Inner Circle* (New York, Oxford University Press, 1984), presented evidence that directors considered themselves part of, and prized membership in, a broader director community. Homogeneity of attitudes, beliefs, and backgrounds cemented together the members of this broader director community.

5. Conformity remains the hallmark of many boards of directors. *See, e.g.,* Jeffrey Sonnenfeld, "What Makes Great Boards Great," 80 Harvard Bus. Rev. 106 (Sept. 2002): "I'm amazed at how common group think is in corporate boardrooms. . . . If you put directors into a group that discourages dissent, they nearly always . . . conform."

6. *See, e.g.,* Douglas M. Branson, "Corporate Governance 'Reform' and the New Corporate Social Responsibility," 62 U. Pitt. L. Rev. 650, 608 & n. 5 (2001).

7. *See* Judith H. Dobrzynski, "When Directors Play Musical Chairs," *New York Times,* Money and Business section, Nov. 17, 1996.

8. Reported in John Farrar, *Corporate Governance in Australia and New Zealand* (London, Oxford University Press, 2001) at 122, citing R. Rhodes-Jones, *Bob Boothby: A Portrait* (Harrisburg, PA, Trinity Press, 1991).

9. One beginning of the movement may be traced to a law reform organization known as the American Law Institute (ALI) and its undertaking to codify or, as many of its critics thought, cut from whole cloth the principles that should govern corporate law and corporate governance.

The ALI is a Philadelphia based organization founded in 1928, consisting of one thousand eight hundred of the leading judges, law professors and deans, and practitioners in the United States with a smattering from England and elsewhere abroad. The institute's products are "restatements" of the law. Restatements attempt to codify in "black letter" principles derived from case law, that is, judge-made law found in appellate court opinions.

In the late 1970s, the ALI convened a series of meetings at Airlie House and at Colonial Williamsburg in Virginia to discuss a formulation of corporate law, or at least those portions of corporate law that remained uncodified, that is, left to case-by-case development rather than statute. Out of those meetings emerged the ALI "Restatement of Corporate Governance," which kicked off with the ALI annual meeting in 1980.

10. The American Law Institute blueprint for good governance is described, *inter alia,* in Douglas M. Branson, *Corporate Governance* (Charlottesville, VA, Michie, 1993) at 227–45. *See also* Douglas M. Branson & Arthur R. Pinto, *Understanding Corporate Law* (New York, Matthew Bender, 2nd ed., 2004) at 87–132.

11. American Law Institute, *Principles of Corporate Governance and Structure* (hereinafter ALI Corporate Gov. Proj.) § 3A.01 (1994)("recommended as a matter of corporate practice that . . . [t]he board of every large publicly held corporation should have a majority of directors who are free of any significant relationship with the corporation's senior executives. . . .").

12. ALI Corporate Gov. Proj. § 3.01.

13. ALI Corporate Gov. Proj. § 3.02 lists as the first function of a board of directors that the board should "[s]elect, regularly evaluate, fix the compensation of, and, where appropriate, replace the senior executive officers."

14. *See* Khurana, *supra,* at 67.

15. These CEO removals are documented as marking a "seismic shift in corporate governance" by, among others, Khurana, *supra,* at 126–27. *See also id.* at 58–60 (CEO appointed between 1990 and 1996 "three times more likely to be fired than a CEO appointed before 1980") & at 67 (de facto twenty-two Fortune 500 CEOs forced from office in 1992–1993 alone).

16. Activist institutional investors were a favorite subject of academic and other writers in the 1990s. *See, e.g.,* Robert Monks & Nell Minnow, *Watching the Watchers: Corporate Governance for the 21st Century* (Malden, MA, Blackwell, 1996); Bernard Black, "Agents Watching Agents: The Institutional Investor as Corporate Monitor," 39 UCLA L. Rev. 811 (1992); John C. Coffee, Jr., "Liquidity versus Control: The Institutional Investor as Corporate Monitor," 91 Columb. L. Rev. 1277 (1991). For a more critical view, *see* Edward Rock, "The Logic and (Uncertain) Significance of Institutional Shareholder Activism," 79 Georgetown L. Journal 445 (1991).

17. *See* Louis Lavelle, "Best & Worst Boards: How the Corporate Scandals Are Sparking a Revolution in Governance," *Business Week,* Oct. 7, 2002, at 104 (cover story)(forth overall ratings by *Business Week* since 1996).

18. *See generally* John Pound, "The Rise of the Political Model of Corporate Governance and Control," 68 NYU L. Rev. 1003 (1993).

19. *See* General Motors Board of Directors, "GM Board Guidelines on Significant Corporate Governance Issues" (rev. ed. 1995).

20. There have been three study committees and reports in England, referred to individually as the Cadbury, Hampel, and Greenbury reports and collectively as the Cadbury Report. See Committee on Corporate Governance, "Committee on Corporate Governance: Final Report" (London, 1998); Committee on the Financial Aspects of Corporate Governance, "Study Group on Directors' Remuneration: Report of a Study Group Chaired by Sir Richard Greenbury" (London, 1995).

21. *See* Brian R. Cheffins, "Current Trends in Corporate Governance: Going from London to Milan via Toronto," 10 Duke Journal of Comparative and Int'l Law 5, at 9 (describing operation of the Yellow Book at the London Stock Exchange).

22. The French efforts are described in James Fanto, "The Role of Corporate Law in French Corporate Governance," 31 Cornell International L. Journal 31 (1998).

23. Australian Institute of Company Directors, "Corporate Practices and Conduct" (Henry Bosch, A.O., Chair)(1993).

24. Committee on Corporate Governance, "Code of Best Practice for Corporate Governance" (Korea)(1999). *See also* Curtis J. Milhaupt, "Privatization and Corporate Governance: Strategy for a Unified Korea," 26 J. Corp. L. 199 (2001).

25. Khurana, *supra,* at 84.

26. Even in 1990 estimated at $200 billion. *See* Gordon Redding, *The Spirit of Chinese Capitalism* (New York and Berlin, De Gruyter, 1990) at 3.

27. *See, e.g., id.* at 25–29.

28. *Id.* at 48.

29. *Id.* at 63.

30. *Id.* at 61.

31. The post-Confucian thesis, with its implications for robust economic growth, is attributed to Herman Kahn, *World Economic Development: 1979 and Beyond* (Boulder, CO, Westview Press, 1979). *See also* Stewart R. Clegg in "'Post-Confucianism,' Social Democracy, and Economic Culture" in *Capitalism in Contrasting Cultures* (Stewart R. Clegg & S. Gordon Redding, eds.)(New York and Berlin, De Gruyter, 1990) at 38.

32. Redding, *supra,* at 52 & 58.

33. Deborah Tannen, *Gender and Discourse* (New York, Oxford University Press, 1994) at 31.

34. *See, e.g., id.* at 32 & 53–60 (what simplistic research records as an "interruption" may be a conversational overlap, a verbal duet, or an aside; a request to pass the food at the dinner table may be regarded as not an interruption at all).

NOTES TO CHAPTER 12

1. Those corporations are listed in an appendix at the end of the book.

2. *Compare* Catalyst INFO Brief, Women Directors in 1999 (11.2 percent) *with* Catalyst Press release dated Dec. 4, 2003 (women held 779 board seats, or 13.6 percent of the total number of seats in the Fortune 500).

3. Charles Peck, Henry M. Silvert, & Gina McCormick, "The Conference Board, Director Compensation, and Board Practices in 2002" at 38 (2003).

4. *See* Sheila Wellington, *Be Your Own Mentor* (New York, Random House, 2001) at 10. As chapter 14 points out, Catalyst, which maintains offices in Toronto, Ontario, Canada, and in San Jose, California, receives its funding from corporate America.

5. Gail Evans, *Play like a Man, Win like a Woman* (New York, Broadway Books, 2000) at 10.

6. An analysis of women on board seats in the 2001 Fortune 500 group is contained in chapter 7 and one of the 2005 group, in chapter 8.

7. Russell Reynolds Associates, "2000 Board Practices Survey: The Structure and Compensation of Boards of Directors of U.S. Public Companies" (Feb. 2000).

8. List of Fortune 500 companies from www.fortune.com. Number of directors from www.fisonline.com.

9. *See, e.g.,* American Bar Association Model Business Corporation Act § 8.03(b) ("The number of directors may be increased or decreased from time to time by amendment to, or in the manner provided in, the articles of incorporation or the bylaws").

10. Data on board size and board size changes was derived from annual proxy statements ("definitive 14As") filed in 2005, available at SEC.gov, and in the historical section of the SEC's EDGAR (Electronic Data Gathering and Retrieval) database.

11. *See, e.g.,* Marleen O'Connor, "The Enron Board: The Perils of Groupthink," 7 U. Cinn. L. Rev. 1233, 1299–1300 (2003)(NYSE rules critiqued).

12. *See* Rakesh Khurana, *Searching for a Corporate Savior: The Irrational Quest for Charismatic CEOs* (Princeton, NJ, Princeton University Press, 2002) at 66.

13. *See* Jonathan Weil, "WorldCom's Ex-Directors Pony Up," *Wall Street Journal,* Jan. 6, 2005, at A-3; Kurt Eichenwald, "Ex-Directors at Enron to Chip in on Settlement," *New York Times,* Jan. 8, 2005, at B-1. *But see* Shawn Young, "Accord with Ex-Directors of WorldCom Fails," *Wall Street Journal,* Feb. 5, 2005, at A-3.

14. *See, e.g.,* Joann S. Lublin, Theo Francis, & Jonathan Weil, "Directors Are Getting the Jitters," *Wall Street Journal,* Jan. 13, 2005, at B-1.

15. Studies purport to find that women are more risk averse, at least in com-

mon stock investments. *See, e.g,* Brad M. Barber & Terrence Odean, "Boys Will Be Boys: Gender, Overconfidence, and Common Stock Investment," 116 Q.J. Econ. 261 (2001); Ammon Jianakoplos & Alexandra Bernasek, "Are Women More Risk Averse?" 36 Econ. Inquiry 620 (1998).

16. U.S. Bureau of Labor Statistics, "Employment and Earnings," Jan. 2000, at 78; U.S. Dept. of Labor Women's Bureau, "20 Facts on Women Workers," Mar. 2000.

17. WWW.Fortune.com (visited January 15, 2005); YahooFinance.com (visited January 16, 2005). *Compare* Catalyst press release, Women CEOs in Fortune 500 Doubles, April 18, 2001 (four women CEOs). *See also* Catalyst INFO Brief: Women CEOs, October 1, 2001 (Anne Mulcahy's elevation to the top post at Xerox); Joan S. Lublui, "CEO's Juggle Love, Power," *Wall Street Journal,* March 7, 2006, at B-1 (Paula Rosput Reynolds became CEO of SAFECO, Inc., on Dec. 7, 2005)

18. *See* Associated Press, "Hewlett-Packard Chairman, CEO Carly Fiorina Resigns, Cites Differences with Board," Feb. 9, 2005, available on Yahoo.Finance.Com (visited Feb. 9, 2005).

19. *See* Pamela M. Moore, "She's Here to Fix the Xerox," *Business Week,* August 6, 2001, at 47 (President Anne Mulcahy expected to be promoted to CEO).

20. For the Fortune 1000 overall, as late 2001, the CEO number was eight and the percentage .08. Catalyst, Inc., "Catalyst INFO Brief: Women CEOs," October 1, 2001, lists the eight, adding to those in the Fortune 500 Crandall C. Bowles at Springs Industries (626), Linda Wachner at Warnaco Group (656), Patricia Gallup at PC Connection (894), and Dorrit Bern at Charming Shoppes (987).

21. It should also be noted that, as of late summer 2005, there are seven female CEOs at publicly held companies in the Fortune 1000: Dorrit Bern, fifty-five, of Charming Shoppes (638), Bensalem, Pennsylvania, women's apparel ($2.33 million), and Patricia Gallup, fifty-one, PC Connection (937), Merrimack, New Hampshire ($434,000), holding over from 2001. The five new CEOs since 2001 are Kathleen Ligocki, forty-seven, Tower Automotive (550), Novi, Maryland, automobile dealerships ($687,000); Dona Young, fifty-one, chairperson and CEO, Phoenix Industries (588), Hartford, Connecticut, insurance, annuities, and asset management ($6 million); Mary Forte, fifty-four, Zale Corp. (657), Irving, Texas, specialty retailer of jewelry ($1.87 million); Meg Whitman, forty-eight, eBay (673), San Jose, California, Internet-based trading community ($2.17 million); and Stephanie Streeter, forty-seven, chairperson and CEO, Banta (891), Menasha, Wisconsin, printing, supply chain management and healthcare ($1.11 million). Linda Wachner, an early pioneer among women CEOs, was removed from her position at Warnaco Group, Inc. (lingerie, Calvin Klein, Speedo) by the board of directors in November 2001. *See*

"Warnaco Outs CEO Amid Its Restructuring," *Los Angeles Times,* Nov. 17, 2001, at C-1.

22. Debra E. Meyerson & Joyce K. Fletcher, "A Modest Manifesto for Shattering the Glass Ceiling," 78 Harvard Bus. Rev. 127 (Jan.-Feb. 2000).

23. *Cf.* Anita Raghavan, "More CEOs Say 'No Thanks' to Board Seats," *Wall Street Journal,* Jan. 28, 2005, at B-1 (in 1997 CEOs of Standard & Poors 500 companies sat, on average, on two other S & P 500 boards; in 2005 the number of outside board seats had fallen to 0.9 percent, according to search firm Stuart Spencer & Associates).

24. Khurana, *supra.*

25. *Id.* at 203, quoting Peter Temin, "The American Business Elite in Historical Perspective," Working Paper, National Bureau of Economic Research, at 34 (1997).

26. *Id.* at 187.

27. *Id.* at 97 & 153.

28. *Id.* at 154.

29. *Id.* at 29, Table 2.1.

30. *Id.* at 105.

31. *Id.* at 113.

32. *Id.* at 116.

33. Esther Wachs Book, *Why The Best Man for the Job Is a Woman* (New York, HarperCollins Business, 2000) at xi. *See also* Ann Crittenden, *The Price of Motherhood* (New York, Metropolitan Books, 2001) at 41 (3 percent of Internet corporate board seats held by women, citing Spencer Stuart, "Internet Board Index" [2000]). Cf. Wellington, *supra,* at 38 (2001)("Seven percent" of Internet startups "have women chief executive officers," citing Spencer Stuart, "Internet Board Index" [1999]).

34. Unless otherwise noted, statistics on women in the law schools come from an annual publication of the American Bar Association published each fall, "Law Schools and Bar Admission Requirements: A Review of Legal Education in the United States," 1972–2004. *See also* American Bar Assoc., www.abanet.org/legaled/statistics/jd.htm.

35. *See generally* Kristin Choo, "Women and the Law: The Right Equation," American Bar Assoc. Journal 58 (August 2001).

36. The actual percentage of female GMAT test takers was 37.6 in 1999, 36.3 in 1998, 34.7 in 1997, 35.7 in 1996, and 36.2 in 1995. The total number of test takers ranged from a high of 142,181 in 1997 to a low of 111,588 in 1999. Graduate Management Admissions Council, "GMAT" (undated brochure 2000).

37. *See* "For Women, Fewer MBAs: Applications Drop as the Degree's Value and Cost Are Questioned," *New York Times,* September 27, 1992; "Female Enrollment Falls in Many Top MBA Programs," *Wall Street Journal,* September 25, 1992.

38. *See* Terry R. Johnson & Steven D. McLaughlin, "Declining Numbers of Female MBAs: An Analysis from the GMAT Registrant Survey," available from Graduate Admissions Council, Suite 1000, 1750 Tysons Blvd., McLean, Virginia, 22102. *Cf.* Catalyst, Inc., "Women and the MBA: Gateway to Opportunity" (2000).

39. All MBA statistics are taken from data produced by the National Center for Education Statistics, http://necs.ed.gov/programs/digest/d02/dt280.asp.

40. American Bar Assoc., "The Unfinished Agenda: Women and the Legal Profession" (2001). *See also* Stephanie Franken, "Women and the Law," *Pittsburgh Post-Gazette,* Nov. 6, 2001, at E-1.

41. *See* Choo *supra.*

42. The average outside director's cash compensation in the largest manufacturing corporations (over $10 billion sales) was $65,430 and for large manufacturing corporations ($5 to 9.9 billion in sales) was $51,750 in 1999. In the service sector, the comparable numbers were $52,000 and $46,500. Kay Worell, "Directors' Compensation and Board Practices in 1999," The Conference Boards, Tables 2 & 7 (2000). Among the highest was Lucent Technology, which paid its directors a flat $100,000 annual retainer plus an option to purchase two thousand five hundred Lucent common shares. Len Boselovic, "Not Just a Pretty Face: Companies Start Demanding More from Board Members," *Pittsburgh Post-Gazette,* Jan. 31, 1999, at F-1.

In the early 1990s, when IBM was experiencing great difficulty entering the Internet age and its fortunes were falling, IBM's directors raised their annual compensation package from $20,000 and $500 per meeting to $55,000 and 100 IBM shares per meeting. In the ensuing case of *Marx v. Akers,* 88 N.Y. 2d 189, 666 N.E. 2d 1034 (1996), the New York Court of Appeals found, "as a matter of law," that in this day and age $60,000–70,000 compensation for a director of a corporation such as IBM was not "waste" of corporate assets. In other words, the justices of that court did not need to read any trial testimony or review expert witnesses' testimony to reach that conclusion.

43. Charles Peck, Henry M. Silvert, & Gina McCormick, "The Conference Board, Director Compensation, and Board Practices in 2002" at 6 (2003)(director cash compensation in top five sectors). When the sample is broadened to include all 616 reporting companies (small, medium, and large capitalization), the numbers are smaller: manufacturing (263 companies), $39,000; financial (104), $31,600; and services (248), $35,700. *Id.* at 8.

The year 1999 was an apogee, with directors at Sun Microsystems ($409,500), Compaq Computers ($362,448), Pfizer ($258,147), and other large corporations receiving pay envelopes fattened considerably by stock and stock option awards for rank-and-file directors. *See* Timothy D. Schellhardt, "More Directors Are Raking in Six-Figure Pay," *Wall Street Journal,* Oct. 29, 1999, at B-1.

44. *See, e.g.,* Schellhardt, *supra* (corporations cut back on stock and options for directors when combined compensation [cash and stock] reached an annual average $133,672 in the Fortune 500 for the year 1999; reporting average cash compensation of $65,246 among two hundred largest corporations in 1999).

45. Russell Reynolds Associates, "1998 Board Practices Survey" (1998).

46. Peck, et al., *supra,* at 6. For all reporting companies (small, medium, and large cap), the combined 2002 cash-stock directors' compensation amounts were as follows: manufacturing, $55,700; financial, $41,450; and services, $48,400. *Id.* at 8.

47. Schellhardt, *supra,* at B-1.

48. Permanent Subcommittee on Investigations, U.S. Senate Committee on Governmental Affairs, "The Role of the Board of Directors in Enron's Collapse," 107th CNG., 2d SSS., at 11 (July 8, 2002).

49. The latest data, compiled by the National Association of Corporate Directors, is that directors of publicly held companies expend 250 hours per year per directorship. *See* Paul P. Brountas, *Boardroom Excellence* (San Francisco, CA, Josey-Bass, 2004) at 19. *Cf.* Schellhardt, *supra* (reporting an average of 190 hours in 1999).

50. *See* "Goldberg Resigns from TWA," *Newsweek,* Oct. 30, 1972, at 42.

51. Kathleen Day, "Soldiers for the Shareholders," *Washington Post,* August 27, 2000, at H-1 (comments of Graef Crystal). *See also* Geoffrey Colvin, "The Great CEO Pay Heist," *Fortune,* June 25, 2001, at 64. The full title of Crystal's book is *In Search of Excess: The Overcompensation of American Executives* (New York, Norton, 1991).

52. Khurana, *supra,* at 201.

53. Statistics on CEO compensation may be obtained from annual proxy statements that publicly held companies file with the Securities and Exchange Commission, available at www.SEC.gov, EDGAR database. They may also be obtained through YahooFinance.com, using the corporation's stock ticker symbol and clicking on "profile."

54. Unless otherwise noted, compensation amounts have been retrieved from company profiles on YahooFinance.com and the SEC's EDGAR database.

55. *See* "Disney's Eisner Tops Pay Chart," *Wall Street Journal,* June 28, 2000, at A-23.

56. *See* Staff, "Who Made the Biggest Bucks," *Wall Street Journal,* April 11, 202, at B-7; Staff, "Oracle's Ellison Has Windfall on Options," *id.,* Sept. 4, 2001, at B-6 ([1] Ellison $706.1 million; [2] Eisner $576 million; [3] Sanford Weil, Travelers-Citicorp, $220 million in 1997). Oracle shareholders sued Ellison in the Delaware Chancery Court, alleging that he profited from insider information and thereby breached his fiduciary duty. In November 2004, the court granted summary judgment to Ellison and his codefendants. *See In Re Oracle Corp. Derivative Litigation,* 2004 W.L. 2756278 (Del. Ch. 2004).

57. *See* Joann Lublin & Kara Scannell, "They Say Jump: SEC Plans Tougher Pay Rules," *Wall Street Journal,* Jan. 11, 2006, at C1.

58. *See* Lucien Bebchuk & Jesse Fried, *Pay without Performance: The Unfulfilled Promise of Executive Compensation* (Cambridge, MA, Harvard University Press, 2004); Jesse Eisinger, "Lavish Pay Puts a Bite on Profits," *Wall Street Journal,* Jan. 11, 2006, at C1.

NOTES TO CHAPTER 13

1. Sheila Wellington, *Be Your Own Mentor* (New York, Random House, 2001) at 20–21.

2. *Id.* at 18.

3. Gail Evans, *Play like a Man, Win like a Woman* (New York, Broadway Books, 2000) at 148–49.

4. Zoe Baird, President, The Markle Foundation, formerly CLO of Aetna Insurance, quoted *id.* at 89.

5. Evans, *supra,* at 19.

6. Wellington, *supra,* at 91.

7. Evans, *supra,* at 69.

8. *Id.* at 113.

9. *Id.* at 71–72.

10. Carol Gallagher, *Going to the Top* (New York, Viking Penguin, 2000) at 143–45.

11. Attributed to Ann Richards, former governor of Texas.

12. Margaret Henning & Ann Jardim, *The Managerial Woman* (New York, Simon & Schuster [Pocket Books], 1977) at 188.

13. Gallagher, *supra,* at 127.

14. Wellington, *supra,* at 21.

15. *Id.* at 47.

16. *Id.* at 55.

17. *Id.* at 74 & 77.

18. Gallagher, *supra,* at 93.

19. Evans, *supra,* at 129–30.

20. Wellington, *supra,* at 88–89.

21. *Id.* at 86.

22. Evans, *supra,* at 39.

23. Dorrit Bern, board chair and CEO, Charming Shoppes, Inc. *Accord:* Evans, *supra,* at 86–87: "Women are brought up to be physically careful, to avoid situations that are potentially dangerous. . . . But you can't get ahead without making risky moves. No one who is content to play safe ever sees her career skyrocket."

24. *See, e.g.,* Esther Wachs's Book, *Why the Best Man for the Job Is a Woman* (New York, Harper Business, 2000) at xii & 2 (women profiled in the book all fit "the new paradigm").

25. *See generally* Deborah Sontag, "Who Brought Bernadette Healy Down? The Red Cross: A Disaster Story without Borders," *New York Times Magazine,* Dec. 23, 2001, at 32.

26. *Id.* at 40.

27. *See* Abigail Goldman, "Beleaguered Mattel CEO Resigns as Profit Sinks," *Los Angeles Times,* Feb. 4, 2000, at A-1.

28. *See* "Fortune's 50 Most Powerful Women," *Fortune,* October 12, 1998, at 76; G. Wayne Miller, "Manager's Journal: The Rise and Fall of Toyland's Princess," *Wall Street Journal,* Feb. 7, 2000, at A38 (in *People* Barad appeared "in a full page spread in which she sprawled on satin bedding with 35 Barbies dressed in bikinis and evening gowns").

29. *See* Kathleen Morris, "The Rise of Jill Barad," *Business Week,* 1998, at 112 ("vicious" and "not a team player"). Between the time she became CEO and September 1999, Jill Barad was featured in 717 stories by the national media. *See* "Princess on a Steeple," *The Economist,* October 9, 1999, at 84.

30. Patricia Sellers, "Women, Sex, and Power," *Fortune,* Aug. 15, 1996, at 44.

31. Kelley Helland & Eric Schine, "Toys 'R' Her," *Business Week,* Sept. 2, 1996, at 47.

32. *See generally* Lisa Bannon, "Mattel Names Jill Barad Chief Executive," *Wall Street Journal,* Aug. 23, 1996, at B-2; "Top Business Women [who] Exceed $1 Million in Pay," *id.,* Dec. 16, 1996, at C-20.

33. Nancy Rivera Brooks & Martha Groves, "Woman to Run the House That Barbie Built," *Los Angeles Times,* August 23, 1996, at A-23.

34. Helland & Schine, *supra,* at 47.

35. On the Tyco acquisition, *see generally* Lisa Bannon & Joseph Pereira, "No. 1 Toy Maker Mattel Agrees to Buy No. 3 Tyco in $755 Million Stock Deal," *Wall Street Journal,* Nov. 19, 1996, at A13; George White, "Mattel Agrees to Buy Tyco for $755 Million," *Wall Street Journal,* Nov. 19, 1996, at D1.

36. Lisa Bannon, "Mattel Cuts Forecast for Yearly Profit in Wake of Toys 'R' Us Restructuring," *Wall Street Journal,* September 25, 1998, at B7.

37. Stacy Kravetz & Jon G. Auerbach, "Mattel Reveals Profit Shortfall," *Wall Street Journal,* Dec. 15, 1998, at B1.

38. Lisa Bannon, "Two Top Mattel Officials to Leave in Reshuffling," *Wall Street Journal,* March 4, 199, at A3; Bannon, "Mattel to Cut 3,000 Jobs as It Posts Loss," *id.,* April 6, 1999, at A3.

39. Lisa Bannon, "Mattel Still Doesn't Grasp Snafu at Learning Company,"

id., Oct. 8, 1999, at A3. *Cf.* Bannon, "Learning Co. Is on Track, Says Mattel," *id.*, Oct. 22, 1999, at A3.

40. Lisa Bannon & Joann S. Lublin, "Jill Barad Abruptly Quits the Top Job at Mattel," *Wall Street Journal*, February 4, 2000, at B1; Constance Hays, "Mattel Chief Quits after Losses," *International Herald Tribune*, February 5, 2000, at 12; Abigail Goodman, "Beleaguered Mattel CEO Resigns after Profit Sinks," *Los Angeles Times*, Feb. 4, 2000, at A1.

41. *See generally* Michael Maccoby, *The Productive Narcissist: The Promise and Perils of Visionary Leadership* (New York, Broadway Books, 2003).

42. Jim Collins, *Good to Great* (New York, HarperCollins, 2001) at 10.

43. *See, e.g.*, Pui-Wing Tam, "H-P's Board Ousts Fiorina as CEO," *Wall Street Journal*, Feb. 1. 2005, at A-1; George Anders, "How Traits That Helped Executive Climb the Ladder Came to Be Fatal Flaws," *id.*, Feb. 10, 2005, at A-1; Richard Karlgaard, "Carly Fiorina's Seven Deadly Sins," *id.*, Feb. 11, 2005, at A-10.

44. Pui-Wing Tam, *supra.* "Yet inside H-P, she was a highly polarizing figure who stirred deep animosity from many veteran employees. Her abrupt—some said autocratic—management style won few fans." *Id.* at A-8.

45. *See, e.g.*, Dennis K. Berman & Almar Latour, "Too Big: Learning from Mistakes—Fiorina's Departure from H-P Reminds Companies about Risks during the Current Merger Boom," *Wall Street Journal*, Feb. 10, 2005, at C-1.

46. Ben Elgin, "Can Anyone Save H-P?" *Business Week*, February 21, 2005, 28, at 35.

47. In September 2000, Mattel announced that it had sold The Learning Company (TLC) to Gore Technology Group of Los Angeles. Mattel, which paid $3.04 billion, sold TLC for no cash and only "a share of future profits." TLC was losing upwards of $1 million per day. An analyst characterized Barad and Mattel's TLC episode as "one of the worst deals in corporate history," rivaling Quaker Oats's bungle in buying Snapple for $1.7 billion in 1994, only to sell it three years later for $300 million. But, pundits noted, at least Quaker Oats got cash. *See* Lisa Bannon, "Mattel to Sell Learning Co. Price Seen as Low," *Wall Street Journal*, April 3, 2000. Bannon, "Mattel, after Learning Co., Faces Big Job," *Wall Street Journal*, October 2, 2000, at B8.

NOTES TO CHAPTER 14

1. *See, e.g.*, David A. Carter, et al., "Corporate, Board Diversity, and Firm Value," 38 Fin. Rev. 33, 51 (2003)("[W]e find statistically significant positive relationships between the presence of women and minorities on the board and firm value"); Steven A. Ramirez, "Games CEOs Play and Interest Convergence Theory: Why Diversity Lags in America's Boardrooms and What to Do about It," 61 Wash. & Lee L. Rev. 1583, 1588 & n. 22 (2004)(same).

2. *See, e.g.*, Catalyst, Inc., Press Release dated Jan. 26, 2004, "New Cata-

lyst Study Reveals Financial Performance Is High for Companies with Women at the Top" (positing 34 percent better return on equity and 35 percent total return to shareholders in firms with a significant number of women executives).

3. Sanjai Bhagat & Bernard Black, "The Uncertain Relationship between Board Composition and Firm Performance," 54 Business Lawyer 921 (1999). *See also* Laura Lin, "The Effectiveness of Outside Directors as a Corporate Governance Mechanism: Theories and Evidence," 90 Northwestern U. L. Rev. 898 (1996).

4. Chapter 11 *supra.*

5. Irving Janis, *Victims of Groupthink: A Physiological Study of Foreign-Policy Decisions and Fiascos* (New York, Houghton Mifflin, 1978).

6. Marleen A. O'Connor, "The Enron Board: The Perils of Groupthink," 71 U. Cinn. L. Rev. 1233, 1257 et seq. (2003).

7. Donald C. Langevoort, "The Human Nature of Corporate Boards: Law, Norms, and the Unintended Consequences of Independence and Accountability," 89 Georgetown L. J. 797, 810 (2001).

8. O'Connor, *supra,* at 1259–60.

9. *Id.* at 1236, n. 19.

10. Adapted from Devon W. Carbado & Mitu Gulati, "Race to the Top of the Corporate Ladder: What Minorities Do When They Get There," 61 Wash. & Lee L. Rev. 1645, 1659–60 (2004).

11. *See, e.g.,* Jeffrey Sonnenfeld, "What Makes Great Boards Great," 80 Harvard Bus. Rev. 16, (Sept. 2000).

12. *See, e.g.,* Langevoort, *supra,* at 814–16 ("Step in the Direction of Compromise: The Search for Mediating Directors").

13. An early work urging that the committee be mandatory for large publicly held corporations is Melvin Eisenberg, *The Structure of the Corporation* (New York, Aspen Business, 1976).

14. *See generally* SEC Schedule 14A, Item 7(d)(2)(disclosures regarding the nominating committee and election procedures). *See, e.g., id.,* item 7(d)(2)(i)("If the registrant does not have a standing nominating committee or a committee performing similar functions, state the basis for the view that is appropriate not to have such a committee. . . ."). Such SEC disclosure requirements come very close, or are tantamount to, direct commands.

15. Rakesh Khurana, *Searching for a Corporate Savior: The Irrational Quest for Charismatic CEOs* (Princeton, NJ, Princeton University Press, 2002).

16. Anne Crittenden, *The Price of Motherhood* (New York, Metropolitan Books, 2001) at 254.

17. *See, e.g.,* Catalyst, Inc., Press Release dated Sept. 5, 2001, "General Motors Donates $300,000 to Sponsor New Catalyst Study on Women in Corporate Leadership."

18. Susan Sturm, "Second Generation Employment Discrimination: A Structural Approach," 101 Columb. L. Rev. 458 (2001).

19. This is an example Professor Sturm uses. *Id.* at 469–71.

20. *See, e.g.,* Louis Lowenstein, "Financial Transparency: You Manage What You Measure," 96 Columb. L. Rev. 1335 (1996).

21. *See, e.g.,* Joan Williams, Cynthia Thomas Calvert, & Holly Green Cooper, "Better on Balance? The Corporate Counsel Retention Project: Final Report," reproduced in 10 Wm. & Mary J. Women & Law 367, at 435–41 & 450–57 (2004)(companies should benchmark usage rate, schedule creep, job and task assignment, and attrition, as well as promotion). *See also* Sturm, *supra,* at 499–518 (Intel Corp. and Home Depot).

22. *See* Piper Fogg, "Female Professors Assail Remarks by Harvard's President, Who Says It's All a Misunderstanding," *Chronicle of Higher Education,* Jan. 19, 2005, at 3.

23. *See, e.g.,* "Sexism at Harvard," *Business Week,* Feb. 28, 2005, at 100 (provable differences between the sexes are at least three, including better male visuospatial skills, variability in intellectual skills, and interests in core subjects).

Bibliography

Adams, Edward S., "Using Evaluations to Break Down the Male Corporate Hierarchy: A Full Circle Approach," 73 U. Colo. L. Rev. 117 (2002).

Ainsworth, Janet E., "In a Different Register: The Pragmatics of Powerlessness in Police Interrogation," 103 Yale Law Journal 259 (1993).

American Bar Association Model Business Corporation Act (Chicago, IL, 1985).

American Law Institute, *Principles of Corporate Governance and Structure* (St. Paul, MN, American Law Institute Publishing, 1994).

Australian Institute of Company Directors, "Corporate Practices and Conduct" (Henry Bosch, A.O., Chair)(Sydney, Australia, 1993).

Axelrod, Robert, "Effective Choices in the Prisoners' Dilemma," 24 Journal of Conflict Resolution 379 (1980).

———, *The Evolution of Cooperation* (New York, Basic Books, 1984).

Barber, Brad M. & Odean, Terrence, "Boys Will Be Boys: Gender, Overconfidence, and Common Stock Investment," 116 Q.J. Econ. 261 (2001).

Baron, Tracy Anbinder, "Keeping Women out of the Executive Suite: The Courts' Failure to Apply Title VII Scrutiny to Upper-Level Jobs," 143 U. Pa. L. Rev. 267 (1994).

Bebchuk, Lucien, & Fried, Jesse, *Pay without Performance: The Unfulfilled Promise of Executive Compensation* (Cambridge, MA, Harvard University Press, 2004).

Becker, Gary S., *Human Capital* (Chicago, IL, University of Chicago Press, 3rd ed. 1994).

Becker, Gary S., & Tomes, Nigel, "Human Capital and the Rises and Fall of Families," 4 J. Labor Economics 43 (July 1986).

Bend, Ruth M., "Male-Female Intonation Patterns in American English," in *Language and Sex: Difference and Dominance* (Barrie Thorns & Nancy Henley, eds.)(London, Stationery Office, 1975).

Bhagat, Sanjai, & Black, Bernard L., "The Uncertain Relationship between Board Composition and Firm Performance," 54 Business Lawyer 921 (1999).

Biskupic, Joan, *Sandra Day O'Connor* (New York, HarperCollins, 2005).

Black, Bernard L., "Agents Watching Agents: The Institutional Investor as Corporate Monitor, 39 UCLA L. Rev. 811 (1992).

Book, Esther Wachs, *Why the Best Man for the Job Is a Woman* (New York, HarperCollins Business, 2000).

Bowman, Garda, & Worthy, N. Beatrice, "Are Women Executives People?" 43 *Harvard Bus. Rev.* 14 (July/Aug. 1965).

Branson, Douglas M., *Corporate Governance* (Charlottesville, VA, Michie, 1993).

———, "The Very Uncertain Prospect of 'Global' Convergence in Corporate Governance," 34 Cornell Journal of International Law 321 (2001).

———, "Corporate Governance 'Reform' and the New Corporate Social Responsibility," 62 U. Pitt. L. Rev. 650, 608 & n. 5 (2001).

Branson, Douglas M., & Pinto, Arthur R., *Understanding Corporate Law* (New York, Matthew Bender, 1999)(2d ed. 2004).

Burmiller, Kristin, *The Civil Rights Society: The Social Construction of Victims* (Baltimore, MD, Johns Hopkins University Press, 1988).

Carter, David A., et al., "Corporate, Board Diversity, and Firm Value," 38 Fin. Rev. 33, 51 (2003).

Central Intelligence Agency (CIA), The World Factbook (2005), available online at http://www.cia.gov/cia/publications/factbook/geos.

Chamallas, Martha, *Introduction to Feminist Legal Theory* (New York, Aspen Law and Business, 2000).

Charny, David, & Gulati, G. Mitu, "Efficiency-Wages, Tournaments, and Discrimination: A Theory of Employment Discrimination Law for 'High-Level' Jobs," 33 Harvard C.R.-C.L. L. Rev. 57 (1998).

Cheffins, Brian R., "Current Trends in Corporate Governance: Going from London to Milan via Toronto," 10 Duke Journal of Comparative and Int'l Law 5.

Claremont, Kevin M. & Eisenberg, Theodore, "Plaintiffphobia in the Appellate Courts: Civil Rights Really Do Differ from Negotiable Instruments," 2002 University of Illinois Law Review 947.

Clegg, Stewart R., "'Post-Confucianism,' Social Democracy, and Economic Culture," in *Capitalism in Contrasting Cultures* at 38 (Stewart R. Clegg & S. Gordon Redding, eds.)(New York and Berlin, De Gruyter, 1990).

Clements, G. E., Lunding, F. J. & Perkins, D. S., "Everyone Who Makes It Has a 'Mentor,'" 56 Harvard Bus. Rev. 89 (July-August 1978).

Coates, Jennifer, *Language and Gender: A Reader* (Malden, MA, Blackwell, 1997).

Coates, Jennifer, & Cameron, Deborah, eds., *Women in Their Speech Communities* (White Plains, NY, Longman, 1989).

Coffee, John C., Jr., "The Future as History: The Prospects for Global Convergence in Corporate Governance and Its Implications," 93 Northwestern University Law Review 641 (1999).

———, "Liquidity versus Control: The Institutional Investor as Corporate Monitor," 91 Columb. L. Rev. 1277 (1991).

Collins, Jim, *Good to Great* (New York, HarperCollins, 2001).

Committee on Corporate Governance, "Committee on Corporate Governance: Final Report" (London, 1998).

Committee on the Financial Aspects of Corporate Governance, "Study Group on Directors' Remuneration: Report of a Study Group Chaired by Sir Richard Greenbury" (London 1995).

Conley, John M., O'Barr, William M., & Lind, E. Allen, "The Power of Language: Presentation Style in the Courtroom," 1978 Duke L. J. 1375.

Coontz, Stephanie, *The Social Origins of Private Life* (New York, Norton,1988).

Cope, David, *Fundamentals of Statistical Analysis* (New York, Foundation Press, 2005).

Crittenden, Ann, *The Price of Motherhood* (New York, Metropolitan Books, 2001).

Dalton, Melville, *Men Who Manage* (New York, Wiley & Sons, 1959).

Delgado, Richard, "Rodrigo's Roadmap: Is the Marketplace Theory for Eradicating Discrimination a Blind Alley?" 93 Northwestern U. L. Rev. 215, 219 (1998).

Denfeld, Rene, *The New Victorians: A Woman's Challenge to the Old Feminist Order* (New York, Warner Books, 1995).

DuBois, Betty L., & Crouch, Isabel, eds., *The Sociology of the Languages of American Women* (New York and Berlin, De Gruyter, 2d ed., 1979).

Eisenberg, Melvin, *The Structure of the Corporation* (New York, Aspen Business, 1976).

Epstein, Richard, *Forbidden Grounds: The Case against Employment Discrimination Law* (Cambridge, MA, Harvard University Press, 1992).

Evans, Gail, *Play like a Man, Win like a Woman* (New York, Broadway Books, 2000).

Fanto, James, "The Role of Corporate Law in French Corporate Governance," 31 Cornell International L. Journal 31 (1998).

Fallows, Deborah, *A Mother's Work* (New York, Houghton Mifflin, 1985).

Farrar, John, *Corporate Governance in Australia and New Zealand* (London, Oxford University Press, 2001).

Fukuyama, Francis, *The End of History and the Last Man* (New York, Simon & Schuster [Free Press], 1992).

Gallagher, Carol, *Going to the Top* (New York, Penguin Books, 2000).

Goffman, Erving, *Gender Advertisements* (New York, Harper & Row, 1979).

Graddol, David, & Swann, Joan, *Gender Voices* (Malden, MA, Blackwell, 1989).

Harris, Robert, "Note on Optimal Policies for the Prisoners' Dilemma," 76 Psychology Review 375 (1969).

Heim, Pat, & Golant, Susan K., *Smashing the Glass Ceiling* (New York, Simon & Schuster [Fireside Books], 1995).

Henning, Margaret, & Jardim, Ann, *The Managerial Woman* (New York, Simon & Schuster [Pocket Books], 1977).

Hetzler, Stanley A., "Variations in Role-Playing Patterns among Different Echelons of Bureaucratic Leaders," 20 American Sociological Review 700 (1955).

Hollands, Jean, *Same Game, Different Rules: How to Get Ahead without Being a Bully Broad, Ice Queen, or " Understood"* (New York, McGraw-Hill, 2000).

Janis, Irving, *Victims of Groupthink: A Psychological Study of Foreign-Policy Decisions and Fiascos* (New York, Houghton Mifflin, 1978).

Jianakoplos, Ammon, & Bernasek, Alexandra, "Are Women More Risk Averse?" 36 Econ. Inquiry 620 (1998).

Kahn, Herman, *World Economic Development: 1979 and Beyond* (Boulder, CO, Westview Press, 1979).

Kanter, Rosabeth Moss, *Men and Women of the Corporation* (New York, Basic Books, 1977).

Karmel, Roberta, "Turning Seats into Shares: Causes and Implications of Demutualization of Stock and Futures Exchanges," 53 Hastings L. J. 367 (2002).

Key, Mary R., *Male/Female Language* (Lanham,. MD, Scarecrow Press, 1975).

Kilduff, Martin, & Day, David V., "Do Chameleons Get Ahead? The Effects of Self-Monitoring on Managerial Careers," 37 Acad. Management 1047 (1994).

Kraakman, Reinier, & Hansmann, Henry, "The End of History for Corporate Law," 89 Georgetown Law Journal 439 (2000).

Khurana, Rakesh, *Searching for a Corporate Savior: The Irrational Quest for Charismatic CEOs* (Princeton, NJ, Princeton University Press, 2002).

Laazear, Edward P., & Rosen, Sherwin, "Rank-Order Tournaments as Efficient Labor Contracts," 89 J. Pol. Econ. 841 (1981).

Lahey, Kathleen A., & Salter, Sarah M., "Corporate Law in Legal Theory and Legal Scholarship: From Classicism to Feminism," 23 Osgoode Hall L. J. 543 (1985).

Laird, Donald, & Laird, Eleanor, *The Psychology of Supervising the Working Woman* (New York, McGraw Hill, 1942).

Lakoff, Robin T., *Language and Woman's Place* (New York, Harper Trade, 1975).

Langevoort, Donald C., "The Human Nature of Corporate Boards: Law, Norms, and the Unintended Consequences of Independence and Accountability," 89 Georgetown L. J. 797, 810 (2001).

———, "The Behavioral Economics of Compliance with Corporate Law," 2002 Columb. Bus. L. Rev. 71.

———, "Overcoming Resistance to Diversity in the Executive Suite: Grease, Grit, and the Corporate Promotion Tournament," 61 Wash. & Lee L. Rev. 1615 (2004).

Lin, Laura, "The Effectiveness of Outside Directors as a Corporate Governance Mechanism: Theories and Evidence," 90 Northwestern U. L. Rev. 898 (1996).

Liu, Jonathan, & Wilson, Doirean, "The Unchanging Perception of Women as Managers," 16 Women in Management 163 (2001).

Lowenstein, Louis, "Financial Transparency: You Manage What You Measure," 96 Columb. L. Rev. 1335 (1996).

MacKinnon, Catharine, & Siegel, Reva P., *Directions in Sexual Harassment Law* (New Haven, CT, Yale University Press, 2003).

Meyerson, Debra E., & Fletcher, Joyce K., "A Modest Manifesto for Shattering the Glass Ceiling," 78 Harvard Bus. Rev. 127 (Jan.-Feb. 2000).

Milhaupt, Curtis J., "Privatization and Corporate Governance: Strategy for a Unified Korea," 26 J. Corp. L. 199 (2001).

Mills, C. Wright, *The American Business Elite: A Collective Portrait* (New York, Oxford University Press, 1963).

Monks, Robert, & Minnow, Nell, *Watching the Watchers: Corporate Governance for the 21ˢᵗ Century* (Malden, MA, Blackwell, 1996).

Morrison, Ann, Van Velsor, Ellen, & White, Randall P., *Breaking the Glass Ceiling* (Cambridge, MA, Perseus Publishing, 1992).

O'Barr, William M., *Linguistic Evidence: Language, Power, and Strategy in the Courtroom* (London, Elsevier Science & Technology, 1982).

O'Connor, Marleen, "The Enron Board: The Perils of Group Think," 71 U. Cinn. L. Rev. 1233 ((2003).

Peck, Charles, Silvert, Henry M., & McCormick, Gina, "The Conference Board, Director Compensation, and Board Practices in 2002" 38 (2003).

Phillips, Susan, et al., eds., *Language, Gender, and Sex in Comparative Perspective* (New York, Cambridge University Press, 1987).

Polacheck, Solomon W., "Occupational Self-Selection," 63 Rev. Economics & Statistics 60 (1981).

Posner, Richard, "An Economic Analysis of Sex Discrimination Laws," 56 U. Chi. L. Rev. 1311 (1989).

Pound, John, "The Rise of the Political Model of Corporate Governance and Control," 68 NYU L. Rev. 1003 (1993).

Preisler, Bent, *Linguistic Sex Roles in Conversation: Social Variation in the Ex-*

pression of Tentativeness in English (New York and Berlin, De Gruyter, 1986).

Ramirez, Steven A., "A Flaw in the Sarbanes-Oxley Reform: Can Diversity in the Boardroom Quell Corporate Corruption?" 77 St. John's L. Rev. 837 (2003).

———, "Games CEOs Play and Interest Convergence Theory: Why Diversity Lags in America's Boardrooms and What to Do about It?" 61 Wash. & Lee L. Rev. 1583 (2004).

Redding, Gordon, *The Spirit of Chinese Capitalism* (New York and Berlin, De Gruyter, 1990).

Reskin, Barbara F., & Roos, Patricia, *Job Queues, Gender Queues: Explaining Women's Inroads into Male-Dominated Occupations* (Philadelphia, PA, Temple University Press, 1990).

Rhode, Deborah L., "Occupational Inequality," 1988 Duke Law Journal 1207.

———, *Speaking of Sex: The Denial Of Gender Equality* (Cambridge, MA, Harvard University Press, 1999), 157.

Rhodes-Jones, R., *Bob Boothby: A Portrait* (Harrisburg, PA, Trinity Press, 1991).

Riesman, David, *The Lonely Crowd: A Study of the Changing American Character* (New Haven, CT, Yale University Press, 1961).

Rock, Edward, "The Logic and (Uncertain) Significance of Institutional Shareholder Activism," 79 Georgetown L. Journal 445 (1991).

Rosen, Ellen Israel, *Bitter Choices: Blue Collar Women in and out of Work* (Chicago, IL, University of Chicago Press, 1987).

Ross, Catherine, "The Division of Labor at Home," 65 Social Forces 816 (March 1997).

Russell Reynolds Associates, "2000 Board Practices Survey: The Structure and Compensation of Boards of Directors of U.S. Public Companies" (Feb. 2000).

Sapir, Edward, *Selected Writings of Edward Sapir in Language, Culture, and Personality* (Berkeley, University of California Press, 1949).

Sarason, Seymour, "Jewishness, Blackness, and the Nature-Nurture Controversy," 28 American Psychologist 962 (1973).

Sills, Beverly, & Linderman, Lawrence, *Beverly: An Autobiography* (New York, Bantam Books, 1987).

Sonnenfeld, Jeffrey, "What Makes Great Boards Great," 80 Harvard Bus. Rev. 106 (Sept. 2002).

Stith, Anthony, *Breaking the Glass Ceiling: Sexism and Racism in Corporate America: The Myths, the Realities, and the Solutions* (Toronto, Warwick Publishers, 1998).

Sturm, Susan, "Second Generation Employment Discrimination: A Structural Approach," 101 Colum. L. Rev. 458 (2001).

Tannen, Deborah, *You Just Don't Understand* (New York, William Morrow, 1990).

———, *Gender and Discourse* (New York, Oxford University Press, 1994).

Taylor, Shelley, & Fiske, Susan, "The Token in the Small Group: Research Findings and Theoretical Implications," in *Psychology and Politics* (J. Sweeney, ed.)(New York, Holt Rhinehart, 1976).

Testy, Kellye, "Capitalism and Freedom—for Whom? Feminist Legal Theory and Corporate Law," 67 Law & Contemp. Problems 87 (2004).

Unseem, Michael, *The Inner Circle* (New York, Oxford University Press, 1984).

Walker, Judith P., & Swiss, Deborah J., *Women and the Work/Family Dilemma* (New York, Wiley, 1993).

Ward, Ralph D., *The 21st-Century Corporate Board* (New York, Wiley, 1997).

Welch, Jack, & Byrne, John A., *Jack: Straight from the Gut* (New York, Warner Books, 2001).

Wellington, Sheila, *Be Your Own Mentor* (New York, Random House, 2001).

Whyte, William H., *The Organization Man* (New York, Simon & Schuster, 1956).

Williams, Joan, *Unbending Gender* (New York, Oxford University Press, 2000).

Williams, Joan, Calvert, Cynthia Thomas, & Cooper, Holly Green, "Better on Balance? The Corporate Counsel Retention Project: Final Report," reproduced in 10 Wm. & Mary J. Women & Law 367 (2004).

Winn, Joan, "Entrepreneurship: Not an Easy Path to Top Management for Women," 19 Women in Management 143 (2004).

Wolff, Kurt, *The Sociology of Georg Simmel* (New York, Wiley, 1950).

Wood, Robert G., Corcoran, Mary E., & Courant, Paul N., "Pay Differences among the Highly Paid: The Male-Female Earnings Gap in Lawyer's Salaries," 11 J. Labor Economics 417 (1993).

Zalokar, Nadja, "Male-Female Differences in Occupational Choice and the Demand for General and Occupation-Specific Human Capital," 26 Econ. Inquiry 59 (1988).

Zelechowski, Deborah D., & Bilimoria, Diana, "The Experience of Women Corporate Inside Directors on the Boards of Fortune 1000 Firms," 18 Women in Management 376 (2003).

Index

About the Author

Douglas M. Branson is W. Edward Sell Chair in Business Law at the University of Pittsburgh School of Law. He is the author and coauthor of several books on corporate law, including *Corporate Governance, Questions and Answers: Business Associations, Understanding Corporate Law,* and *Boardroom Chronicles.*